SLA

Anthropology, Culture and Society

Series Editor:
Dr Jon P. Mitchell, University of Sussex

RECENT TITLES

SLAVE OF ALLAH

Zacarias Moussaoui vs. The USA

KATHERINE C. DONAHUE

Pluto Press

LONDON • ANN ARBOR, MI

First published 2007
by PLUTO PRESS
345 Archway Road, London N6 5AA
and 839 Greene Street,
Ann Arbor, MI 48106

www.plutobooks.com

British Library Cataloguing in Publication Data
A catalogue record for this book is available from
the British Library

Hardback
ISBN-13   978 0 7453 2620 7
ISBN-10   0 7453 2620 X

Paperback
ISBN-13   978 0 7453 2619 1
ISBN-10   0 7453 2619 6

Library of Congress Cataloging in Publication Data applied for

10   9   8   7   6   5   4   3   2   1

Designed and produced for Pluto Press by
Chase Publishing Services Ltd, Fortescue, Sidmouth EX10 9QG, England
Typeset from disk by Stanford DTP Services, Northampton, England
Printed and bound in the European Union by
CPI Antony Rowe Ltd, Chippenham and Eastbourne, England

CONTENTS

To Donald S. Pitkin, Professor Emeritus, Anthropology, Amherst College
You showed me how to see the person behind the ethnographic data.

ACKNOWLEDGEMENTS

I owe thanks to many people who have made this project possible. Anne Beech of Pluto Press offered encouragement, Sophie Richmond provided consistency, and Bonnie Holcomb made a significant connection that led to my attending the trial. Many people gave up their time to think about this project. I thank Melanie Adrian, Harvard University; Iain Edgar, Durham University; Dale F. Eickelman, Dartmouth College; Patricia Heck, Professor Emeritus at the University of the South, Sewanee; Melissa Rich Herman; Stacy Lathrop, editor of *Anthropology News*; R. John Matthies, Brigham Young; Suzanne Nothnagle and Kenneth Colby; Paulina Ochoa, Yale University; Fran Oscadal, reference librarian, Dartmouth College; Susan Parman, California State, Fullerton; Stephen Reyna, University of New Hampshire; Andrew Shryock, the University of Michigan; Andrea Smith, Lafayette College.

Michael Sheridan, Middlebury College; Peter Allen, Rhode Island College; John Cole, Professor Emeritus, University of Massachusetts; and the late Estellie Smith made valuable comments on the chapter on "Islam without Borders." I thank Terry and Jay Rixse for their kind hospitality, Paula Schwartz, Deborah Losse, Bridget Healy, and Connecticut College classmates; Captain Tom Williamson of American Airlines; Aïcha el-Wafi; Larry Haley, Stefan Mosley, Nadia Bilbassy-Charters, Deirdre Blake, Phyllis and Orlando Rodriguez, and members of the Washington press corps for answering my questions. I thank the staff of the Alexandria Federal District Court for their courtesy.

My colleagues at Plymouth State were helpful in many ways: I thank former provost Virginia Barry for the sabbatical needed to write this book, David Beronä, Marcia Blaine, Khuan Chong, Scott Coykendall, Brian Eisenhauer, Krisan Evenson, Grace Fraser, Robert Heiner, Thaddeus Gulbrandsen, Rebecca Noel, Filiz Otucu, Meg Petersen, Leonard Reitsma, Sheryl Shirley, David Starbuck, and David Switzer for their comments on various concepts and chapters. I also thank the Plymouth State students who helped me think through some of the issues discussed here.

Without the help and advice of my husband, William J. Donahue, and my sons Thomas, Samuel, and James, this project would not have been possible. Nor would it have happened without my parents, Will and Jane Curtis, and my uncle Donald S. Pitkin, whose comments, encouragement, and support started me on this path.

Versions of the Introduction and Chapter 8 have appeared in *Anthropology News* (vol. 47, issue 7, 2006, copyright 2006), with the permission of the American Anthropological Association.

Portions of Chapter 5 appeared in "The Language of Violence, Race, Racism, and Culture in France," published in Bernhard Dieckmann, Christoph Wulf, and Michael Wimmer (eds) *Violence – Racism, Nationalism, Xenophobia*, pp. 187–203 (New York: Waxmann Münster, 1997). Versions of this project have been discussed at length and extensively revised with my husband's help; without his legal knowledge, clarity of thought, and patience in working through the details of this complicated case, it could not have been written. Any errors are, however, my own.

INTRODUCTION

THE UNITED STATES INDICTS ZACARIAS MOUSSAOUI

On Tuesday afternoon, December 11, 2001, United States Attorney General John Ashcroft entered the US Justice Department's conference room and faced the press. The reporters were about to receive headline news. With FBI Director Robert Mueller and Assistant Attorney General Michael Chertoff at his side, John Ashcroft said:

Today, three months after the assault on our homeland, the United States of America has brought the awesome weight of justice against the terrorists who brutally murdered innocent Americans. The first indictment has been brought against the terrorists of September 11. Al Qaeda will now meet the justice it abhors and the judgment it fears. (Ashcroft, 2001)

Ashcroft continued:

This morning, a grand jury in the Eastern District of Virginia charged Zacarias Moussaoui, a native of France, of Moroccan ancestry, with conspiring with Osama bin Laden and Al Qaeda to murder thousands of innocent people in New York, Virginia and Pennsylvania on September the 11th. (2001)

He went on to name as unindicted co-conspirators Osama bin Laden, al-Qaeda's[1] second in command Ayman al-Zawahiri, and Ramzi bin al-Shibh, who, Ashcroft said, had sent money to Moussaoui. Ashcroft also listed those hijackers who were beyond indictment, each one incinerated in the planes that hit the twin towers, the Pentagon, and the field in Shanksville, Pennsylvania. He then said that for "those who continue to doubt Al Qaeda's role in the murders of September 11" the indictment contained "30 pages of chilling allegations of Al Qaeda's campaign of terror" (2001). There were six counts against Moussaoui; the first four could carry the death penalty. These counts were conspiracy to: one, commit acts of terrorism transcending national boundaries; two, commit aircraft piracy; three, destroy aircraft; four, use weapons of mass destruction. The other two counts were conspiracy to: five, murder United States employees, and six, destroy property.

The indictment handed down that morning in the Virginia courthouse meant that Attorney General Ashcroft, with the approval

1

of President Bush, had decided that Zacarias Moussaoui was to be tried in Alexandria Federal District Court in Virginia. The court was close to the Pentagon. It was just across the Potomac River from the Washington headquarters of the US Justice Department and the FBI. The trial would not be in New York City, where thousands had died at the World Trade Center, and not in a military tribunal, even though John Ashcroft had vigorously supported President George Bush's executive order of November 13, 2001, allowing military tribunals to try alleged non-American terrorists.

Ashcroft took questions. One reporter asked him about his recent testimony in Congress and his comments to the press concerning the usefulness of military tribunals for terrorists:

Attorney General, last week, when you testified about the tribunals, you talked about you didn't want to see defendants with flamboyant defense attorneys and a long – and people with, you know, a talk show of their own. Aren't you now going to see a very long, expensive trial, since Moussaoui will be afforded two defense lawyers since he's facing the death penalty? (2001)

Ashcroft responded:

We look forward to this trial and the presentation of the evidence, which I think the indictments clearly indicate the direction in which we will move, and to go beyond the indictment now and try and describe the trial it would not be appropriate for me to do that. (2001)

No one could have predicted that the case of the United States of America against Zacarias Moussaoui would not go to trial until four years later; that Moussaoui would represent himself for more than a year; that the judge would rule that the prosecution forfeited the death penalty because they refused to compel defense witnesses to appear at trial; that this ruling would be reversed; that there would be no trial on guilt or innocence, but only for what penalty would be imposed; that a government lawyer would tamper with witnesses; that the judge would threaten to throw out the trial completely. The judge would say she thought Moussaoui had a better command of the law than many lawyers in her courtroom. The press and the blogosphere would call Moussaoui crazy. Family members of the victims of the attacks would call for his blood. Moussaoui would curse all those in the courtroom with him, would continue to refuse to stand when all others rose as the judge entered or left the room, and would habitually ask God to bless al-Qaeda.

In April of 2005, Moussaoui pleaded guilty to all six counts against him. The trial, finally held in March and April 2006, was to determine which sentence he would receive: death, or life in solitary confinement without possibility of release. On May 3, 2006, the jury delivered its verdict: Zacarias Moussaoui would spend the rest of his life in solitary confinement. He avoided a sentence of death only because one juror held out for life. The following morning Judge Brinkema formally sentenced him to life in prison. On May 12, 2006, he was flown by the US Marshals Service on a small jet operated by the Justice Prisoner and Alien Transportation System, more commonly known as "Con Air," to the Administrative Maximum security facility, or "Supermax" prison in Florence, Colorado. He now spends 23 hours a day alone in a cell, with another hour alone in exercise space.

Questions Raised, An Opportunity Missed

How did this happen? There is no evidence to show that Moussaoui was part of the planning of the September 11, 2001 hijacking.[2] In fact, he was not the twentieth hijacker, and the prosecution did not make that claim.[3] Moussaoui was in custody by August 16, 2001, because he had overstayed an immigration visa. When asked what he was doing in the United States, he said that he wanted to learn to fly for his personal enjoyment. The case against him was reduced to the following: if he had told the FBI that he was taking flight lessons in order to attack the United States, steps could have been taken to find the other hijackers and the attacks might have been avoided. Moussaoui went to prison for life, in solitary confinement, because he lied about his reason for being in the United States.

What can, and should, we learn from the case of the *United States v. Zacarias Moussaoui*? The trial revealed remarkable details about the American justice and intelligence systems, the FBI and Federal Aviation Administration (FAA), American foreign policy, and the fear and, some might say, the obsession, with which Americans focus on the attacks of September 11. In many ways, Moussaoui was a scapegoat for those attacks. A close look at evidence used in the trial shows how slim the government's case against him was. The Justice Department's initial decision to prosecute him was based on the need to show progress on the home front in the new war on terror. As the case unfolded, the CIA and the FBI were shown to have had difficulty in sharing information, with disastrous results. For a while the FBI seemed to be on trial, not Moussaoui.

What could be learned about Moussaoui? The United States missed an opportunity. During the trial Moussaoui was depicted as being a heartless monster by the prosecution, as a paranoid psychotic by the defense. The lawyers were doing what their jobs required of them, to prosecute and to defend him. Both sides of the justice system built their cases as they wished the jury to see Moussaoui. However, policy planners and analysts for the United States and, by extension, the West, could have used the evidence it did have to piece together the sociocultural ties, the belief systems, the importance of dreams, the conversion experiences of an al-Qaeda member in order to understand the acts he did undertake. They could have learned from the details of his life important information about his reasons for joining al-Qaeda. These lessons could have been useful to those who make foreign policy and who analyze intelligence reports. Rather than dismiss Moussaoui as the hapless terrorist who failed in his mission, one can, through his story, understand what leads people to *jihad*. Moussaoui brought his jihad to the American courtroom, confounding the American justice system and at times bringing it to a halt.

Was he guilty? To be clear about the case against him, Moussaoui did plead guilty, against the advice of his lawyers, to six counts of conspiracy, including conspiracy to commit acts of terrorism, to hijack planes, and to destroy aircraft. He was somewhat truthful, as he did plan to commit such acts, but not the acts of September 11. Instead, the prosecutors argued that Moussaoui's actions in attending flight school, buying knives, working out in gyms, and receiving money from abroad were similar to those of the hijackers. They introduced evidence showing that Moussaoui traveled to Afghanistan, Pakistan, and Malaysia, where he met with Osama bin Laden and Khalid Sheikh Mohammed, the planner of the attacks. But, according to this same evidence, Mohammed and some of his Malaysian associates thought Moussaoui was too unreliable to be trusted. Indeed, Mohammed disavowed any connection between Moussaoui and the attacks. Thus the government had no evidence to prove that Moussaoui was part of the plot. How then could the government persuade the jury to condemn Moussaoui to death for conspiracy to commit the acts of 9/11? The prosecution's strategy was to argue that if Moussaoui had not lied about why he was in the United States the FBI and FAA could have taken steps to ensure that the hijackers of 9/11 did not board those planes. Moussaoui's lie, which concealed his hope of future martyrdom, was sufficient to support the death penalty.

Again, to be clear, during the trial Moussaoui did not want the jurors' sympathy. Whenever he could he mocked the pain of family members and the horror felt by survivors of the attacks. He made obvious his contempt for America and Americans. His courtroom utterances, made daily as he left the courtroom, were consistently unrepentant. "God curse America" and "God bless Osama bin Laden" were only a few of his comments. The press duly noted his statements, conferring with each other to make sure they heard him correctly. He knew they were reporting his words, and he knew that his testimony and pleadings were available to the world through the court's public website.

IMPORTANCE OF THE TRIAL

If Zacarias Moussaoui was considered a secondary and relatively unimportant player before, by the time of the trial he had the world's attention. Reporters from the major American newspapers, television, and radio networks, as well as the BBC, the London *Times*, the French newspapers and radio, and the Arabic-language television networks Al Arabiya and Al Jazeera were there – their cameramen and satellite trucks waiting across the street for the reporters to emerge for sound-bites. Andrew Cohen (2006), a CBS legal analyst, called the trial: "the government's most important single trial over the century." *USA Today* said it was: "one of the most important criminal cases in decades" (Johnson and Levin, 2006). National Public Radio called it: "the (untelevised) trial of the century" (Smith, 2006). In a letter to family members of the victims of 9/11, assistant US attorney David Novak said that: "in many ways, this trial will serve as a historical record of the events of September 11" (2002). By the end of the trial, al-Qaeda was shown to be checking the court's public website. Osama bin Laden, in an audiotape message, presented what he called his own testimony on the subject of the "honorable brother Zacarias Moussaoui," who, he said, was not involved in 9/11. According to a reporter for the *New York Daily News*, Ayman al-Zawahiri, al-Qaeda's second in command, used one of the photos of a bearded Mohammed Atta from the trial's website in a July 2006, videotaped broadcast (Meek, 2006).

PURPOSE OF THE BOOK

Putting Zacarias Moussaoui, and people similar to him, in context is an important project for the following reasons. The trial of Moussaoui opened the door to understanding the way in which the FBI, the CIA, and al-Qaeda worked before September 11. The 9/11 Commission's report and investigations by congressional committees used, and condensed, information on the missed opportunities and the planning for 9/11. The trial made many of the actual documents available to the press and the public. Those documents shed light on the workings of the justice, intelligence, and investigatory systems of the United States, revealing the imperfections of those systems. Most important, however, a member of al-Qaeda was hidden in plain sight. The trial produced evidence of Moussaoui's life in France and Britain. Moussaoui talked of his travels to Afghanistan, Chechnya, Malaysia, and back. His testimony concerning his connections to al-Qaeda was corroborated by evidence from the FBI, French intelligence, and al-Qaeda associates.

There is no evidence that Moussaoui ever participated in the events of 9/11, but the evidence in his case revealed what the United States and the West generally speaking should have known before 9/11, and what it faces from newly radicalized Muslim militants in the developed and the developing world. Why did Zacarias Moussaoui become a member of a terrorist group that conspired to blow up major American buildings and oppose the United States government in every possible way? Unless we answer that question, we can't answer two more important questions: Why is there so much alienation and discontent among young Muslim men and women living in the West? Why do hundreds, even thousands, of people in North America and in Europe join fundamentalist Islamic groups which offer them a role in the global jihad? No matter how many trials we have, no matter how much surveillance we conduct, no matter how many wars we wage, these attacks will not stop until we can answer those two questions.

Questions Answered

The case of Zacarias Moussaoui provides a window into the life experiences which led this intelligent man – a man who has a master's degree in international business – from conventional success to jihad against the United States. An investigation of Moussaoui's life shows how French racism and exclusion blocked him from following his dream to become well educated, to become a businessman or at the very least a sales technician, to be involved in Franco-British trade with the Middle East, to marry his French girlfriend – in short, to have a happy, "normal" life. According to his brother Abd Samad he was "stuck" (Moussaoui, 2003: 87) in that regard, and so he chose to change his life and move to London. He learned English. He worked on, and received, his master's degree there. But according to his friend Nil Plant: "He had all these dreams and ambitions, and thoughts, mapped out, roaring to go, nothing to channel his intelligence and his dreams and all the things he had in his head ... " (2005). When he found that dream blocked, he rejected it and substituted a fundamentally different dream: he would join the global jihad. He would join the cause of protection of the *ummah*, the Muslim community. He would resist what he believed was the Western world's campaign to destroy or obstruct the creation of the ummah. He would follow his dream to fly a plane, into the White House, or to Heathrow, or to Afghanistan with the blind sheikh Omar Abdul Rahman, who was serving a life sentence for the plan to blow up the World Trade Center in 1993. He had to learn to fly. But he was blocked in that regard as well.

This discussion of Zacarias Moussaoui provides a close look at one of the people described in Marc Sageman's *Understanding Terror Networks* (2004). Sageman's well-regarded work[4] provides social network analysis of the ties that connect and bind different clusters of the global Salafi jihad. In many cases these are ties of friendship and family. Countries of origin figure in this analysis, and Sageman placed Moussaoui in the Maghreb, the North African, cluster. Sageman suggested (2004: 92–93) that one common characteristic was the exile, or emigration, experienced by members of the different clusters, not only the Maghreb cluster but also the core Arab cluster, which includes Osama bin Laden, Ayman al-Zawahiri, and many of the imams in France and Great Britain. The experience of exile or emigration was central to Moussaoui. He was the child of Moroccans, born in France, and when in London he was separated from his French family and friends. His connection in London to French converts to Islam, in some cases also of North African descent, helped form the bonds of brotherhood that led him to the training camps of Afghanistan and military action in Chechnya that only served to reinforce those ties.

This interpretation is a psycho-social one that places an individual, Zacarias Moussaoui, in context with a set of social and cultural factors that excluded and blocked him in some of his choices, and which opened the door to others.

ALTERNATIVE EXPLANATIONS ARE EXPLORED

In the following chapters, I will address alternative possible explanations for Moussaoui's actions, explanations which, I argue, are not adequate to the task. These alternative explanations are as follows:

1. Moussaoui and people like him are evil-doers. This explanation has frequently been used in American anti-terrorist rhetoric, not only by members of the Bush administration but also by certain Christian groups, the press, and relatives of the 9/11 victims. Objections to this explanation are discussed more fully in Chapter 2.
2. Moussaoui is crazy, delusional, or psychotic. It was a strategy of the defense to argue that he is mentally ill. It is the case that some members of his family have a record of mental illness. Even before the trial, the press depicted him as unbalanced. Jonathan Turley (2006), a law professor at George Washington University, called Moussaoui a "barking lunatic." Objections to this alternative explanation are discussed in Chapters 2, 3, and 4.
3. A related explanation would hold that Moussaoui is a failed, unreliable, "wannabe" terrorist, distrusted even by the planners of September 11. This explanation was a favorite of the conservative press and blogosphere, safely reducing Moussaoui to insignificance. Objections to this explanation are discussed more fully in Chapters 3 and 4.

4. What we have is an example of the clash of civilizations. This explanation is the commonly held view of Samuel Huntington's hypothesis (1993, 1997). In that view, there is a clash between the West and the rest (of the world) because of Western attempts to spread its political ideology and its control over nuclear power. This explanation, and arguments against it, is discussed more fully in Chapters 5, 6, and 7.

5. The cause is structural economic conflict and unemployment. In this view, Moussaoui joined al-Qaeda because he was North African, and North Africans are generally unable to find employment in Western countries. True, it is the case that unemployment levels in France are the highest for North and West Africans. Unemployment and consequent marginalization of young residents of the poor suburbs of France are said to have led to the riots of October and November 2005. But an economic answer is not sufficient. Many young French North and West Africans do not turn to jihad. Objections to this explanation are discussed in Chapters 5 and 6.

Eyewitness Information

I was there for a third of the trial. I attended part of the jury drawing in February 2006; three days in March of the eligibility phase (the presentation of evidence to determine whether Moussaoui was eligible for the death penalty) and three days in April of the penalty phase (the presentation of evidence to determine whether he would receive life or death). Seats were scarce and security was extremely tight, but it was possible to be in the main courtroom if one arrived at the courthouse very early in the morning. I have also had access to the court transcripts, to all the unclassified evidence, and have interviewed lawyers and observers of the trial. The court's website provides not only Moussaoui's own handwritten pleadings when he represented himself but also French orphanage records, FBI presentations, statements by al-Qaeda members, videotaped testimony from an *imam*, his sisters, and a French friend. Moussaoui's psycho-social history and the life events leading him to jihad can be pieced together. Using his pleadings and testimony in the trial one can understand his own identity, his representations of self, and the importance of his dreams of jihad. Those dreams did not end with his arrest. His arrest only served to give his jihad a new direction, one that would put Zacarias Moussaoui in the public's eye. As early as January 2002, it was clear that he was determined to work the American justice system to his own ends. He refused to enter a plea, so the judge entered it for him. He insisted on representing himself, and he did so for 17 months. He refused to remain standing while the judge entered and left the courtroom, so the judge arranged it so that both she and Moussaoui would enter and leave the courtroom at the same time. His pleadings, for a while feared to be coded messages for al-Qaeda, were rich with word play, revealing his frustration, anger, and sense of humor. His testimony, often erratic and contradictory, reveals the person behind the courtroom presentations of him.

PLAN OF THE BOOK

The book is structured as follows: the first three chapters move from a description of the case brought by the US Justice Department against Moussaoui, to the evidence and the proceedings, to his 17-month-long representation of himself, to the trial and the final verdict. The following four chapters discuss Moussaoui's life, place his experiences in context with those of others who experience exclusion, analyze the attraction of an Islam without borders, and then place Moussaoui in context with the evidence we have. The final chapter discusses the lessons that should be learned from the case of Zacarias Moussaoui, and the applications to policy that these lessons can produce.

Methods Used

The book includes eyewitness information drawn from seven days of observation of the jury selection and of the trial. I have talked with, among others, lawyers who worked on the case and with members of the press who covered the trial. These reporters were from the American, British, French, and Arabic-language news media, both print and broadcast. I have interviewed family members of victims of the September 11 attacks, as well as people who were present in the Pentagon and in the area of the World Trade Center. I also use the extensive evidentiary material posted on the court's website for information gathered by the American, British, and French intelligence services. I have drawn from academic sources as well, especially anthropologists and political scientists who have worked in and on the Middle East.

The book is written from an anthropologist's point of view. The discussion draws on anthropological fieldwork I have carried out in eastern France and in Paris at various times since 1989 in order to understand the social and cultural setting in which Moussaoui grew up. I use the legal situation in which he found himself in order to understand, and explain, the life events that led him to jihad. I move from the description of the courtroom proceedings to discussions of him as an individual to the social and cultural settings he experienced on his route from France to British mosques to training camps in Afghanistan.

Outline of Chapters

Chapter 1, "The Legal Process Begins," describes Moussaoui's arrest, the charges brought against him by the US Justice Department, and the proceedings leading up to the trial and his guilty plea. The chapter describes the members of the bar, including District Judge Leonie Brinkema, the US attorneys representing the government, and Moussaoui's federal defenders.

Chapter 2, "Slave of Allah: Zacarias Moussaoui's Struggle to Represent Himself," explores the period from June 2002, to November 2003, when he represented himself, despite the advice of his defense lawyers.

Chapter 3, "Courtroom 700, Alexandria, Virginia," discusses the selection of the jury, the two different phases of the trial – the eligibility phase and the penalty phase – and the verdict. The analysis includes discussion of the testimony by witnesses from the FBI, the flight schools, Western Union and American Telephone and Telegraph (ATT), and the FAA, as well as testimony by mental health experts and relatives of 9/11 called by both sides. It also describes members of the press, family members, and spectators who were members of the general public.

Chapter 4, "Zacarias My Brother: The Making of a Terrorist," uses court evidence, press reports, and interviews to describe Moussaoui's life in France, the social and economic problems he faced, his friendships and disappointments, his decision to move to London, his subsequent conversion, his commitment to jihad, and his travels to Afghanistan, Malaysia, and ultimately the United States.

Chapter 5, "Why Can't They Be More French?" uses background ethnographic material including fieldwork I have done in France since 1989. This discussion places Moussaoui in context as a French citizen of North African descent. The chapter examines ways in which membership in a state's polity is constructed and maintained by concepts of inclusion and exclusion. French concepts of race, ethnicity, and culture are explored in order to understand more fully why people such as Zacarias Moussaoui have experienced exclusion.

Chapter 6 discusses the meaning of an Islam without national borders. Zacarias Moussaoui disavowed his French citizenship. He told the court "I am al Qaeda," and that he is a slave of Allah. His adherence to an extra-state religious belief system – in particular one that endorses forms of resistance which are at once symbolically and physically violent – is indicative of the issues which face Western nation-states.

Chapter 7, "By Word and Bullet: Language and Symbolic Violence," explores Pierre Bourdieu's formulation (1991) of the concept of symbolic violence, of the dominance and submission enforced through control of speech and language in order to understand Moussaoui's actions. This formulation helps to explain why Moussaoui became a "slave of Allah," as he called himself in court documents, and explains some of Moussaoui's actions during the proceedings against him. The chapter explores the context in which choices are made not to submit to the domination of a state, but to offer submission to a group or institution beyond the state. In so doing, it places Zacarias Moussaoui in context with others much like him: disaffected members of Western nation-states.

Chapter 8, "What the West Should Learn from the Case of Zacarias Moussaoui," argues that the United States and the West in general should learn important lessons from the case of Zacarias Moussaoui. The trial testimony and evidence revealed the way in which the FBI and the US Department of Justice uncovered its evidence and built the case against Moussaoui. The administration learned that a trial such as this one can be cumbersome, lengthy, and expensive. More important, through analysis of Moussaoui's own statements, and the evidence about him, we can learn about the decisions made by young European neo-Muslims who Khosrokhavar (2002, 2005) calls "Allah's New Martyrs." Moussaoui's case reveals what the United States should have known before 9/11, what the West faces in the form of both symbolic and physical violence from newly radicalized Muslim militants, and what it could do to alter its policies to help lessen the appeal of the call to jihad against the West.

What This Book Does Not Do

There are several things this book is not designed to do. Although it is a thorough presentation of the proceedings against, and trial of Zacarias Moussaoui, it is not a complete history of all the motions and legal nuances of the case. That task is better left to a legal scholar. This book is not an analysis of the issues of language and power in the courtroom. There is a rich literature on this topic. Exchanges between lawyers and witnesses, lawyers and defendants, judges and lawyers and juries are often highly codified but rich with meaning (see, for instance, Cotterill, 2003). Analysis of courtroom interaction, while fruitful, is not a focus here. I look more narrowly at one aspect of the courtroom interactions. This aspect concerns Moussaoui's insistence on representing himself, and the ways in which he chose to do so. In that vein, I focus on the way in which he used his opportunities to represent himself, and the unexpected uses he made of those opportunities. I use courtroom testimony and evidence to understand more fully Moussaoui's road to jihad. It is not possible to interview him. Therefore I have had to rely on testimony, evidence, interviews, and press reports to gather information about his life.

Also, although Islam framed Moussaoui's life after conversion, this is not a text on Islam as a whole, nor is it a text on political or radical Islam, nor is it a text on Islam in the West. Those topics are discussed successfully by others (al-Zayyat, 2004; Esposito, 1998a [1988], 1998b, 2002; Karam et al., 2004; Kepel, 1997).

This book is a discussion of one man's journey into a particular form of Islam, and the meaning it had and still has for him. The book places the life of Zacarias Moussaoui into context, in order to explain the attraction of global jihad to its adherents. Jihadis are not necessarily evil, nor crazy, nor ineffectual loners, nor are they the unemployed, ill-educated, marginal people often characterized in the press. Who, then, are they? Who, then, was Zacarias Moussaoui? *Slave of Allah* provides answers to that question.

1 THE LEGAL PROCESS BEGINS

MOUSSAOUI'S ARREST

It was Monday, August 13, 2001. Clancy Prevost had a new flight student. He was surprised that Zacarias Moussaoui had so little flight time under his belt. Usually, pilots came to the Eagan, Minnesota, flight school with thousands of hours in the air. Moussaoui had only 55. Prevost was a simulator flight instructor. Pilots came to Pan Am International Flight Academy for training on simulators in order to upgrade to bigger jets or to move to better jobs. Pan Am used Northwest Airlines' facilities to offer training on Boeing 747-400 and 757 jet simulators. It was not odd that Moussaoui was a foreign national; Pan Am trained many pilots for foreign airlines. But Moussaoui's lack of flight time was going to be a challenge.

Prevost was to be Moussaoui's ground school instructor. The plan was to use a PowerPoint demonstration to introduce Moussaoui to the fundamentals of how the 747-400 simulator worked. Prevost would take care of that. Moussaoui would then spend time as an observer in the simulator. Finally he would train in the simulator himself. He was to finish training on August 20, 2001. Never before had Prevost worked with someone who had so little flight time. He assumed Moussaoui was a person with too much money who was, like those who go to major league baseball camps, "just fulfilling a dream" (*US v. Moussaoui*, tr. March 9, 2006, page 741, line 11).[1] In fact, Moussaoui had emailed Pan Am on May 23, 2001, saying that he wanted to know if the flight school could help him "achieve my 'Goal' my dream ... to be able to take off and land.... to be able successfully to navigate from A to B (JFK to Heathrow for example)" (Prosecution Exhibit, MN00151). The flight school set up a schedule for him, Moussaoui paid a deposit on his Visa card, and Prevost was then assigned to work with him.

Moussaoui had arrived in Norman, Oklahoma, from London in February 2001. He enrolled at Airman Flight School in Norman, where he planned to learn to fly a single-engine Cessna. Moussaoui was an attentive student in ground school but less capable when in the air. His instructor at Airman later testified that Moussaoui managed to fly the plane when in flight training space, but when returning or taking off, when there was a good deal of chatter on the radio and planes were coming and going, he had difficulty banking and maintaining control of the plane. In May, the instructor moved on to other students. The flight school told Moussaoui that he was not progressing satisfactorily. On May 23, 2001, Moussaoui sent the email to Pan Am in Minnesota to ask for multi-engine jet training on a flight simulator.

The person Prevost met on August 13 was wearing loafers, a baseball hat, and casual pants. He wasn't dressed like the sort of person who had money. Moussaoui told Prevost he was a businessman from Britain and that he wanted to impress his friends with this training. The PowerPoint demonstration Prevost was supposed to give was not working properly, so Prevost talked Moussaoui through a display, a mode control panel. When discussing the simulator training Moussaoui was to have several days later, Prevost told him that the following could happen: Moussaoui is sitting in a 747-400. The pilots have had a bad meal and are incapacitated. A flight attendant comes through the plane asking if anyone can fly it. Moussaoui, said Prevost, would be able to do so. Moussaoui replied: "I would rather take a parachute and jump out the door" (tr. March 9, 2006, page 756, lines 11–12). Prevost told Moussaoui that he would not be able to open the door because the plane would be pressurized. By way of explanation, Prevost told him about an unfortunate *"hajj* charter," a plane filled with pilgrims headed to Mecca. The plane caught fire while still on the runway, but the doors could not be opened because the flight engineer did not depressurize the cabin. All were burned to death. Prevost then said: "hajj, Ramadan, what is that? Are you Muslim?" According to Prevost's testimony, Moussaoui's voice changed, and he answered: "I am nothing." Prevost decided not to continue the questioning (tr. March 9, 2006, page 757, lines 1–9).

Moussaoui's decision to learn to fly a 747 using a simulator did not seem especially odd. Simulators are routinely used by pilots because it is too expensive to use a real plane. The plane, which brings in revenue for an airline, would have to be taken out of service. A person with some experience flying in a small plane could, with simulator training, learn to fly a much larger plane. Later, during the trial, Prevost testified: "If you know how to work the mode control panel, you know how to fly a 747-400" (tr. March 9, 2006, page 775, lines 11–18.). Unlike Mohammed Atta, who the flight school personnel in Florida called "the little terrorist" (Susan de Santis Hall, testimony, March 21, 2006),[2] Moussaoui did not himself draw suspicion, however. During the trial, defense attorney Kenneth Troccoli asked Prevost: "Is it safe to say, Mr. Prevost, that it was fairly obvious to you at least at the end of the first day that this was a very suspicious guy?" Prevost replied:

No, I was never suspicious of Zac until I – even when I thought we should do a background check, I was not suspicious of him. I thought that there should be a protocol in place that if they're going to have somebody like this come through, that, that they should have some kind of a mechanism to do a background check. I was not suspicious of Zac. (tr. March 9, 2006, page 776, lines 17–25)

In fact, Prevost said Zac was "a pretty genial guy" (tr. March 9, 2006, page 763, line 12). Prevost did say he was concerned that this was a person who did not have a pilot's license, who did not work for an airline, and who had not been vetted in any way. Once Prevost told the story about the hajj flight to Moussaoui, he made the connection that Moussaoui was probably Muslim, that hijackers had been from the Middle East, that "we should have a background check here before we teach somebody how to fly a commercial airliner" (tr. March 6, 2006, page 771, lines 16–19; page 772, lines 3–19). At the end of the first day, Prevost learned that Moussaoui had paid his $6800 for training in hundred dollar bills. He testified that he told some of his supervisors that the FBI should be contacted, but they didn't seem especially concerned.

Clancy Prevost was not the only one who thought Moussaoui's presence at Pan Am raised questions. Tim Nelson was the Pan Am flight school manager, and his curiosity was aroused. He wanted to meet this man Moussaoui, who had said his desire to learn to fly a 747 was "an ego thing." Nelson had just watched a video of a Japanese hijacking. The hijacker had stormed the cockpit with a knife. He had wanted to fly the plane. Nelson had that event in his head, knew that Middle Easterners had recently been responsible for hijackings, and watched Moussaoui talk with two Syrian flight students, in Arabic (Arena, 2006).

THE FBI AND "THE WALL"

Tim Nelson called the Minneapolis FBI. Agent Harry Samit, an investigator with the Joint Terrorism Task Force of the Minneapolis FBI, then called Clancy Prevost on August 15. The Minneapolis FBI opened an intelligence investigation and, because it was reported that Moussaoui was French, contacted the FBI legal attaché in Paris. The Immigration and Naturalization Service (INS) checked his date of entry into the US. Moussaoui had arrived on February 23, 2001, using a French passport. He had been in the US more than the 90 days allowed for visitors from countries such as France. He could be arrested and deported. On August 15, Agent Samit and other FBI and INS personnel went to Pan Am. They then met with Prevost at his motel on August 16. That afternoon Moussaoui was picked up at his hotel by FBI and INS personnel and taken into custody for overstaying his visa waiver. On August 17, the FBI asked the US State Department to check on visa application information on both Moussaoui and his Oklahoma roommate, Hussein al-Attas, who had accompanied him to Minnesota. Meanwhile, al-Attas was being interviewed about Moussaoui's religious beliefs. Moussaoui believed in jihad, al-Attas said, and talked a great deal about the role of the United States in causing difficulties in the Muslim world.

The intelligence investigation was well under way. In Paris, the FBI legal attachés Jay Abbott and his boss Enrique Ghimenti were investigating what the French knew about him. Ghimenti had been in Paris for three years and had a working relationship with French counter-intelligence. On August 21, Ghimenti went to the French version of the FBI, the Direction de la Surveillance du Territoire, or DST, for information on Moussaoui. They had information.

The FBI wanted permission to search Moussaoui's bags of belongings as well as his Toshiba laptop, which were stored with the INS. To do so they would need to open up a criminal investigation on Moussaoui, in addition to the intelligence investigation. In order to perform the search a judge would have to issue a warrant. Colleen Rowley of the Minneapolis FBI said in an email of August 22 that, while it might be possible to get the judge to sign a search warrant, the US Attorney's Office there in Minneapolis seemed to have an even higher standard for evidence, blocking them from proceeding with the criminal investigation (Defense Exhibit 56). At the time, once an FBI intelligence investigation was under way, information could not be exchanged with the FBI's criminal investigators. The law had created a "wall" between intelligence investigations and criminal investigations, and information could not be shared across that wall, even within the FBI. The purpose of this wall was to prevent prejudicing the case of someone who was accused of a crime.

Meanwhile, the Paris FBI had learned that the French had a file on Moussaoui. He was linked to Ibn Khattab, a Chechen rebel leader, who had connections to Osama bin Laden. On August 28, 2001, FBI legal attaché Jay Abbott was asked to check the French white pages (i.e. residential telephone directory) for the name "Zacarius (sic) Moussaoui" in order to learn the likelihood that this Moussaoui was the same as the Moussaoui known to the French police. Abbott emailed back that such a task might be "tooo tall of an order" (emphasis his) but that he had the Paris white pages and was checking it (Defense Exhibit 332).

By August 30, Jay Abbott had more information on Moussaoui. The French police had been thorough. Moussaoui had been friends with a French citizen, Xavier Djaffo, who had gone to London, converted to radical Islam, and had joined Ibn Khattab, the Chechen leader. Djaffo, who had changed his name to Masood al-Benin, had died in

Chechnya in April 2000. Moussaoui, the French said, was reported to be cold and cynical – and a strategist. His commitment to radical Islam was of long standing (Defense Exhibit 59B).

The 9/11 Commission and the Inspector General for the Justice Department later reported that the wall was a major impediment to learning of the 9/11 plot. Furthermore, FBI headquarters staff in Washington had not encouraged pursuit of the Moussaoui investigation. The Foreign Intelligence Surveillance Act, or FISA, set standards for approval of investigations which the FBI headquarters staff thought would prohibit an investigation of Moussaoui. FISA approvals were concerned with "foreign powers." The Chechen rebels were not thought to be a foreign power or a terrorist group. Harry Samit tried to link Moussaoui to Osama bin Laden through Moussaoui's friendship with Djaffo, who had fought along with Ibn Khattab, the Chechen leader, who was linked to Osama bin Laden. Michael Maltbie at FBI headquarters said the Minneapolis agents were getting people "spun up" about this case (Hill, 2002: 21).

FBI headquarters denied the Minneapolis FBI's request for a FISA search warrant because there was no apparent link between Moussaoui and a foreign power. According to Senate hearings, and Samit's later testimony, his immediate boss called FBI headquarters and said he was "trying to make sure Moussaoui did not take a plane and fly it into the World Trade Center" (Hill, 2002: 21). On August 28, 2001, Samit was told that his request to search Moussaoui's belongings was not approved. On August 31, 2001, he drafted a "Letterhead Memorandum" to go from the FBI to the FAA and any other governmental agency, warning that Moussaoui seemed to fit the profile of a hijacker, that he had received flight training, that he had trained at a gym, that intelligence had reported he had "fully embraced Radical Islamic Fundamentalism" since 1995, that he had been in Pakistan shortly before coming to the US, and that he believed in jihad (Defense Exhibit 810). By September 5, 2001, a teletype had gone out to the FAA reporting on the threat. Blocked from receiving a FISA warrant to search Moussaoui's belongings, Samit instead decided to work with the French, who agreed to receive Moussaoui and search his belongings once he arrived on French soil. On the afternoon of September 10, Samit received approval to send Moussaoui to France. He started work on Moussaoui's deportation (tr. March 9, 2006, page 948, line 1).

The next day, the case completely changed. Immediately after learning of the attacks of September 11, Samit got permission from a US magistrate in Minneapolis to search Moussaoui's bags (tr. March 9, 2006, page 951, lines 14–25; page 952, lines 1–2). The search revealed three knives, all under four inches long, boxing gloves, shin guards, the phone number of someone in Germany, and Western Union receipts for wire transfers of money. A notebook contained phone numbers for flight schools and Blackwater Training, a private military training company based in North Carolina. Next to phone numbers for an Abdel Kader was a shopping list for 7UP, orange juice, and an oven dish (Prosecution Exhibit MN00601). He used another notebook for keeping track of the flight lessons at Airman. In that notebook, together with an outline of living expenses, he wrote: "Plan Omar" and then "mental preparedness, concept of *hijra* [exile]," "difficulty in travel, patience," followed by "What to do with family," "Discret[e], not to say." The following page had a phone number for Pan Am International Flight Academy (Prosecution Exhibit MN00666). There were other, less sinister items in Moussaoui's belongings. Later, during the trial, Defense Exhibit 922 listed them as: "Inventory of items seized from Moussaoui." The items included Warner Brothers' Scooby-Doo boxer shorts (Defense Exhibit 922). The FBI agent was careful to note that they were made in Pakistan.

Moussaoui was photographed. He was wearing an orange prison jumpsuit and had a neatly trimmed beard. On his forehead was a brown spot, a small sign of religious devotion. In Arabic it is a *zabib*, a "raisin." It is a callus acquired from the type of prayer in which one kneels forward and lowers one's forehead to the ground.

THE PROCEEDINGS BEGIN

On September 14, 2001, Moussaoui was flown in a small private jet to New York to face American justice in one of the areas where the attacks had occurred. Another passenger on the plane was Al-Bader al-Hazmi, a Saudi medical resident in radiology who had been picked up in Texas on September 12. Al-Hazmi later reported, after he was released, that Moussaoui seemed very calm on the plane, that he joked with the others and said that they all should not worry. Moussaoui said they, and he, would soon be released as they all had nothing to do with September 11 (*San Antonio Express News*, 2006). Meanwhile the FBI and the US attorneys in New York and Washington were assembling evidence and building their case against Moussaoui.

In November 2001, President Bush signed an executive order allowing military tribunals to try terrorist suspects who were not Americans. A debate, described later by John Ashcroft (2006), ensued. Where was Moussaoui to be tried? Michael Chertoff, at the time the head of the Criminal Division at the Department of Justice, wanted to try Moussaoui in a US court, not in a military tribunal. To some in the Justice Department, the Federal District Court in the Southern District of New York, in Manhattan, seemed the logical choice. Kenneth Karas, an assistant US attorney there, had experience with terrorism cases. He and his assistant US attorneys had just tried, and sent away for life in prison, men connected with the bombings of the US embassies in Kenya and Tanzania. The twin towers, where more people had died than any other place on 9/11, were just down the street. Senior officials in the Defense Department lobbied for a military tribunal, where the burden of proof and the rules of evidence were less rigorous than in US criminal courts. However, public criticism was growing over the use of military tribunals. Ashcroft agreed with the recommendation of Chertoff and others that Moussaoui be tried in a US criminal, or civilian, court. But the Department of Justice was going to ask for the death penalty, and the New York court had deadlocked on the death penalty for two of the East African embassy bombing suspects. A court near the Pentagon would more likely decide for the death penalty. The Alexandria Federal District Court was chosen for the trial. On Monday, December 10, President Bush agreed to the recommendation (Van Natta and Weiser, 2001).

On Tuesday, December 11, 2001, Attorney General John Ashcroft announced to the press and the public the indictment of Zacarias Moussaoui on six counts of conspiracy to commit terrorist acts. Citing the similarities in behavior between Moussaoui and the 19 hijackers, Ashcroft said that "Al Qaeda will now meet the justice it abhors and the judgment it fears" (2001). Moussaoui was charged with four counts which could bring the death penalty. Those were conspiracy to: one, commit acts of terrorism transcending national boundaries; two, commit aircraft piracy; three, destroy aircraft; four, use weapons of mass destruction. The other two counts were conspiracy to murder United States employees and conspiracy to destroy property.

On December 13, 2001, Moussaoui was transported to Alexandria, Virginia, where he would face trial in the Federal District Court of the Eastern Division of Virginia, close to the Pentagon, close to the main Department of Justice in Washington. He was placed in the Alexandria Detention Center, less than a mile away. Soon thereafter, John Walker Lindh, the "American Taliban" arrived, picked up in Afghanistan. The US Marshals Service, charged with securing and protecting prisoners, courthouses, and judges, began working out security measures for the Alexandria courthouse. Fox News reported on the day Moussaoui was transported:

The trial, which will take place in Alexandria, promises to be one of the most closely watched cases in recent memory and has already sparked safety concerns. "This will make the Timothy McVeigh case look like kindergarten," said Drew Wade, spokesman for the U.S. Marshals Service, responsible for security at the courthouse. (Fox News, 2001)

By December 19, 2001, Moussaoui was in the Alexandria courthouse listening to the charges against him. On January 2, 2002, he was brought back to the courthouse to enter his plea.

THE COURTHOUSE

The walls of Courtroom 700 are paneled with wood. Half-globe white lights hang from the high ceiling. There is blue carpeting on the floor. Behind the judge are the flags of the United States and the State of Virginia. The witness stand is on the left of the courtroom, the jury box on the right. Behind it, a door opens into the jury room. To the left, when facing the judge and the bench, are two doors. People chatted quietly, waiting for Moussaoui to enter his plea. They fell silent as court officers took their positions. "All rise," said a court official. The two doors opened. Leonie Brinkema entered through the door closest to the bench, Moussaoui entered through the other door – the door closer to the seats used by the press, family members, and the public. Moussaoui was wearing a green jumpsuit with the word "Prisoner" on the back. Wearing a black robe, glasses perched on her nose, graying hair pulled up in a bun, Judge Brinkema took her seat at the bench.

When Judge Brinkema asked Moussaoui how he pleaded, he said: "In the name of Allah, I do not have anything to plea. I enter no plea. Thank you very much." She said she assumed this was a plea of not guilty. Frank Dunham, Moussaoui's federal public defender, agreed that it was, and a plea of not guilty was entered (tr. January 2, 2002, page 1, lines 7–8, 10).

Moussaoui refused to stand when the judge entered, nor would he stand when she left the courtroom. Over time, a compromise seemed to be reached. The two would enter at roughly the same time, meaning that the US Marshals would have to time his entry with hers. This was a bit difficult, for when he was out of the courtroom he was detained inside what sounded like a cell, given the metal clanking one could hear from the courtroom.

Judge Leonie Brinkema was appointed to the case in December 2001, by Chief Judge Claude Hilton. A graduate of Rutgers University, she had worked in the criminal division of the US Department of Justice, and had served as a US Magistrate Judge in this same court. Magistrate Judges serve eight-year terms. They are overseen by the federal district court judges, who serve life terms. In 1993, President Clinton appointed Brinkema to the position of federal district judge. The Alexandria court was known for its fast action, the "rocket docket," which may have helped in the Attorney General's decision to send the case there and not to New York. There were other reasons as well. The courthouse was in a conservative district, close to the Pentagon and next to Washington, DC. Jury members would be drawn from a pool of people employed by or otherwise connected to governmental agencies such as the Department of Defense. The Fourth Circuit of Appeals in Richmond, Virginia, to which cases from this court are appealed, is known to be steadfastly conservative. Judge Brinkema, considered to be somewhat more liberal than some of her colleagues on the federal district court bench, nevertheless was known to move things along, firmly but politely, and to keep a strong hand on court proceedings. Yet she would be willing to give Moussaoui leeway longer than many other judges. She took pains to make sure that he received a fair hearing and a fair trial.

The prosecutors in this case came from the US Attorney's offices in Virginia and New York. Paul McNulty was the US Attorney for the Eastern District of Virginia. He took office three days after September 11, having been selected over Edward MacMahon of Middleburg, Virginia, for the position. In one of the many ironies of this case, MacMahon would become one of Moussaoui's defense attorneys. By the time of the actual trial, the members of the prosecution were three assistant US attorneys, two from the Eastern District of Virginia, one from New York. Robert Spencer, tall and slim, was from the Alexandria office, and was chief of the Eastern District's Criminal Division. Called by one source "among the most ethical and persuasive assistant U.S. attorneys in the nation," he had experience with violent crime and terrorism prosecutions (Kelley and McLure, 2006). David Novak, shorter and tenacious, had come up from the Richmond office. Formerly a federal prosecutor in Texas, Novak spent hundreds of hours interviewing family members of the victims of 9/11. Kenneth Karas came down from the Southern District of New York, and was later replaced by David Raskin, also from New York, where he had served on the organized crime and counterterror unit. He was part of the team which prosecuted 70 members of the New York Genovese crime family (Kelley and McLure, 2006). The prosecution had support from a number of other attorneys and investigators, some of whom would attend the proceedings of the trial.

Frank Dunham, the Federal Public Defender for the Eastern District of Virginia, was to see the defense of Moussaoui through some difficult times. He had been sworn into office in March of 2001, and charged with setting up offices in Norfolk, Richmond, and Alexandria, Virginia, including hiring the lawyers to staff them. When he received a phone call from the secretary of the chief judge of the Alexandria Federal District Court asking him to represent Moussaoui, he had no real office or staff in Alexandria. Previously in practice with a large Washington law firm, he had defended Mark Felt of the FBI, who had been charged with wiretapping. Years after Watergate, Felt revealed that he was Robert Woodward and Carl Bernstein's "Deep Throat," the source with whom the two *Washington Post* reporters would meet to receive information about the Watergate affair, which led to the resignation of President Richard Nixon.

In short order, Dunham assembled a team which included Gerald Zerkin, an assistant federal public defender with experience in death penalty cases from the new Richmond office, Anne Chapman, assistant federal public defender in the new Alexandria office who also had death penalty experience, and Kenneth Troccoli, assistant federal public defender who had prior experience in a public defender office in Alexandria. Because this was a case which could carry the death penalty, Moussaoui was entitled to two different teams of lawyers. On December 11, 2001, Chief Judge Claude Hilton appointed Edward MacMahon to Moussaoui's defense team. Later, while Moussaoui was representing himself, Judge Brinkema appointed Alan Yamamoto as a standby lawyer for Moussaoui.

On January 7, 2002, Special Administrative Measures (SAM) were imposed on Moussaoui. The only visitors he could receive would be attorneys or his family. Telephone calls would be allowed only from lawyers or their staff or his family. Those calls would be monitored. Translation would be necessary if the calls were in another language. No visitor would be allowed to talk with him except at a distance. There was to be no communication with other prisoners. By April 12, 2002, his defense lawyers were asking for relief from these restrictive measures of confinement. According to their motion, he had been moved from a larger cell to a smaller one when another high-profile defendant arrived in the Alexandria Detention Center. He had a steel toilet and sink, space for a mattress on a shelf. Lights were on 24 hours a day so he could be monitored. No pens or pencils were allowed. He was in solitary confinement even though he was supposedly presumed innocent. He had no space for a desk nor access to a computer. It would be difficult, even impossible, for him to have access to the stacks of documents being prepared in the case against him (Docket No. 94). Frank Dunham later (2004) said that the case was the largest FBI investigation in US history (180,000 interviews by 7000 agents) comprising all of the 9/11 documents and evidence accumulated by the FBI. Approximately 1400 CD ROMs were used to hold all FBI information. Lawyers call this "boxcar discovery" because the material in a case sometimes appears to come in by the boxcar load, particularly from large, well-funded law firms and from the government. On July 29, 2002, Moussaoui wrote:

Allah u akbar. In its constant effort to win by cheating the US gov is flooding (my cell) with CD, tape, and video, blank. The quantity is so enormous already that nobody could load all the CD before trial. (Docket No. 369)

He asked for help from his lawyers, and for an internet hookup from his cell connecting to an internal website established for the lawyers in the case.

In fact, even the court was expecting logistical problems in handling the voluminous pleadings and the transcripts of hearings. The press and the public wanted access to the court documents. Court personnel would find it hard to make those documents easily available. The broadcast media had already been told that they would not be permitted in the courtroom. However, a ruling by the Judicial Conference of the United States allowed for the creation of websites in cases of high public interest. On March 21, 2002, Judge Brinkema ordered that all documents in the case were to be submitted in both paper and electronic versions. There remained a concern with a Protective Order entered on January 22, 2002, regarding classified materials. Such materials were to be reviewed, and certain materials could not be placed on the website. Some documents would be redacted, meaning that they would be censored (Docket No. 88). Both parties would have to comply with proper handling of classified documents. The website was created.

On March 28, 2002, the Department of Justice issued a Notice of Intent to Seek a Sentence of Death. Attorney General Ashcroft announced that the US intended to seek the death penalty for each of the first four counts (conspiracy to commit acts of terrorism transcending national boundaries, conspiracy to commit aircraft piracy, conspiracy to destroy aircraft, conspiracy to use weapons of mass destruction). Moussaoui had, the notice said, intentionally participated in an act of violence, contemplating that the life of a person would be taken, and that participation "constituted a reckless disregard for human life and the victims died as a direct result of the act" (Docket No. 89). The Federal Death Penalty Act sets up specific procedures for trials in which the death penalty is sought, and lawyers specialize in death penalty cases because of the complications of procedural issues. Moussaoui, however, was ready to demand that his defense lawyers be removed from the case.

MOUSSAOUI MOVES TO REPRESENT HIMSELF

Moussaoui's profound distrust of American lawyers and the American legal system was becoming apparent. He insisted on finding a Muslim lawyer who could advise him on procedure. Barring that, he would represent himself. A hearing was held on April 22, 2002, on his claim that he had a right to self-representation. At that hearing, Moussaoui read a long statement concerning his views on the American justice system.

In the name of Allah, I, Zacarias Moussaoui, today the 22nd of April, 2002, after being prevented for a long time to mount an effective defense by overly restrictive and oppressive condition of confinement, take the control of my defense by entering a pro se defense set for presentation in order to mount a significant defense of the defense of the life that Allah, the most masterful, has granted to me. (tr. April 22, 2002, page 4, lines 3–10)

He continued: "I, slave of Allah, Zacarias Moussaoui, reject completely" the lawyers the court has imposed on him. "I, slave of Allah, Zacarias Moussaoui" will engage in action against the "U.S. Department of so-called Justice" for a "very serious misconduct reason" he would discuss in court. "I, slave of Allah, Zacarias Moussaoui" intend to hire a Muslim lawyer in the shortest time possible (tr. April 22, 2002, page 4, lines 11–24).

He was concerned about the sheer volume of material he expected to receive from the government. He said that he was reading the transcript of the New York trial in the case of the US embassy bombings in Kenya and Tanzania, and saw how the government overwhelmed the proceedings with details in that trial. Given the possibility that the government would use the same tactic in his case, he wanted a trial by judge, because, he said, a jury might lose sight of the main points. He was also uncomfortable with the idea of defense lawyers he did not trust "going freely all over the world and trying to meet with people that I know" (tr. April 22, 2002, page 59, line 62). When the judge questioned his ability to handle the complexity of the case on his own he said that he was well acquainted with the Western system of justice; he was French and was well educated and knew the Anglo-Saxon system as well because he lived in London (tr. April 22, 2002, page 62, lines 23–25; page 63, lines 1–5).

In order to ensure his competence to represent himself, Judge Brinkema ordered a mental examination, to which he strongly objected. He did meet with a psychiatrist for the prosecution, Dr. Raymond Patterson, but would not meet with mental health experts for the defense. The government psychiatrist thought that Moussaoui was competent. At a hearing on June 13, 2002, the judge ordered that he could represent himself. She appointed Alan Yamamoto as his standby local counsel. "Given the total break-down of the attorney–client relationship between defendant and his former counsel," Edward MacMahon was dismissed from the case and ordered to turn over all non-classified materials to Yamamoto (Docket No. 186). Frank Dunham asked that the federal defenders be relieved from the case. Judge Brinkema said they would remain on the case on a standby basis until new counsel could be found. After the hearing, Frank Dunham said:

If he just wanted to represent himself and didn't have this fixation that we were trying to harm him, I would be more than delighted to take a standby role. It's just that I don't think he should be subjected to having a standby counsel that he can't stand. (Jackman, 2002)

According to one lawyer close to the case, the thought of removal from the case was disappointing. A great deal of effort had already been expended in this high-profile case, and it would be hard to let it go, despite the difficulty of their intractable client.

Moussaoui's mother, Aïcha el-Wafi, had arrived from France. She was in the courtroom that day with a lawyer she had retained for her son. Randall Hamud, a Muslim and an Arab-American lawyer from California, went to Virginia during the last week of May 2002, to see Moussaoui. Moussaoui refused to see him, even though Moussaoui's mother had given Hamud a letter of introduction. Moussaoui's decision to represent himself was, in Hamud's opinion, "a one-way ticket to the death chamber" (CourtTV, 2002). During the June 13 hearing the judge asked if Hamud was present, and Hamud said he was. Moussaoui turned around, waved, and said, "Hello, mama." He told the judge that he would not accept Hamud as a lawyer, and that his mother was well-intentioned, but did not speak English and did not understand the case. "My mother, she's a mother. She wants to help her son," Moussaoui told the judge. "I would prefer to have my own choice." His mother said afterwards that she had not seen him in five years. He looked thin and tired, she said (Jackman, 2002).

That evening, Philip Shenon of the *New York Times* told Gwen Ifill of the Public Broadcasting Service (PBS) of his own observations of Moussaoui in the courtroom:

He is a very intelligent man, very articulate, he has a very strong command of English. He speaks in heavily accented English, but it is very clear. And he has an understanding of an awful lot of the vocabulary of the legal community and demonstrated that he's done an awful lot of reading about the law. In many ways, he is more intelligent than a lot of lawyers we see practicing in a lot of courthouses around the country. (Shenon, 2002)

On June 18, 2002, Judge Brinkema asked Alan Yamamoto, a solo practitioner in Alexandria, to join the defense team in representing Moussaoui. Someone close to the case speculated that he was engaged in hopes that his non-American roots (his father had been a Japanese "intern," held as an alien in a detention camp during World War II) would help in easing the defense lawyers' relations with their difficult client. To no avail. Moussaoui refused to see him (Hirschkorn, 2002).

A Muslim lawyer Moussaoui did trust and who he wished to represent him refused to apply for admission to practice in the Alexandria court. Apparently the lawyer, Charles Freeman from Texas, would not agree to the requirements of the court for admission as an attorney there. Charles Freeman filed a protest with the court, "IS THIS HOW ALEXANDRIA DIVISION TREATS ITS GUESTS?" saying

that the court had called the detention center to deny Freeman access
to Moussaoui (see Docket No. 228).

The following month, on July 16, 2002, the Alexandria grand
jury returned a superseding indictment which, in its last two pages,
augmented and strengthened the death penalty case against him
(Docket No. 340). Two days later, at a hearing concerning that
superseding indictment, Moussaoui said that previously he had tried
to plead no contest, "dictated by the fact that I am an affiliate of
Muhammad that I will not commit perjury." Now, on July 18, 2002,
he said: "I enter formally today a pure plea and affirmatively plea." In
other words, he said he was pleading guilty to the charges against him
(tr. July 18, 2002, page 64, lines 23–24). Brinkema gave him a week
to reconsider. Moussaoui also used the occasion to ask for a better
computer and more time for preparation in the case. The prosecutors
said they were sending him 70,000 pages of hard copy – from the
Minnesota and Oklahoma investigations – so that he would not have
to download the documents from a computer. Moussaoui's prediction
of the government's tactic was proving to be right. There was more
material than one person could manage. A computer presented
difficulties, particularly if it was given to him by the defense, whom
he still did not trust. Also, Moussaoui was convinced that the FBI
and the CIA had conducted electronic surveillance of him before
August 2001. Information gained from that surveillance might be
useful to him in court. He asked for confirmation of this surveillance.
The judge told the prosecution that she wanted an affidavit from
each agency involved, to affirm or deny that such surveillance had
happened (tr. July 18, 2002).

MOUSSAOUI TRIES TO PLEAD GUILTY

At the hearing the next week, on July 25, 2002, Judge Brinkema ruled
that Moussaoui was competent to plead guilty to the six charges.
Again, his mother was in court, this time with another Muslim
lawyer, Professor Sadiq Reza of New York Law School. In a hearing
that National Public Radio called "stormy," Moussaoui tried to plead
guilty to four counts, but the judge was not convinced he understood
the process. The judge said:

But what you will not be able to do during the penalty phase of this trial
is to come in and say that you were not – if I have found you guilty of the
offense, that you were not part of that conspiracy. Do you understand that?
That argument will not – it is not consistent with an adjudication of guilt.
(tr. July 25, 2002, page 37, lines 20–25)

Moussaoui replied: "That's, that's your, your interpretation" (tr. July
25, 2002, page 38, lines 1–2). The judge then said:

No, no, that's how the trial will be run. If you – you can argue a mitigating role. You can argue that ["]I was on the periphery of this conspiracy,["] but the jury will get this case with an explicit instruction from the Court that you have admitted being guilty of the conspiracy. (tr. page 38, lines 3–7)

The exchange between them continued. Here it is reproduced from the court transcript. The Defendant is Moussaoui, The Court is Judge Brinkema, and they are discussing the conspiracy charges:

THE DEFENDANT: Which one?
THE COURT: Count 1, 2, 3, 4, whatever counts we accept, or all four of them.
THE DEFENDANT: You, you will tell me where in the indictment it is alleged, at which in the indictment, which point in the indictment it's alleged that I even, I knew about September 11.
THE COURT: Well –
THE DEFENDANT: It's not even alleged.
THE COURT: We're going to move on to –
THE DEFENDANT: No, but this is not to be moved. This is essential, okay, in order people to understand my position, okay? I plead guilty to what is in the indictment. I cannot plead guilty to what the, the government is going to allege during trial, okay? Today I have been given a document, a precise document. I read it, and I say that according to Rule 11, I can truthfully say that I had, I had some guilt in the alleged fact who are in this document. (tr. July 25, pages 38, lines 8–25; page 39, line 1)

He went on to say that the government alleges that he worked in an al-Qaeda guest-house. He said he could accept this. The government alleged that he provided training; this he could also accept. There were many allegations he said he could accept, but "certain of them are not possible." None of this meant, he said, that he was on the plane. The judge responded:

I explained to you in the letter that was sent to you that the law of conspiracy basically punishes people who join in a common scheme or plan to do something the law forbids. Remember I explained that to you, that what a conspiracy is, it's an agreement between two or more people to do something which the law forbids. (tr. July 25, 2002, page 39, lines 11–16)

Moussaoui said that he did understand the conspiracy law, that: "it's an agreement between two or more people to carry on some action by legal or illegal mean, and the object of the action is, is illegal" (tr. July 25, 2002, page 39, lines 20–25). He said he could plead guilty to terrorist activity, to working in an al-Qaeda guest-house, to providing training.

This is all in the indictment, so I'm truthful. I don't cheat, I don't lie, I don't evade. I'm saying yes, I might at some time have engaged in this kind of thing, okay? But it doesn't mean that I'm on the plane. (tr. July 25, 2002, page 40, lines 3–6)

Moussaoui and Judge Brinkema seesawed over the meaning of his intentions to plead guilty. Moussaoui withdrew his pleas.

UNLAWYERLIKE BEHAVIOR

A hearing was held August 29, 2002, to decide, among other matters, whether Moussaoui objected to public hearings soon to be held by Congress's Joint Inquiry Investigative Committee, which was looking into the intelligence community's activities before 9/11. Hearings for that portion of the inquiry were to start in September 2002. This did not appear to be a problem for Moussaoui. But, he said:

I'm being used in this country as a scapegoat for the inefficiency of your government, and people want to look at it, and the government want to, to prevent them. That's what they are usually doing, the government, preventing people to know the truth. (tr. August 29, 2002, page 7, lines 10–14)

Judge Brinkema had a warning for him:

... you are, as I have said many times before, an obviously intelligent man, and you write very well, but I have to tell you that I am granting the government's motion to keep all of your pleadings under seal from here on out unless you tone down the rhetoric and simply address what the real issue is. (tr. August 29, 2002, page 34, lines 13–17)

She continued: "Your rhetoric about the United States, about jihad, about all this stuff, you've said it a million times, but you're wasting my time having to read those pages, your own time writing it ..." (tr. August 29, 2002, page 34, lines 23–25; page 35, line 1). She said that she would never permit an attorney to write the things in pleadings that he wrote. She told him he had damaged his case, and she would no longer permit him to do so. From then on his pleadings would remain under seal, meaning that the public would not be able to see them. "If you want your motions to be read by the public, you're going to have to write them in a proper manner" (tr. August 29, 2002, page 35, lines 8–15). Pleadings were to be written properly, in a lawyer-like manner, without editorial comments.

Given that Moussaoui was representing himself, Frank Dunham asked again that the defense lawyers be dismissed. The judge again ordered that they remain on standby, and they continued to work, not without considerable abuse from Moussaoui. Among other names, Moussaoui called Dunham a "Megalopig," Zerkin received abuse because he was a Jew, and Moussaoui called MacMahon a member of the KKK (see, for instance, Dunham, 2004).

THE RIGHT TO QUESTION WITNESSES

At the end of January 2003, Judge Brinkema ordered that an "enemy combatant," now detained, give testimony by satellite hookup from an undisclosed location, which testimony would be videotaped and played at trial. Ramzi bin al-Shibh, who had wired money from

Hamburg to Moussaoui and to Mohammed Atta, had been captured in September 2002, and Moussaoui had several times moved for access to him. The "enemy combatant" was most likely bin al-Shibh. The prosecution appealed her decision to the Fourth Circuit Court of Appeals in Richmond, Virginia. On February 12, 2003, Brinkema postponed the trial until the issue of access was resolved. In April the appeals court remanded the case – or sent it back to the district court – to see if a substitution could be made in lieu of the proposed videotaped testimony (see Docket No. 832). Judge Brinkema, however, rejected the government's proposed substitution, taken from military and intelligence reports, on the grounds that the material was unreliable. The government attempted to appeal this decision as well, but the Fourth Circuit dismissed this appeal because the question was of the sort routinely raised during litigation in a trial court, and thus was inappropriate for appellate review at that time (*United States v. Moussaoui*, 4th Cir. 333 F.3d 509, 517 [2003]).

By early March 2003, Khalid Sheikh Mohammed, often called the mastermind of the September 11 attacks, was captured in Pakistan, along with Mustafa al-Hawsawi. Mohammed in particular would be an important witness for Moussaoui, since Mohammed knew most of the details of 9/11. Al-Hawsawi had sent money to Ramzi bin al-Shibh and to some of the 19 hijackers, and therefore might have useful information for Moussaoui as well. The judge had rejected the government's proposed "substitution" for "Witness A," or Ramzi bin al-Shibh, and a stalemate arose when, on July 13, 2003, the Justice Department refused to let Moussaoui question that witness. On August 29, 2003, the judge ordered that Moussaoui have access to Witnesses B and C, presumably Khalid Sheikh Mohammed and Mustafa al-Hawsawi, directing the government to file proposed substitutions for their testimony, and for defense counsel to file a response to those substitutions. Both sides did so, but the judge rejected the government's substitutions on the same grounds as she had for Witness A. The government then told the judge that it would not follow the judge's August 29 order giving Moussaoui access to witnesses.

Both sides were told to prepare arguments as to what steps should be taken against the government. Both the government and the defense presented arguments that dismissal of the case could be an option, but on October 2, 2003, Brinkema barred the government from seeking the death penalty as a sanction for its blocking Moussaoui's access to the witnesses. Furthermore, she ruled that, since the government did not have to prove that Moussaoui was involved in 9/11 in order to get his conviction, and since these witnesses might prove that he had no involvement, she barred the government from presenting any argument or evidence concerning Moussaoui's involvement in

9/11. She also refused to let the government present to the jury what promised to be heart-rending details from the attacks of 9/11: airplane cockpit recordings, photos of 9/11 victims (which the government had been collecting since spring of 2002), and videotape of the collapse of the twin towers (see *United States v. Moussaoui*, 382 F.3d 453 [4th Cir. 2004]). The government appealed to the Fourth Circuit Court.

Senate Judiciary Committee Hearing

Congressional members signaled that they were taking notice of the proceedings. On October 21, 2003, Attorney General Ashcroft did not make an appearance at a US Senate Judiciary Committee hearing. This was not a rare occasion, according to the committee chair, Patrick Leahy, Democrat from Vermont, and he vented his spleen. The hearing was on "Protecting Our National Security from Terrorist Attacks: A Review of Criminal Terrorism Investigations and Prosecutions." Leahy commented on his irritation that Attorney General John Ashcroft was not present; in fact, Leahy said, Ashcroft had only been to one congressional hearing:

I expect the Attorney General to participate in these hearings, and I am disappointed that we will not be hearing from him today. Unlike other senior Administration officials who regularly participate in oversight hearings, Attorney General Ashcroft has appeared before this Committee only once this year, and then only for a short time. (Leahy, 2003)

Instead of Ashcroft, Christopher Wray, Assistant US Attorney and Chief of the Criminal Division at the Department of Justice, who had replaced Michael Chertoff in that position, appeared at the committee hearing. Wray told the Senate Judiciary Committee about the successes resulting from the Patriot Act. He listed the captures of al-Qaeda members and the money seized from charities aiding terrorist causes. Patrick Fitzgerald, US Attorney for Northern Illinois, and Paul McNulty, US Attorney for the Eastern District of Virginia, also spoke of how well prosecutions were going in the war on terror.

Patrick Leahy's statement further expressed his frustration:

I would like to hear about the progress in prosecuting Zacarias Moussaoui. I want to better understand why the Department [of Justice] so sharply criticized the Federal judge who instead imposed lesser sanctions for the Administration's refusal to follow the law and abide by court rulings. (Leahy, 2003)

SELF-REPRESENTATION REVOKED

Judge Brinkema finally ended Moussaoui's self-representation on November 14, 2003. Despite her warnings, he had persisted in submitting abusive briefs, insulting not only her but also his defense attorneys and most of the rest of the American court system and the press. The defense team was once again in control of the case.

On April 22, 2004, the Fourth Circuit Court of Appeals ruled that the death penalty was to be reinstated as a possible sentence. The court argued that the need for national security prevented the appearance of witnesses such as Khalid Sheikh Mohammed, but that Moussaoui's defense team would be able to use summaries, prepared by the government, of statements made by these witnesses (*United States v. Moussaoui*, 365 F.3d 292 [4th Cir. 2004]). The defense asked for a rehearing. In September 2004, the Fourth Circuit handed down its decision; the judges agreed with Judge Brinkema that Moussaoui should have access to statements from the witnesses, and agreed that the government's proposed substitutions had been inadequate. They found that all three witnesses had knowledge that could be beneficial to Moussaoui's case. As to Witness A, or Ramzi bin al-Shibh, although he believed that Moussaoui might have been involved in 9/11, "a witness's 'belief' is not admissible evidence," and they noted that he also provided exculpatory evidence for Moussaoui. Given the need for national security, "a substitution is an appropriate remedy when it will not materially disadvantage the defendant." Their statements could, with care, be crafted. The judge, the defense, and the government were to work together in doing so (see *United States v. Moussaoui*, 382 F.3d 453 [4th Cir. 2004]).

On January 10, 2005, Moussaoui's lawyers appealed to the US Supreme Court in a challenge to the Fourth Circuit Court of Appeal's decision that Moussaoui could be tried, and possibly be put to death, without the ability to question the potential al-Qaeda witnesses. On March 21, 2005, the Supreme Court refused to hear the appeal (*Moussaoui v. United States*, 161 L. Ed. 2d 496, 2005). The following month, Moussaoui decided to plead guilty to all the charges against him. Three years before, in July 2002, Moussaoui had attempted to enter guilty pleas to the charges against him, but then Judge Leonie Brinkema had ruled that he did not understand those charges. Now, she was assured that he did understand. She issued a court order on Wednesday, April 20, 2005, saying that for the reasons stated on record in a sealed (closed) hearing that day, she found that: "the defendant is fully competent to plead guilty to the indictment." She ordered that a change of plea (from not guilty to guilty) was to be held on Friday, April 22. Judging from his statements at the plea hearing, Moussaoui considered this to be a trial tactic which might get his case back before the Supreme Court. Randall Hamud, still identified as Moussaoui's mother's lawyer although Moussaoui himself had not seen him, said on Thursday, April 21, that the change of plea was "death by court," similar to "death by cop," because Moussaoui was being held in "odious" conditions. Hamud said that Moussaoui thought that by getting a jury trial, somehow proceedings would move more quickly for him (Hemmer, 2005).

MOUSSAOUI PLEADS GUILTY

On Friday, April 22, 2005, security at the Alexandria Federal District Court was extremely tight. Two dogs and their handlers patrolled the street outside the courthouse, sniffing people's briefcases and purses for explosive devices. People entering the courthouse passed through a nuclear materials detector positioned just outside the doors. Up on the seventh floor, Courtroom 700 was closed off until 1:30 p.m. Some people waited in the second floor cafeteria, drinking coffee and chatting. One of the family members, whose father and step-mother had died on Flight 93 in Pennsylvania, said he was there "to see raw evil." "I just want to see him face-on," said Arnold Ostrolenk, a retired dentist from Alexandria (McCrummen, 2005). The press was there, the sound trucks had pulled up, the cameras were positioned across the closed street from the courthouse. At precisely 1:30 p.m. the guards let people take the elevators up from the second floor. The lawyers, press, family members of 9/11 victims, and the curious began to file in, again passing through another security checkpoint. IDs were checked, briefcases were x-rayed, people walked through metal detectors, men pulled their pant legs up to show that they had nothing hidden in their socks. At exactly 3:30 p.m. Judge Brinkema and Zacarias Moussaoui both entered the courtroom. Proceedings began. Judge Brinkema said to Moussaoui:

"You understand that all answers to this court's questions must be truthful?"
"It is understood."
"You are aware that the first four counts essentially expose you to the possibility of a death sentence . . . ?" Brinkema asked.
"Yes, I read the document."
"Now, you do understand that you have the right to plead not guilty ... ?" the judge asked.
"I do understand that," Moussaoui said.

Each of the six charges was read to him, and the judge asked how he pleaded. "Guilty," he said, to each count: "Guilty" to conspiracy to commit acts of terrorism transcending national boundaries, "Guilty" to conspiracy to commit aircraft piracy, "Guilty" to conspiracy to destroy aircraft, "Guilty" to conspiracy to use weapons of mass destruction, "Guilty" to conspiracy to murder United States employees, and "Guilty" to conspiracy to destroy property (McCrummen, 2005).

Assistant US Attorney Robert Spencer said that Moussaoui should be made to pay restitution to the September 11 victims' families.

When the judge told Moussaoui he might have to pay a $250,000 fine, he said: "I wonder where I will get the money." The government prosecutors had written a statement of facts, laying out the claims against him they expected to prove. "Finally I get a pen," Moussaoui said. He stood to read it, and then asked to sit down. Moussaoui signed his name "20th Hijacker," and underneath, he wrote "Zacarias Moussaoui," "a/k/a Abu Kaled Al Sahrawi," "a/k/a Shaquil" (tr. April 22, 2005 [Defense Exhibit 954]; Docket No. 1264; CourtTV, 2005).

The US Department of Justice had its first, and only, guilty plea in the attacks of September 11, 2001. Four years after Moussaoui had been indicted with the conspiracy charges, he pleaded guilty to them all. Alberto Gonzales, who had replaced John Ashcroft as US Attorney General, made a statement congratulating the government lawyers for successfully convicting Moussaoui (Gonzales, 2005a).

The next step was to determine whether Moussaoui received the death penalty or life in prison without the possibility of release. That summer, Moussaoui's defense team moved to have the death penalty struck from count one (conspiracy to commit acts of terrorism that transcend national boundaries) and count two (conspiracy to commit air piracy) (Docket No. 1314). Three days before jury selection was to begin, Judge Brinkema issued an opinion and an order striking the death penalty from count two, but not from count one. Moussaoui could still face the death penalty on counts one, three, and four (Docket No. 1508 and 1509).

In October 2005, Moussaoui's lawyers moved to have the trial proceed in separate phases. Death penalty trials are usually bifurcated into two phases. In phase one, sometimes called the "guilt phase," the jury determines whether the defendant is guilty or innocent. In phase two, the jury determines the penalty. In this case, Moussaoui had already pleaded guilty, removing the need for a guilt phase to determine his guilt or innocence. The problem was how to present in a balanced manner the aggravating and mitigating evidence required in federal death penalty trials. The defense, by submitting a "motion *in limine*," argued that they thought the government would be able to use evidence that would only serve to inflame the jury's emotions in making their decision. His lawyers argued that the trial should proceed in separate hearings. There should be a hearing on the threshold factor, to determine Moussaoui's mental state (whether he contemplated that death would result from his actions). Then, they said, there should be separate hearings, on statutory aggravating factors, and for determination of the actual sentence (Docket No. 1377).

The government agreed that the trial could be split, or bifurcated, into an eligibility phase and a phase that would allow for presentation of the aggravating factors (Docket No. 1346). The judge heard the two sides' arguments and granted the defense's request to have a separate threshold hearing, limited to finding whether Moussaoui: "'intentionally participated in an act (lying to agents about his knowledge of September 11), contemplating that the life of a person would be taken or intending that lethal force would be used with a person, other than one of the participants in the offense, and the victim died as a direct result of the act,' in violation of 18 U.S.C.§ 3591 (a) (2) (C)" (Docket No. 1372).

In that first phase, the jury would only decide whether he was eligible to receive the death penalty. In the second phase, the jurors would hear testimony from the government witnesses and victims concerning what would be termed aggravating factors, the factors that could lead to imposition of the death penalty. The defense could introduce evidence which could "mitigate" that penalty, or in which they could argue that there are reasons why the jury should not impose the death penalty.

Jury selection was set to begin on February 6, 2006. The level of investigation and collection of evidence intensified. The press became part of the effort as interviews were published and articles written. Patrick Baudouin (2006), a human rights lawyer in Paris who worked closely with Moussaoui's mother, published an article in *Le Monde Diplomatique*. Moussaoui's mother was interviewed many times over. The French government was surprisingly silent on his case, and Moussaoui's mother, and Baudouin, commented on this several times through the coming trial. Alberto Gonzales, the US Attorney General, gave a speech to the Council on Foreign Relations in New York in which he highlighted the successes of the Department of Justice, and underscored the continuing dangers from al-Qaeda.

Another important tool we have in the fight against terrorists is our criminal justice system. Many of the Department's prosecutorial efforts are familiar to you. There was Zacarias Moussaoui, who admitted his role in a plot to crash airplanes into prominent buildings in the United States. (Gonzales, 2005b)

But, he went on, new investigations and prosecutions are continuing. We are safe, but not safe enough, he said.

The media attention to the Moussaoui case was going to be intense, and the world was watching. Lawyers, investigators, and staff for both the defense and the government had spread out across the United States, Great Britain, and France, and beyond, gathering information. The defense arranged a number of witnesses, including a social worker and mental health experts. Videotaped interviews were conducted with Moussaoui's two sisters, several friends, and his former imam in London. The government was also lining up witnesses: there were to be agents and supervisors from the FBI, personnel from the Federal Aviation Administration (FAA), Western

Union, American Telephone and Telegraph (ATT), flight school managers and instructors, a psychiatrist, people who survived the 9/11 attacks, and family members of those who did not survive. Both sides reached out to the families of the victims. Since a 1991 Supreme Court decision, victim impact testimony is now permissible in federal death penalty cases. The "victim impact project" involved thousands of family members, and David Novak and others had already spent hours interviewing, and consoling, them. Some family members contacted the prosecutors to ask to be witnesses, other family members contacted the defense, depending on their feelings about what should happen to Moussaoui. Moussaoui, however, was placing his fate in the hands of Allah. His zabib, or prayer callus on his forehead, was growing more noticeable.

2 SLAVE OF ALLAH: ZACARIAS MOUSSAOUI'S STRUGGLE TO REPRESENT HIMSELF

Ne t'inquiète pas, ils vont essayer de fabriquer des preuves et des témoins mais moi j'ai des vraies preuves et témoins et Allah, in Shah Allah, ridiculisera leur complot. ["Don't worry, they are going to try to fabricate the truth and the witnesses but I have the real proof and witnesses, and Allah will make their plot look ridiculous."] (Zacarias Moussaoui, letter to his mother, October 2001 in Chambon, 2001)

I am learning the hard way that every word count [sic] in this life. (*United States v. Moussaoui*, Docket No. 272, July 3, 2002)

JIHAD IN THE COURTROOM

Moussaoui's arrest and detention transformed his jihad against America, but did not stop it. He could no longer wage war in a physical sense. Instead he would wage a war of words in court. The problem for Moussaoui was that courtroom procedure, and the conditions under which he was held, limited his war of words. His defense lawyers were supposed to speak for him. This was repugnant to Moussaoui for a number of reasons. First, in December 2001, he was assigned defense counsel without his permission. Second, those lawyers were not Muslim; even worse, Gerald Zerkin was Jewish. Third, he wanted a chance to speak for himself. The Special Administrative Measures (SAM) under which he was confined meant that he could not make statements from the detention center. No reporters could interview him. Communication with the world outside the detention center was impossible. The courtroom was the one place where he could speak. Representing himself would allow him to say what he wanted to say.

On April 22, 2002, Moussaoui moved to represent himself and to waive counsel (Docket No. 112). District Judge Brinkema granted that request on June 13, 2002, but kept his lawyers on as standby counsel. He represented himself until November 14, 2003, when the judge vacated that request. His standby counsel was now Moussaoui's counsel of record. Nevertheless, for 17 months he had said and written some extraordinary things. His pleadings, and later testimony, were not designed to ensure his release nor even to save his life. They did, however, provide a way to understand his thought processes, as odd as they may have appeared to the press. Whenever given an opportunity, he spoke and wrote of his contempt for America, for the American justice system, for his lawyers, and later, for the victims of 9/11 and their family members. But this was part of his jihad. Against the advice of his lawyers, he insisted that he be able to testify during his trial, and he did so twice. When he was on the witness stand, he said:

I have been fighting. I thought my understanding about the fight that was whether or not you can put me to death, that's another matter, okay? I fight because this is jihad, okay? And I'm not concerned with the death penalty because I don't believe that you have or the government or this 12 juror or 18 juror will have more say in my death than anybody else sitting there. (tr. March 27, 2006, page 2381, lines 13–19)

His defense attorney Gerald Zerkin then asked Moussaoui: "As you sit here now, have you given up jihad?" Moussaoui replied: "Never" (tr. March 27, 2006, page 2382, lines 17–18).

He was speaking not only to the judge, the lawyers, and jury. He was speaking to the rest of the world, in particular to the Muslim world. He made clear that he knew he was doing this:

I knew that my pleadings were being put on the Internet. You have a war of propaganda to say that I'm crazy on this. I carry on my war of propaganda. You might not understand it, I know that some people Muslim around the world have read my pleadings and have been probably motivated or happy to see that I don't give in. I fight on. (tr. March 27, 2006, page 2378, lines 19–24)

What can we learn about this jihad, and about Moussaoui? Moussaoui's self-representation in a legal sense allowed him to represent himself in a social and personal sense. That self-representation allowed him to represent himself as part of the Muslim community, the ummah, in particular the jihadi part of the ummah. Representing himself opened the door for the Western press to label him as someone in search of martyrdom, or crazy. Why else would he write pleadings such as the ones he wrote? Why else would he not submit to the American judicial system? Understanding his motives, and what his messages were, is not a trivial pursuit. One can look beyond his anger at his isolation and the system of justice that was keeping him there, to see how he interpreted the power and, to his mind, the unfairness, of an America that was holding a slave of Allah in a court that he would defy every chance he got.

REPRESENTATION

The word "representation" often indicates something that stands for something else, as with a metaphor, or to present oneself to others in some way. "Representation" or "representations" are here defined as the interconnected ways in which humans understand, explain, and go about living in the world (see Searle, 1995: 150–51). Similar to conceptions of "culture," which also see human beliefs and actions as interconnected – the "holistic" view – "representation" includes ways in which humans use language, meaning, and metaphor. How one represents oneself indicates the interconnected ways in which that person makes sense of her or his world. Through representation one constructs and exhibits a conceptual reality for him or herself. Language is only one of the ways in which representation occurs. Body language, clothing, preferred foods, daily rituals, dance, all those things an anthropologist calls "culture," are also representations.

The Zacarias Moussaoui case provides a window on the way in which he used language to create representations. This is about all we have, because access to him is so limited. There can be no interviews. The attorney–client privilege keeps information-gathering at bay. Moussaoui's writings, his comments in court, and his testimony during trial provide evidence for how he represented himself during the four and a half years of the proceedings against him. To that end, the term "representation" is used in three ways: first, Moussaoui's legal self-representation in the court system; second, Moussaoui's representation as part of a social system, in which he drew on his identity in a religiously based social community (Islam), and in which he is himself given an identity by a different social community (the US Department of Justice and the media; in this different community, he was identified as an "enemy combatant"); and third, his representation in terms of his own personal identity, the self that he created after leaving his family and education in France. The focus here is primarily the period during which he "represented" himself, in other words, the period when he was serving as his own lawyer. But there were other, earlier parts of his life when he faced what could be called a crisis of representation, when he had to rethink who he was and what he wanted to become.

Crisis of Representation

The term "crisis of representation" here refers to points in Moussaoui's life which led to a break or rupture with his former life, in which he was forced to create a different representation. Such crises create turning points that lead a person to represent him or herself in a different way from the previous life. These various references have important, underlying, philosophical and semiotic underpinnings which enable the construction of social reality. By understanding these representations, one can understand the important relationships between language and power (Bourdieu 1990a, 1991, 1998a). By looking at a person's particular use of language, and the settings and circumstances in which that language is used, one can glimpse that person's construction of social reality. Moussaoui's life story, revealed quite fully during the course of the trial, demonstrates a series of crises of representation. Several of his friends and family members noted that he felt "blocked" or "stuck," when he was in France and again when he was in London (see Moussaoui, 2003: 87; Plant, 2005). In each instance, he chose another way to create his social reality, another way to represent himself. In the discussion that follows, the 17 months in which he represented himself illustrates the way in which Moussaoui used language to present himself not only to the federal district court but also to the world through the court's website and through the press. Faced with the death penalty, Moussaoui insisted on presenting himself as he wanted to be seen in the Muslim world.

LEGAL REPRESENTATION

In the legal sense of the term "representation," Moussaoui had the right to representation by legal counsel in United States courts (*Gideon v. Wainwright*, 372 U.S. 335, 1963). Legal representation included his right to represent himself in court, and to refuse legal counsel (*Faretta v. California*, 422 U.S. 806, 1975). On April 22, 2002, Moussaoui wrote:

I, Slave of Allah, Zacarias Moussaoui, having been prevented for a long time, to mount an effective defense by overly restrictive and oppressive condition of confinement, take the control of my defense by entering a Pro Se Defense (self representation) in order to mount an effective defense of the life that ALLAH the Most Merciful has given to me.
I, Slave of ALLAH, Zacarias Moussaoui, reject completely the imposition of the US, so called appointed lawyers ... (Docket No. 112)

He was not beyond some measure of politeness. On the back of the last page he wrote: "Not being sure if I gave you this letter that I read to the court on 22/04 here is the original. (Could you send it back) Thank you" (Docket No. 112).

By the end, there were over 270 hand-written pleadings by Moussaoui, which initially resembled court pleadings that an American lawyer might submit. Over time, his frustration with the power of the court, with the American justice system, and with his inability to connect with the outside world, led to increasingly vituperative pleadings. His invective was transferred from the FBI and John Ashcroft to Judge Brinkema.

Why Represent Himself?

There is a common saying in the legal profession that someone who represents himself has a fool for a client. Criminal defendants who choose to represent themselves make court systems wary. Trial lawyers generally, and public defenders in particular, are suspicious of self-representation, not only because these lawyers make a career of representing defendants, but also because they know the deadly pitfalls in court procedure and trial tactics that lie ahead. A petition filed in the US Supreme Court revealed the level of that concern. In the case of *Egwaoje v. US*, No. 03-691, Egwaoje petitioned for a writ of certiorari, i.e. he asked the Supreme Court to review his case. In his filing Egwaoje contended that allowing self-representation would "undermine confidence in the criminal justice system," and he cited the prosecution of Zacarias Moussaoui "as an example of self-representation run amok" (*Egwaoje v. US*, No. 03-691).[1]

Even when in detention in New York, Moussaoui had asked to defend himself, or to be assigned a Muslim lawyer. Both requests were denied. Once moved to Alexandria, on April 22, 2002, Moussaoui moved for permission to represent himself and to waive counsel (Docket No. 112). District Judge Brinkema allowed him to do so until November 14, 2003, when she moved to stop him from representing himself in court. She had had enough. She declared that Moussaoui used "contemptuous language that would never be tolerated from an attorney and will no longer be tolerated from this defendant" (Docket No. 1120). Until Judge Brinkema's decision to deny him self-representation, his hand-written pleadings were available to the public through the District Court's website. After that date, if they were posted, they were "under seal," meaning that they were not available to the public, although the title or topic was posted.

Moussaoui went through most of the proceedings without talking with his defense counsel (see Dunham, 2004). After his right to self-representation was removed, the defense counsel's role was to represent him in court, not only in District Court in Alexandria, VA, but also in appeals to the Fourth Circuit Court of Appeals in Richmond, VA. They also asked for the US Supreme Court to review (a "writ of certiorari") a decision by the Fourth Circuit Court of Appeals (that the death penalty could be applied when the defendant cannot directly interview witnesses). The US Supreme Court denied the review. In April 2005 Moussaoui asked, in a motion signed "ak/47 Zacarias Moussaoui," to have two members of his defense counsel, Frank Dunham and Edward MacMahon, removed from his case

(Docket No. 1277). Unfortunately, Dunham did remove himself from the case because of illness.

From the point of view of a defendant, self-representation can have advantages. Despite what appeared to be erratic behavior, and despite refusing advice from his defense counsel, Moussaoui managed to focus media attention on himself and on the inconsistencies of the government's case against him (e.g. Hersh, 2002; Novak, 2003; Guy Taylor, 2005). Granted, his hand-written pleadings, or "motions," were full of abuse of District Judge ("Dirty Joke" and "Death Judge") Brinkema, of Federal Public Defender Frank Dunham ("Fat Megalo Dunham") (Docket No. 847), of his defense counsel generally (they were the "Death Squad" and the "bunch of blood suckers") (Docket No. 772). Attorney General Ashcroft, who announced the indictment against him, was the "WTC," or "World Top Criminal" (Dunham, 2004; Docket No. 847). In other pleadings, Leonie Brinkema was "Lie-onie Brinkema," the US Fourth Circuit Court of Appeals was the "United States Court of Appall for the Ultimate Circus," the US Department of Justice was the "U.S. Sickness of Justice," the FBI was the "Fascist Bureau of Inquisition," and, finally, the United States was the "United Sodom of America" (Dunham, 2004; Docket No. 796, 803).

There was one attorney who met with Moussaoui's approval, and this attorney's failure to qualify with the court tells of the effectiveness of Moussaoui's own self-representation.

Charles Freeman, a Muslim lawyer and member of the Texas bar, refused to apply for standing as an attorney in the federal courts of Virginia. A lawyer must apply to practice in the court in which he or she tries a case. Freeman would not do so. The Fourth Circuit Court of Appeals considered whether Freeman should be allowed to represent Moussaoui, or to act as "out-of-court advisory counsel." The government argued that Freeman should not be allowed to do so because, among other reasons: "Moussaoui has proved himself very capable of filing pleadings on his own behalf" (*United States v. Moussaoui*, Fourth Circuit Court of Appeals No. 02-4571, Opposition to Petition). Judge Brinkema also saw Moussaoui as an effective advocate for himself. On April 22, 2005, while she was accepting his guilty pleas, the judge said: "Mr. Moussaoui is an extremely intelligent man. He has actually a better understanding of the legal system than some lawyers I've seen in court" (tr. April 22, 2005, page 23, lines 10–12). In short, through insisting on self-representation, Moussaoui had achieved recognition from both the judge and the prosecution for effective self-advocacy, even in the face of his surface representation as unstable, abusive, and erratic.

SOCIAL REPRESENTATION: NATIONALITY AND RELIGION

In this section, I explore the various ways in which Moussaoui has represented himself as a social being, as part of a society, whether it is through legal standing as a French citizen, or ethnically as a Moroccan, or in the religious sense, as a Muslim, and the ways in which those various entities have treated him. These representations have also gone through some crises, or turning points, particularly when, as a young teenager, he learned that he was not exactly considered to be French, slightly later when he met his Moroccan cousins, and again as a young adult, when he was increasingly drawn to Islam. What follows here is a brief discussion of his youth in France.

Moussaoui was born in St. Jean-de-Luz, France, on May 30, 1968. His parents had migrated to France from Morocco. They divorced three years later. According to Moussaoui's brother's memoir (Moussaoui, 2003), Aïcha el-Wafi, Zacarias's mother, took the four children north to the Dordogne, where they lived for a while in an orphanage. They then lived with their mother in Mulhouse, in north-eastern France. When Zacarias was 12, they moved to Narbonne, in the south. They had only occasional contact with their father (Beaud and Masclet, 2002: 164). During the time in Mulhouse, Zacarias became very proficient in handball, and dreamed of becoming a coach. The move to Narbonne disrupted that dream. According to Moussaoui's brother, life was happy in Mulhouse, but life after the move to the south of France was not. Students in Narbonne were quick to pick up on Zacarias's differences in ethnicity (Moroccan), in accent (he had acquired a northern French accent), and religion (he was a Muslim, though not a practicing one, in a predominantly Christian school system). Food avoidances were openly mocked by the school cafeteria personnel (Moussaoui, 2003). Nevertheless, the situation for Moussaoui was not so different from that of many other immigrants to a new country, and the French educational system did give him opportunities, in the form of scholarships to high school and university. While in Narbonne, Zacarias had a French girlfriend. They went to parties and discos, and entered dance contests together. Zacarias and his brother Abd Samad both received their baccalaureates, and Zacarias passed his entrance exams for the technical and commercial advanced vocational diploma in Perpignan, where he decided to study mechanical and electrical engineering (Beaud and Masclet, 2002; Moussaoui, 2003).

A Moroccan cousin, Fouzia, came to stay with the family, who remarked how French the Moussaouis had become. She discussed with the brothers the proper way of dressing as a modest Moroccan woman, and talked about Islam with them. Zacarias apparently listened. While studying in Perpignan, he spent increasing amounts of time with practicing Muslims from West and North Africa. In London, while working on his master's degree in international business, he began attending mosques in Brixton and in Finsbury Park, where he attended the speeches of Abu Hamza al-Masri, a fiery Egyptian who was later removed from the mosque by the London police. Moussaoui briefly returned home with a beard and robes, and then disappeared. Abd Samad married Fouzia, his first cousin. He began attending a mosque in Montpellier. He now teaches in the French educational system (Beaud and Masclet, 2002; Moussaoui, 2003).

So, what led Zacarias Moussaoui to the mosques of London, to Chechnya, Afghanistan, and, later, Malaysia? What led him to train with al-Qaeda, to attend flight schools in Oklahoma and Minnesota, and, ultimately, to a Supermax prison in Colorado? These questions are especially interesting when one considers the quite different choices made by his brother.

These different views of the world and the ways in which life should be lived are what Searle refers to as "conceptual relativity." There can indeed be different ways of representing the same reality (Searle, 1995: 151). These various conceptual schemes can be influenced, or determined, by any number of sociocultural factors. For Moussaoui, the transition from one to another happened several times, and it is on the border between social and personal representations of conceptual schemes that insights into one's self can be found. His shifting representation of himself was apparent, for example, in his taking of new Arabic names to represent his oath of *bayat*, or fealty to al-Qaeda and Osama bin Laden. In court he said that Shaquil is "my name in … the western world," while Abu Khaled al Sahrawi is "my war name, my jihad name" (tr. April 22, 2005, page 4, lines 11–13). Renaming to represent oneself as a slave of Allah is common among young converts to fundamental Islam. These transitions indicate not only the fluidity of selfhood but also the difficulty of knowing just who one is at various points in time.

The Many Names of Zacarias Moussaoui

Viveca Novak, in an article in *Time* titled "How the Moussaoui Case Crumbled," reported that when Moussaoui heard in April 2003

… that the government, in a closed hearing, had presented a new theory of his role in 9/11 – that he was meant to pilot a fifth plane into the White House in a separate attack – he called on Brinkema to send Ashcroft a multiple-choice question asking how he saw Moussaoui. "Death Judge you must force Ashcroft to tick the box," he scrawled. Each choice had a blank box next to it: "20th Hijacker," "5th Plane to Dark House," "I, Ashcroft don't know" and "Lets just kill ZM." (Novak, 2003)

Moussaoui used at least five names when referring to himself. In his hand-written pleadings and in court he was, alternatively "Zacarias Moussaoui," "Slave of Allah," "Shaqil," "al Sahrawi," and "Abu Khaled al Sahrawi." He said, when testifying on March 27, 2006 (tr. page 2318, lines 9–13), that he also used the names "Abdullah" when he was in Jalalabad, Afghanistan, and on occasion "Yousuf." He signed his pleadings with names such as "20th hijacker" and "AK/47." This variety of names seems odd, problematic, and disjointed. Why would he use so many names? What can be learned from his choices of names? Does that variety of choice indicate mental instability, or is something else at work here?

Moussaoui was not alone in using multiple names. The list of 14 high-level al-Qaeda detainees, or "alien enemy combatants" transferred to Guantanamo Bay, Cuba, in late summer 2006 showed that some of them had used as many as six or seven different names (*Washington Post*, 2006). The FBI and CIA call these names "aliases," and have found it difficult to identify the "real name" of each captured al-Qaeda member. Some of these names were used to disguise their real identities, while other names reveal identities, as I will explain below. Not all the names were chosen as aliases, but names can and do accrue.

A review of the names used by Moussaoui reveals patterns common to the naming practices found in Islam. There is a system of using given names, last names, and acquired names, all of which have some similarities to, and some differences from, the Western system of naming. In order to understand these practices it helps to think first about naming practices in Europe and North America. In the West, people may have as many as three or four different names. They have: first, or personal, names, sometimes referred to as the given name; last, or family names; and sometimes middle names and nicknames. The first, or personal, name often appears to be freely chosen. The name is occasionally the same as that of a past or present relative, or is chosen because the name is liked. While first name choices in Western societies appear to be limitless, in practice the popularity of first names changes with the times. In English-speaking countries Michaels and Jennifers have replaced Roberts and Dorothys in popularity. In some countries, such as France, first names have often been saint's names, and the birth registry has been known to ensure some degree of conformity, although North and West Africans are able to give their children Arabic and African names. In much of the West the last name is often but not always the last name of the father (the "patronymic"), or the mother ("metronymic," sometimes called the "matronymic"). Middle names are either last names or a chosen name. In the West people also acquire nicknames. Nicknames are sometimes shortened versions of their given names, often of their first name. Stephen becomes Steve. Elizabeth becomes Liz or Beth or Betty. MacIntyre becomes Mac. Occasionally nicknames indicate a physical characteristic, such as Shorty or Slim or Red. Nicknames are sometimes acquired later in life.

There is a wide range of naming practices in Muslim societies, and it is difficult to make generalizations about them. However, the work of Eickelman (1977, 2002) on Middle Eastern practices, Geertz (1979) on Moroccan naming in particular, and Bulliet (1978) and Sublet (1991) are helpful. The primary practices include the choices of personal, or first, names (in Arabic, *ism*), nicknames (*laqab*), names of occupation or origin (*nisba*), teknonyms (sometimes referred to as *kunya*), patrifiliative names (*nasab*), and "family" names (also referred to as *kunya*). The word *kunya* is also used by the Western press to mean war name, or *nom de guerre*, and that concept includes the use of nicknames, names of origin, teknonyms, patrifiliative names, and "family" names.

In Islam, personal names are frequently chosen from a particular set of possibilities. Islam is an overarching theme in name choice.[2] Personal, or first, names reflect four important Muslim concepts such as a close relationship to Allah; the names of Mohammed, his family, and his companions; the names of prophets, of saints, or pious people; and the names of desirable qualities. In the first instance, the name may be drawn from one of the 99 names of Allah. These names may be a variant on the concept of *abd* meaning "servant or slave of" one of those names or qualities of Allah. Abdullah is "the slave of Allah." Moussaoui said in testimony that he used the name Abdullah in Afghanistan, particularly when he knew no one (tr. March 27, 2006, page 2318, lines 9–13). Abd Samad, the name of Moussaoui's brother, means "slave of the eternal" or of the "absolute." Second, the names of the Prophet Mohammed, and his family members, and companions are not only given by parents but are often chosen later in life, particularly when that name connotes an historical event in the history of Islam. Geertz, working in Morocco, found that in a sample of 982 male names, 156 were "Mohammed" (1979: 342). Ali, the Prophet's son-in-law, is also popular. Moussaoui's mother's name, Aïcha, was the name of one of the Prophet's wives. Third, the name may come from the Koran or the Old Testament (Yusuf for Joseph, Maryam for Mary). Moussaoui's own first name, Zacarias, was that of an Old Testament prophet. This name was given to him by his family, at birth. Fourth, a personal name may indicate a desirable quality, such as hope, in Arabic, "Amal."

Nicknames (*laqab*-s) draw on features which represent something about the person. They are given to a person, and can be either positive or negative in connotation. Nicknames are often given to a young child, even several weeks after birth, at an official ceremony.

Nicknames can be acquired later in life, and there may be a ceremony associated with that event as well. Nicknames have been chosen by jihadis when out in the battlefield. Moussaoui's friend Xavier Djaffo was given the name Masood or "happy," which his friends reported as an attribute when in France. At some point Moussaoui received the name Shaqil, or "handsome." He used that name in Oklahoma; his roommate Hussein al-Attas claimed when he was first detained that Shaqil was the only name he knew for Moussaoui. Moussaoui said in his testimony that Shaqil was his name in the West, but that it was a new name, used only within the last year or two (tr. July 25, 2002, page 17, lines 17–20).

Names of occupation or origin (*nisba*) are given when a person is out of his or her own geographic area. In Morocco, such names were given to people who had arrived from elsewhere in Morocco, or from a particular city. In the newer context of jihad, people arrive from throughout the Muslim world to fight in Bosnia or Chechnya or Afghanistan, or now Iraq. Geographic names of origin are frequently used. The now-dead leader of al-Qaeda in Iraq, al-Zarqawi, was from the Jordanian town of Zarqa. Moussaoui's friend Xavier Djaffo became not only Masood, but also chose the name al-Benin in preference to the name al-Francee, his country of birth, or al-Britani, his place of most recent residence. Djaffo's father was from Benin; this became Djaffo's last name. While fighting in Chechnya, he was known as Masood al-Benin. Moussaoui used the name al Sahrawi, a name representing the fact that his father was from southern Morocco, at the edge of the Sahara. In court, he said that it was the name of his father's tribe. Moussaoui did not choose a name which denotes Morocco as a whole, nor the name for the west of North Africa, the Maghreb, or al-Maghrebi. The latter was not uncommon for jihadis from Algeria and Morocco, much as al-Masri, for Egypt, has been used by jihadis of Egyptian origin. His choice of name may have included a political statement, since the Sahrawi are also people dislocated from the contested territory of Western Sahara, living in refugee camps in Algeria and Morocco. Abu Khaled al Sahrawi is the name he used as a signature in many of his hand-written pleadings.

The teknonym (the word comes from the Greek for child, *teknon*) refers to a name associating a person with the name of his or her child. This is often referred to as the *kunya* (e.g. Schimmel, 1989). In Arabic, *abu* is "father"; Abu Ali is "father of Ali." Mother is *umm*, and Umm Ali is "mother of Ali." Moussaoui has had no children, but, according to him, he wanted to indicate the possibility: in court documents he used – and the court accommodated him – the name Abu Khaled al Sahrawi, or father of Khaled al Sahrawi. The teknonym is a term of honor, an honorific.

The concept of patrifiliation (*nasab*) is a means of indicating a chain of generations. In Arabic, *ibn* means "son." A person could be called Ali ibn Abdullah ibn Mohammed, or "Ali, son of Abdullah, son of Mohammed." Moussaoui referred to himself occasionally in court documents as "ibn Omar," son of Omar, who is his father.

Eickelman (1977, 2002) uses the term *kunya* for family names which the Moroccan government made obligatory in the 1950s. Hermansen (2004) equates *kunya* with the patronymic (as in "son of"). Others use the term in the sense of the teknonym ("father of").

The concept of the *nom de guerre*, a war name chosen to hide identity, is not new, but Palestinian rebels created such war names using the concept of the teknonym. On occasion the name is not the soldier's real child's first name but instead a symbolic term. Yasser Arafat was Abu Ammar, drawn from the name of Ammar ibn Yasser, a companion of the Prophet. Abu Nidal, another Palestinian leader, was "father of the struggle." The name by which al-Zarqawi was known in Iraq was based on geographic origin, the *nisba*. He was often referred to as Abu Musab al-Zarqawi, father of Musab, from Zarqa. Similarly, Moussaoui used al Sahrawi as a war name. He claimed that he used it when making satellite telephone calls from Kandahar, Afghanistan, and from London to Chechnya. Alternatively he was Abu Khaled al Sahrawi, father of Khaled, from the Sahara.

Lawrence Wright describes one use of these names. According to a controversial *hadith* – a story or tradition – widely discussed on the internet, the Mahdi, the leader in the end-times, will come out of Khorasan or present-day Iran, Afghanistan, and Central Asia, accompanied by soldiers carrying black flags. These soldiers will bear names from the cities and geographic areas of their origin. Wright suggests that al-Qaeda and jihadi belief systems place their own soldiers in those roles, recreating the prophecy (2006: 233). These *noms de guerre* change as the field of battle changes, and as people acquire new roles and levels of command. Khalid Sheikh Mohammed had several dozen names attributed to him and was also known as Mukhtar, meaning "head" or "chief." Understanding these names and name changes can lead to significant information about changing roles and emerging statuses among al-Qaeda members and their associates. For Moussaoui, they were names that continued to be important when he was in detention, and he used them to represent who he was.

PERSONAL REPRESENTATION

Slave of Allah

When asked his religion by Clancy Prevost, the flight instructor at the Pan Am Flight Academy, Moussaoui is reported to have replied:

"I am nothing" (Hersh, 2002). He was, one might argue, metaphorically nothing, having submitted his will as a slave to Allah. In his
hand-written pleadings, written from 2002 to November 2003,
Zacarias Moussaoui frequently referred to himself, in English, as
"Slave of Allah." He continued to sign himself in English as "Slave
of Allah" and "Abu Khaled al Sahrawi" in Arabic script, from April
2002 through August 2003 (see Docket No. 1024). Gradually, the
term "20th hijacker" took over, but even with his later pleading,
written on April 22, 2005, he used the term "Slave of Allah" five
times (Docket No. 112).

The word "slave" has such charged meaning in the West that it
is difficult to see beyond it to its meaning in Islam. The word *'abd*
in Arabic is translated as "servant" or "slave" in English. Talal Asad
(1993) and John Esposito (2003) both translate the word *'abd* as
"slave," while others translate it as "servant." Asad argues that:

> by employing the metaphor of slavery to describe the human relation to
> God, the Islamic rhetorical tradition stands in powerful contrast both to the
> figure of kinship (God as Father) and the figure of contract (the covenant with
> God), which are part of Judeo-Christian discourse. As God's slaves, humans
> do not share any essence with their owner, who is also their creator, nor can
> they ever invoke an original agreement with him. The relationship requires
> unconditional obedience. (1993: 221–22)

This obedience is also difficult for secular Westerners to understand.
In fact, disobedience is permitted or at least understood to be part of
human development in the West. It is perhaps easier to understand
being a slave of love, or of chocolate than being a slave of Allah. To
call oneself a slave of Allah hints at things Westerners, often wrongly,
think they know about Islam. This person must have no mind of her
own. Why can't she think for herself? And how could one possibly
be a slave of God? Aren't responsible believers supposed to think
about the sources of religious authority? What is the role of free will?
Where is the individual who is a thinking self?

For eight years I have done an informal survey in a course on
anthropology of religion which I teach. Students with regularity
report that they are not currently practicing the religion in which they
grew up. Many report practicing no religion at all. Their responses
imply that, now they are in college, they are thinking for themselves
and have left their parents' religious beliefs behind. It must be said
that these are students at a university with no religious affiliation
in the north-east of the United States. If students wanted to have
a religious education, or at least an environment in which religion
was regularly practiced, this would not be the place of choice. These
university students are in a place where new ideas and personas are
tried on, to see if they fit.

Zacarias Moussaoui's experience in his 20s was not much different. There is no evidence that he practiced Islam when he was growing up in France. The French concept of secularism, or *laïcité*, ensures the separation of Church and state in its educational institutions. According to both Moussaoui's mother and his brother, religion was not discussed nor practiced in the Moussaoui household. The boys' experience with Islam was primarily acquired when they went to Morocco on summer holidays to visit family, when they would occasionally attend a Koranic school. Abd Samad said that he himself did not practice Islam until 1992, about the time that Moussaoui was planning to move to London. When Moussaoui came home from London in 1993, Abd Samad said Zacarias refused to go to the mosque with him, preferring to go into town (Moussaoui, 2003: 94). Yet Moussaoui did start to attend mosque regularly while he was a graduate student at South Bank University in the early 1990s. Nil Plant (2005), his friend there, reported that he regularly attended Friday noonday prayers at a mosque in central London. Regular attendance, however, does not a slave of Allah make.

In London in the early 1990s there were many opportunities for Moussaoui to learn about Islam, including radical interpretations of it. But at first he chose to attend a moderate mosque in Brixton, which was primarily attended by converts from non-Muslim backgrounds. These were converts from places like the Caribbean, not Arabic-speaking practicing Muslims who had grown up in Islam. The chairman of the Brixton mosque was Abdul Haqq Baker, a Jamaican convert. What was the path to becoming a slave of Allah? How could Moussaoui, in every way a Westerner, become a slave of Allah? I do not use the term "decide" to become a slave of Allah, as people do not always have choice in the paths they follow. However it came about, Moussaoui identified himself in the courtroom as slave of Allah. He labeled his pleadings "Slave of Allah," he signed the pleadings "Slave of Allah," and he called himself a "Slave of Allah" during hearings. He clearly thought of himself as a slave of Allah, but he also used the term to separate himself from the court system. If he was a slave of Allah, then he could not be judged in a legal system which was clearly so separate from Allah. He said he could not take an oath in the courtroom, because that was not part of the teachings of Islam. Given the high level of his knowledge of English, he would know what effect the term would have on an American courtroom. It was his way of bringing jihad into that courtroom. The choice of words also reflected the concept in which he put his faith. While American prosecutors strove to put him to death, Allah would be his sole source of support.

The work of Farhad Khosrokhavar (1997, 2002) on Islam in France offers important insights into choices made by the second- and third-

generation French who are of North African descent. His analysis
indicates the differences between those descendants and the original
migrants. The search for something other than a life in a high-rise
French industrial suburb has led some to seek the structure, and also
the transformations, of a life dedicated to a different belief system.
Khosrokhavar told Seymour Hersh of the *New Yorker*:

Islam is the only plausible identity they can endorse. To accept their identity
as French might mean accepting the inferiority they feel in their daily life
as a second-rate citizen. The inevitable result is a hatred for France and, by
extension, for the West. (Hersh, 2002)

Moussaoui may not have felt inferior when he was growing up. But
he did rage against the unfairness of French attitudes toward North
and West African "immigrants." The conversions to an active form of
Islam, often in prison, of these children of immigrants, and the "new
martyrs of Allah" whom Khosrokhavar (2002, 2005) has studied,
indicate the important relationships among language, symbolism,
power, and action, of the symbolic violence, and, I argue, the crisis
of representation experienced in their lives.

John Searle (1995) argues that language is a constituent part of
social reality. Humans can be social without using language, living
together in cooperative groupings, but the "institutions" they create,
such as marriage and money, religions and court systems, even wars,
are constructed through the use of symbols, meaning, and metaphor
(something that "stands for" something else). Humans agree that
these things have meaning; when they stop behaving as though they
exist, they no longer exist, but this behavior is dependent on the use
of meaning and symbol, and these are linguistic acts (Searle, 1995:
59–78). These different views of the world and the ways in which life
should be lived are Searle's "conceptual relativity." He suggests that
there can be "any number of different systems of representations
for representing the same reality" (1995: 151). Zacarias Moussaoui,
I argue, has moved through several different systems of representation, which we are able to observe through his life story and his own
courtroom pleadings.

Pierre Bourdieu's work frequently (1990a, 1990b, 1991, 1998a,
1998b) explored the relationships among education, class, status,
language, and power. He argued that educational systems, such as
those in France, mainly reproduced the current elite (in *The Inheritors*
[Bourdieu and Passeron, 1979], see Reed-Danahay, 2005). Symbolic
violence occurs when individuals and social groups are invisibly and
quietly denied power and speech. Thompson, in his introduction
to Bourdieu's *Language and Symbolic Power* (1991), noted the irony
of the fact that political systems, supposedly intended to represent
individual citizens and groups of citizens, actually deny those groups

a voice. Members of subordinate groups often "misrecognize" the fact that they are denied access and control, and participate in the systems of which they are a (subordinate) part. This is what Bourdieu called "symbolic violence." Bourdieu defined symbolic violence as: "gentle, invisible violence, unrecognized as such, chosen as much as undergone" (1990a: 127). He argued that symbolic violence occurs in a wide range of relationships between individuals and groups. Such violence is worked out in various social fields such as in gift exchange, in educational institutions, and in policies of states. Unlike physical violence, symbolic violence is hidden behind a veil of normalcy and acquiescence.

All trial proceedings in the United States hinge on the assumption that the defendant will acquiesce, that he will acknowledge the authority of the court to pass judgment on his actions. Self-representation is assumed to work in this particular field of social action, but the assumption collapses if the defendant refuses to accept the rules of that field of social action. Moussaoui would not submit to the ways in which language and testimony were expected to be used in court. For that he was silenced throughout the trial except when he demanded to exercise his right to testify. Yet Moussaoui was willing to submit to Osama bin Laden, and in particular to Allah. This submission was an important part of his identity.

Identity is created with the assistance of language and metaphor. There is a large social psychological literature on identity (e.g. Erikson, 1980), some of which has been used to try to explain choices made by the accused terrorists such as Moussaoui (see Beaud and Masclet, 2002). That literature is helpful and compelling, but the focus here is on the expression of Moussaoui's identity as seen through his own pleadings. As Hill and Wilson, in "Identity Politics and the Politics of Identities," say:

Investigating the form and content of cultural performances and representations often provides important insights into the power relations embodied in and shaped by social identities. (2003: 5)

Hill and Wilson see "'identity politics' as discourse and action within public arenas of political and civil society" (identity from the top down), while the "politics of identity" (overlapping, but more likely from the bottom up)

... can take place in any social setting, and are often best and first recognized in domains of the private, the subaltern, the subversive, where culture may be the best way or means to express one's loss or triumph, whereas identity politics depend to a great deal on institutions and application of economic and political power ... (2003: 2)

Moussaoui engaged in both identity politics *and* the politics of identity, for he framed his identity in the contexts of the very public arenas of law, politics, international, and extra-state relations, while he is using culture (through his use of language, metaphor, word play, and acronyms) to present himself to the world, and to resist the metaphorical symbolic violence which he faced in court. Moussaoui's search for identity ranged across the globe, from France to England to Afghanistan to Malaysia, with several stops in between. His relationship to al-Qaeda, and specifically to Osama bin Laden (his "brother in Islam," his "father in jihad"), gave him a spiritual home. Thanks to his self-representation in a legal sense, we are able to understand his social and personal selves. That personal self is revealed over time. Through his hand-written pleadings, we are able to see that much of the legal sparring with his defense counsel and with the prosecutors at the US Department of Justice stems from a vision he had of himself in the social sense, as an al-Qaeda member, as part of a global struggle for power, but also as an individual, in a search for redemption, for purity, for a place. These social and personal representations are reflections of the life of Zacarias Moussaoui, and explain much about his choices and those made by others quite similar to him.

ALTERNATIVE EXPLANATIONS: EVIL OR CRAZY?

His self-representations provide an opportunity to consider two of the alternative explanations for Moussaoui's behavior discussed in the Introduction to this book. The first was that Moussaoui and his colleagues are evil, the second that Moussaoui is crazy, psychotic, or delusional.

Evil and Evil-Doers

We cannot know Moussaoui's mind, but his pleadings and courtroom interactions give one an idea of his sense of identity and of how he thought of himself. Furthermore, his efforts at legal self-representation and his own pleadings removed for a time the often obscure legal linguistic parlance used by defense counsel, allowing those who followed his case to learn a great deal about him and his use of language. The analysis of Moussaoui's sense of identity, and his representation of it, is essential to the discussion of his case. It is this representation which must be understood, and which has been neglected in the rhetoric of the "war on terror." This close look provides a window into how the "enemy" sees him- or herself, and chooses to represent himself. Such analysis parts the veil applied by the terms "enemy" or "evil-doer," revealing and representing the person behind that veil. Naturally, the choices made by members of groups such as al-Qaeda are viewed with great suspicion and little sympathy by the US Department of Justice; al-Qaeda is, after all, accused of causing the deaths of close to 3000 people in the attacks of 9/11, and has been accused of responsibility for the insurgency in Afghanistan and Iraq, as well as the Madrid bombings of March 2004 and the London bombings of July 2005.

In 2005 President Bush said of Islamic terrorists: "Evil men obsessed with ambition and unburdened by conscience must be taken very seriously, and we must stop them before their crimes can multiply" (Sandalow, 2005). David Raskin, one of the prosecutors in the Moussaoui case, said during the trial, in the government's closing statements to the jury, that Moussaoui represented "unforgivable evil" (Hirschkorn, 2006d). In September 2006, the National Security Council and the Bush administration released its "National Strategy for Combating Terrorism," which said of the terrorists: "Islam has been twisted and made to serve an evil end, as in other times and places other religions have been similarly abused" (National Strategy for Combating Terrorism, September 2006, page 15). As the fifth anniversary of 9/11 approached, Bush gave a speech to the Military Officers Association of America. On September 5, 2006, Bush said: "The terrorists who attacked us on September the 11th, 2001, are men without conscience – but they're not madmen. They kill in the name of a clear and focused ideology, a set of beliefs that are evil, but not insane" (Bush, 2006b).

Evil is not a cause for behavior; it is a result. Seeing evil as a cause for behavior removes any need to understand why terrorists act as they do. There are reasons why people like Moussaoui, and Osama bin Laden, and Khalid Sheikh Mohammed think and act as they do. These reasons have social causes. They are to be found in the affairs of humans, not in a Manichean struggle of evil against good. It is clear that the young men and women of England and the European continent who join Islamic fundamentalist groups are searching for something meaningful in their lives, no matter how horrible this may seem to the Western sensibility. Islam, and in particular, adherence to the Wahhabi and Salafist versions of Islam favored by Islamic "militants," offers a structure and belief system different from the Western religious and social milieu in which many European-born "terrorists," including Moussaoui, grew up. It must be understood. The appellation of "evil-doer" implies that these people are wicked, that they like to do evil, for evil's sake. However, a thorough look at Moussaoui's statements in court and his pleadings reveals not that he reveled in evil for evil's sake. Instead, his goal was to fight against a world power, the United States, which he saw as a representation of Satan.

Power can beget evil. Anything that can have power over a person, or a group of people, can effect evil results. In Christian ideology, Satan has control over evil, a dark power which entices people to be led astray. Satan figures in Islam as well, and Moussaoui was not shy about attributing Satan's characteristics to American power, and to the men who wield it. He referred to himself as "the Slave of Allah" in opposition to John Ashcroft, to whom he referred as "the Slave of Satan" and "the Slave of Bush." He saw the United States of America as the "United Satan of America." The World Trade Center, for Moussaoui, was a source of metaphor. The "World Tyran Court" was allied against him in "the World Tyran Conspiracy," and the "World Top Conspiracy." And this was all in just one pleading (Docket No. 972).

Over the course of the trial, evidence was released which showed Moussaoui as a man who felt his causes strongly. A sister commented on his support for Martin Luther King Jr., and his stand against racism (Nadia Moussaoui, 2005). An acquaintance at South Bank University in London spoke of his anger at globalization and the colonial policies of the West, especially those of France (Newman, 2001). For Moussaoui, Islam's promise of social justice provided a path to righting the many wrongs of the world. America became his target because of its economic power, which, he thought, was creating social injustice. His thoughts and actions were not a sign of evil. They were a sign of commitment to a cause of global jihad. This cause is threatening to many in the West for it has caused horror, death, and destruction. The intent of global jihad seems evil. The actions of jihadis stem from what moderate Muslims consider to be misinterpretations of the Koran. But Zacarias Moussaoui, who was of the West, took on this cause because it gave him a role in the fight for social and economic justice.

Was Moussaoui Crazy?

When Moussaoui moved for the right to represent himself, Judge Brinkema ordered that he be evaluated as to his mental competence to do so. Dr. Raymond Patterson, a psychiatrist enlisted by the government, reported that Moussaoui appeared to be mentally competent. Therefore, Moussaoui's motion for self representation was granted by District Judge Brinkema at the hearing on June 13, 2002. His mother, when she saw him in court, observed that he did not appear to be himself, but thought his behavior was due to long periods of time in isolation (e.g. Dominus, 2003; Hersh, 2002; Guy Taylor, 2005). He used derogatory names for his defense team. Frank Dunham, the lead defense attorney, was a "Megalopig." Moussaoui played several times on the relationship between Dunham's size, and the fact that his last name contained the letters "ham." Alan Yamamoto, of Japanese parentage, was a "geisha." Edward MacMahon, from the southern US, was "KKK." The judge came in for a great deal of abuse. Among other things, he referred often to her as "Death Judge" and wondered about her gas chamber. Ashcroft and Bush were targets. Lawyers, judges, and presidents were not his only targets. He referred to the Queen of England as "the Bitch of Buckingham" (see Defense Exhibit ZM010). The people he blessed were members of al-Qaeda and dead Chechen rebels.

The question of Moussaoui's mental state continued to be an issue throughout the proceedings and into the trial. Mental evaluations were something the prosecution did not want, and the defense did. The government claimed that such an exam would "pattern" Moussaoui's later responses to the prosecution's questions (Dunham, 2004). The defense would go on to use psychological and psychiatric evaluations of Moussaoui in the trial. Moussaoui resisted all these attempts at evaluation. When District Judge Brinkema ordered a mental exam before she would allow him to represent himself, Moussaoui replied on July 11, 2002, with a motion titled: "Do you think that I am crazy to see your Doctor Frankenstein?" (Docket No. 314). He used the mental health experts' own language in a list of what he implied were Judge Brinkema's mental symptoms:

Mental State Examination
Axis I: Acute symptom of Islamaphobia with complex of gender inferiority
Diagnostic impressions
Legal pathological killer instinct with ego boosting dementia to become Supreme
Conclusion and Recommendations
Immediate Psychiatric hospitalization to specialist Unit.
I propose UBL Treatment Center (of course UBL stand for unique best location).
(Signed) Slave of Allah (Docket No. 314)

It is no wonder that he spent his time working out acronyms, for according to the Special Administrative Measures memo ordering the conditions of Moussaoui's detention (see, for instance, Dockets No. 94 and 95) and, according to a lawyer close to the case, his isolation was virtually complete. There was to be no contact with other inmates. No talking with them. Any possible conversation with them was to be recorded. There were to be no visitors except for family members, legal counsel and an imam. Family members were to notify the center in writing that they intended to visit. The imam was not to come within touching distance for fear that Moussaoui would take him, or any other visitor who came too close, hostage. His telephone conversations were to be limited to family and legal counsel. Finally, for a number of reasons including the security strictures on telephone calls – advance notification had to be given, a French–English translator had to listen in – his mother stopped trying to call him (see Docket No. 794).

Not surprisingly, he worked over the multiple connections that words and acronyms made to his own plight. Not only did the Special Administration Measure (SAM) keep him in solitary confinement. Pleadings included reference to "Uncle Sam," the United States, of course, but he also equated "SAM" with "Sanction Against Moussaoui," "Sensured Against Moussaoui," and "Sensured Against Muslim" (e.g. Docket No. 1082). "Uncle Sam," he wrote, was part of the "Wicked Anglo Sionist [sic] Prosecution" ("WASP") (Docket No. 1117).

When, in October 2003, District Judge Brinkema apparently ordered that Moussaoui not have access to CNN and other media, he wrote an appeal asking her to

... order delivery and connection to the Crusader Nasty Network (a/k/ CNN); the Big Bullshit Company (a/k/ BBC); the Wicked Propagand (a/k/ WP), and the Nasty Yankes [sic] Times (a/k/ NYT).

All of these news sources, he wrote, are "World Anglo-Satan Propaganda" or "a/k/ WASP." This pleading was signed "ZM, The Global 20th One" (Docket No. 1082).

Moussaoui's use of acronyms and his general play on words both hindered and helped his case. It helped his case, in that his verbal sparring kept the court off balance. From the point of view of the defense, it helped his case in that his mental state could therefore be questioned. But Moussaoui resisted that strategy. He commented in his hearings that he highly resented statements to the media by defense counsel that, in their opinion, he was crazy. At his plea hearing in 2005, he said:

So I don't see how on earth I'm receiving effective assistance of defense lawyer. Except that Dunham, he have his day with the journalists, you know, going around and saying Moussaoui is crazy, Moussaoui is crazy. He's crazy to want to defend his life, that's what he's crazy for, an ex-prosecutor, who is doing the job of the prosecution ... (tr. April 22, 2005, page 32, lines 16–21)

As soon as he pleaded guilty, and the judge accepted that plea, legal experts offered a variety of explanations for his decision. Al Jazeera interviewed several American defense attorneys shortly after the plea. One Washington defense attorney, Richard Hibey, was quoted as saying:

"he was deprived of his martyrdom and feels the only way he can achieve that lofty state is simply to admit to the crimes," and another defense attorney, David Schertler, said Moussaoui defies any conventional sense of what a defendant is and what a defendant is trying to accomplish. It seems that he is using the system to make a political statement regardless of what implications it has for him. (Al Jazeera, 2005)

Further evidence of Moussaoui's mental competence was revealed during the trial. After it was over, the lawyer with whom he had the most contact, Alan Yamamoto, said in an interview that he had found his client difficult, but not crazy (Townsend, 2006). The jury had agreed with that assessment, and had not been swayed by the mental experts' testimony. Moussaoui's court pleadings, his testimony, and comments were more a fact of his jihad than they were of his mental unbalance.

WHAT CAN WE LEARN?

The case of Zacarias Moussaoui, and the ways in which Moussaoui represented himself, provide us with a view into the workings of language, metaphor, and the politics of identity in representation of the self. The various conceptual realities that are represented in the above discussion allow us to see ways in which humans create meaning, and try to lead meaningful lives. Those conceptual realities may change at critical junctures, in periods of crisis, and new conceptual realities are formed. While Moussaoui's pleadings may at first seem irrational (at least, from a legal point of view), it was through the creation of his own conceptual reality that Moussaoui was actually able to speak for himself, and with effect. It was his own, singular voice, and his ability to keep the court off-balance, which to an odd degree worked in his favor. He argued that he wanted to plead guilty, yet few believed him guilty of complicity in the September 11 attacks. He verbally attacked the judge, yet she sanctioned the federal prosecutors for refusing to allow Moussaoui to depose three witnesses he considered important to his defense. By November 2003 she had had enough. But Moussaoui's three crises of representation, legal, social, and personal, provided him with opportunities to work out a sense of who he actually was, and to resist as best he could the symbolic violence of state control and manipulation. The person who was Zacarias Moussaoui may not always have been clear to those close to his case, or to the press, and that legal, social, and personal representation was not orthodox. But its very heterodoxy provided him with a fertile ground for confounding those involved in the proceedings against him.

In April 2005, the day Moussaoui pleaded guilty, he said:

I have not a chance to have my voice being speak [heard] because they know that I've being held in this cave, in Alexandria Detention cave, and nobody speaking for Moussaoui, okay? And this is my last time, I'm sure, that I have the opportunity because I am not my lawyer. The only reason I have the right to speak today is because I'm pleading guilty. Otherwise, I will be silenced. (tr. April 22, 2005, page 31, lines 21–25; page 32, line 1)

He would come out of his cave to speak at his own trial, much as Osama bin Laden would later come out of his own metaphorical cave to speak for Moussaoui.

3 COURTROOM 700, ALEXANDRIA, VIRGINIA

You are America – the defense, the judge, the attackers. These people are
American. I'm al Qaeda. I'm a sworn enemy of you. (Zacarias Moussaoui
at hearing, tr. February 14, 2006, page 6, lines 18–20)

SELECTION OF THE JURY

Jury selection began on February 6, 2006. The court had sent
summonses to 500 potential jurors selected from the cities and
counties of the Alexandria Division of the US District Court of Eastern
Virginia. The Alexandria Division included the city of Alexandria and
counties in the Washington, DC area.[1] On that day, the 500 potential
jurors took elevators to ninth and tenth floor courtrooms at staggered
intervals in groups of 125. They were given a 50-page questionnaire
asking their views on the death penalty, their knowledge of the case,
and if they knew any victims of the attacks. The questionnaire asked
how they felt about flying, whether any of their relatives had been
victims of crimes, and whether they belonged to organizations such
as the Rotary Club, about their hearing and eyesight. They were
asked if they had any negative feelings or opinions about Muslims or
people of North African descent and if they believed Islam endorses
violence more than other religions.

Beginning on Wednesday, February 15, the potential jurors were
to arrive in smaller groups for individual questioning, or *voir dire*, in
order to create a pool of 85 potential jurors. On the first day of the
trial, March 6, twelve jurors and six alternates would be chosen for
the final jury panel. The alternates would be available should a juror
become ill or have to leave the trial for some reason.

Moussaoui is Removed

On February 6, Moussaoui saw his opportunity and took it. Four
times the groups entered the courtroom. Four times he rose to berate
his lawyers: "I'll have nothing to do with them," and to declare his
affiliation: "I am al Qaeda"; and to foreshadow what he would say

later: "For four years I have waited," he said. "I will testify." Four times he was removed by the US Marshals. Each time he went quietly, hands over his head.

Judge Brinkema held a hearing on Tuesday, February 14, to determine if he would remain quiet when the jurors were brought in for individual selection. Wearing a white Muslim skullcap for the first time, Moussaoui read a statement in which he accused the lawyers for both sides and the judge of planning his death. He said he was not French: "I am a Muslim, and I have nothing to do with a nation of homosexual Crusaders. And I am not a frog" (tr. February 14, 2006, page 4, lines 23–25). He went on:

As for the hearing, okay, you say that I misbehaved. What on earth is the problem for the jurors to know that this defense doesn't belong to me? You own everything. You are America – the defense, the judge, the attackers. These people are American. I'm al Qaeda. I'm a sworn enemy of you. You, you, you, you, for me you are enemy. And your own commander in chief says he want to launch a revenge against terrorists. (tr. February 14, 2006, page 6, lines 16–22)

"Mr. Moussaoui," the judge said. "You are the biggest enemy of yourself." He was told he would watch the proceedings from the cellblock on closed circuit TV. He was removed from the courtroom. "God curse you," he said as he left. The judge told the court reporter that his last comment should be reflected in the record of the proceedings (tr. February 14, 2006, page 8, line 14; Seper, 2006).

Surprisingly, he was in the courtroom the next day, the first day for *voir dire*. There was no explanation from the judge, but the press speculated that he was wearing a stun belt (Powell, 2006). He would save his comments for breaks in jury selection and in the trial itself; one in the morning, one at lunchtime, one in the afternoon, and one at the end of the day. "God bless Osama," "God curse this courtroom," "God bless Moussaoui," he would say.

Jury Selection Continues

After five days of *voir dire*, 67 of the possible 85 jurors had been selected. On Thursday, February 23, as members of the groups of jurors arrived, some stood in line outside the courthouse, some sat in their cars, drinking coffee until the courthouse opened.[2] A fast-moving convoy of police cars brought Moussaoui's vehicle from the detention center into the courthouse's underground garage. Only one cameraman was permitted to film his arrival. Footage of his arrival was then shared with the press pool. Two guards and a German shepherd worked the public entrance to the courthouse. Briefcases were placed on a wooden pallet for the dog to sniff. Lunches were forbidden. Cell phones and all electronic equipment were banned. Some people raced back to their cars to put them away. Across the street, the deli ran a thriving business in holding cell phones and laptops for $2 a day.

The public entrance to the courthouse did not open until 8 a.m. Outside, a line formed early. Entry into the courthouse took time. Identity cards were checked. All coins and metal objects went into a dish, bodies went through the metal detector, wands searched for suspicious objects. Coins, cards, and keys went back into pockets, only to come out again at the entrance to the seventh floor courtroom for the procedure to be repeated. No one was allowed on that floor until 9 a.m. The courthouse coffee shop on the second floor did good business while people waited. There was time to buy a newspaper and some coffee. Upstairs, some guards thought newspapers were not allowed into the antechamber of the courtroom, even if kept in briefcases. Those newspapers disappeared into the trash. Not a briefcase entered Courtroom 700.

Two US Marshals entered the courtroom from the courthouse's cellblock promptly at 9 a.m. One marshal poured water into a cup and placed it on a desk to the left of a podium facing the bench. One brought in a pad of paper, and left it with a blue-covered book for Moussaoui. The book was on trial techniques (Sniffen, 2006a). The bald marshal sat in the chair, and looked under the desk. Then, more courtroom security members entered. One sat below the judge's bench to her left, the other to her right. One guarded the door to the jury room. Almost all of them had wires in their ears.

The front row of the benches was reserved for the lawyers and their staff members. Some benches were set aside for family members of the victims of 9/11, others for the public and the press. Guards sat at the back of the courtroom. During jury selection the spectators were primarily members of the press. Reporters and producers from the *Washington Post*, the *New York Times*, CNN, NBC, Associated Press, and Agence France-Presse were present. Later, during the trial, competition for seats would become fierce, but during jury selection seats were easy to find.

At 9:30 a.m. the judge's judicial law clerk intoned: "All rise. The Honorable Judge Leonie Brinkema ... " All rose. Two doors opened; the judge entered from one door, and at the same time Moussaoui entered from the other. The judge walked up the steps and sat down behind the bench. Moussaoui slipped behind his desk. Stocky and serious in demeanor, he wore a white knit cap and a green jumpsuit with the word "prisoner" on the back. The judge started the proceedings, and the day's first of four groups of potential jurors filed in and found seats in the jury box. Moussaoui would look at each juror in turn and survey the courtroom. Each member of the panel had been given a number. For security reasons their identities were kept secret. The press had been told not to identify them or to interview them, and the sketch artists had been told not to draw their faces.

Judge Brinkema explained the procedure for selection. She then asked if it would affect the jurors if the defendant was to watch the proceedings on closed circuit television from the cellblock in the courthouse, should he be removed from the courtroom. No, they said. The judge said the case may go to Passover or Easter, would that affect you? No. Will school holidays affect you? No. The group was then asked to return to the jury room, with the exception of the day's first person to be questioned individually.

Juror number 313 was asked to stay in the courtroom and was told to go to the witness stand. Judge Brinkema looked at the questionnaire and then asked her about her search for work. Number 313 said she had been sick but was now actively looking for a job with the House of Representatives. There would be a problem if she got an offer and couldn't take it because of the trial. She left the courtroom. Judge Brinkema said "This is a problem." Robert Spencer of the prosecution had no objection to excusing her. Gerald Zerkin, for the defense, also had no objection. Juror number 313 was brought back in to stand by the jury room door. She was excused. She was to tell the clerk downstairs that she would not be on the panel. She left the courtroom. Juror number 323 was called. A woman in her 30s, with blonde hair and a brown dotted shirt, she appeared to be nervous. Had she read the news? Yes, WTOP, on the computer screen. She admitted that she looked at it after she filled in the questionnaire; the jurors had specifically been told no news should be read or listened to during the proceedings. Number 323 said she was "frazzled" but thought she should do her civic duty. Could you continue to avoid the news? asked the judge. She would do her best. It was quickly apparent that she was trying to get off the jury. There was no objection to that from anyone, and she was excused.

Juror number 330 was a male with dark hair, wearing a blue shirt. He appeared to be in his 30s. He worked in the private sector as an accountant. The judge asked about the news: "Have you seen or read it?" "No," he replied. But he said it was difficult to stay away from it. Fortunately, the Winter Olympics helped. Has anyone talked to you about the case? No. Have you talked with anyone? Your wife? Would it be difficult to avoid conversation? No. Have you told your employer? No. Could you follow instructions as to the law? Yes. Would your religious beliefs keep you from deciding fairly? No. Could you set aside your religious beliefs in deciding this case? Yes. Could you decide for life or death, depending on the facts? Yes. Do you have any opinion of the defendant and whether he should face life or death? No. There were no objections. He was on the panel of 85, and was later selected as a member of the final jury panel.

Number 336 knew an employee at the Pentagon who had burns on 80 percent of his body from the attack. He also knew of one person who had been killed. Both victims were from his church. The judge asked: Knowing all this, won't it affect you? No, he said. He would make a decision based on facts. Brinkema replied "You think so? The law won't tell you what to do; the jury will have to decide." He did say he has a friend in the CIA. "Are you open to criticism of the CIA?" He was. His CIA friend has been in Pakistan and Afghanistan. He left the courtroom. Defense attorney Zerkin wanted him removed from the panel. Then, with some frustration, he said the court "can't keep stacking the jury with people who have connections." The judge agreed. Juror number 336 was excused.

Before juror number 345 entered the courtroom the judge asked the attorneys to approach the bench. A white noise machine was turned on. Moussaoui, still sitting at his desk, was given a pair of headphones so he could listen. The attorneys talked with the judge, some tilting their heads to see her at the bench. The attorneys then returned to their seats, the noise machine was turned off, and juror number 345 was called. A white male in his late 40s, he was excused from the jury pool without discussion.

Juror number 356 entered. He said he was looking for a job and was concerned that he may receive an offer soon. He said he would like to talk with the judge. Again, the white noise machine was switched on; again, the attorneys approached the bench and Moussaoui was given headphones. He could not hear the conversation, shook his head, and took the headphones off. Juror number 356 was excused because of financial hardship. Kenneth Troccoli of the defense team leaned over and whispered to Moussaoui, presumably about the juror.

One potential juror knew of a person killed in the World Trade Center and had attended the funeral. The judge asked the potential juror if he thought the FBI had performed well before 9/11. Yes, he said. After 9/11? Yes. On your questionnaire, Judge Brinkema noted, you said life imprisonment is not sufficient punishment. Would you be open to considering life? Yes. He left the witness stand. The judge said he would be excused because he was too close to 9/11. David Novak of the prosecution stood up to address her: "Is it useless to fight or not?" The judge said it was useless to fight. The juror was excused, as was another juror who knew personally a young man killed in the World Trade Center. The prosecution objected. Judge Brinkema did not change her mind.

Juror number 659 was asked if she had been listening to or watching the news. She said "I don't do news." A mental health researcher, she knew a person who was on the list of potential witnesses. They

saw each other at meetings, and were in a similar field of work. She
was told by the judge that she could not be a "shadow expert" on
mental health if she was a member of the jury. She was in the pool,
and later served on the jury panel.

The judge stopped the proceedings for lunch. "All rise ... "
Moussaoui did not rise. The judge left the courtroom. Moussaoui
got up, saying: "God curse Troccoli and Zerkin and America. God save
Osama bin Laden and al Qaeda." His voice rose on the last word, as
the door closed behind him. The reporters huddled, compared notes,
and wrote down what he said. Gerald Zerkin said: "You are always
writing, taking notes." The reporters asked each other about the
exact relations of the potential jurors to the victims at the Pentagon
and the World Trade Center, and took notes. They headed for the
elevators and the floor was cleared. Some reporters went to file a
story, others to have a cigarette, still others to have lunch. Then back
they came, through the two security checks. The benches filled up.
It was 2 p.m.

"All rise." Judge Brinkema and Moussaoui entered simultaneously, and jury selection continued. One person was a member of
the American Civil Liberties Union, and worked as a lawyer for them.
He was excused. A woman who worked for a regional airport security
agency was not. Juror number 402 entered. A tall, well-dressed man
in his late 40s or 50s, he was in the military reserves. When asked
about the news, he said he missed the newspaper, but could get
along without it. The government attorneys asked to approach the
bench, and once more the noise machine was switched on. The judge
then proceeded with the questioning. Juror 402 had no problem
considering the possibility of life in prison without release. He was
in the pool of 85, and sat on the final jury panel. During one pause,
as the attorneys were huddled at the bench and the noise machine
was on, several of the reporters chatted quietly among themselves.
This brought the court security officer over to chasten them. "No
talking, please." At the afternoon break Moussaoui exited saying:
"God curse Zerkin and MacMahon; God kill America. God bless
Osama bin Laden." Edward MacMahon heard this and grimaced.

More jurors were added to the pool. One had friends in counter-
terrorism. He was excused. Another, in the airline industry at Dulles
International Airport, was working on 9/11. The judge wanted to
know how it affected her. Well, after 9:30 a.m. we weren't laid off, she
said. There was nothing to do. The judge asked again, how did 9/11
affect you? She responded that she didn't think people should be able
to live on through long appeals of their sentences. Gerald Zerkin said
he was troubled by her response, but she was added to the pool.

That one day yielded three of the final panel members. The final
members of the pool were selected by Friday, February 24. It had taken

seven days. Eighty-six people, one more than planned for, had been chosen from the original group of 500. Sixteen of the 86 were chosen over the defense's challenges, six over the prosecution's challenges. The judge excused some for a variety of reasons; one woman had child-care issues, to which the judge was sympathetic. The final panel of 18 would be selected at the beginning of the eligibility phase of the trial, Monday, March 6, 2006. As Moussaoui left the courtroom he said: "God bless Osama bin Laden, al Qaeda, and Moussaoui" (Cratty, 2006).

THE ELIGIBILITY PHASE BEGINS

The first phase of the trial was to determine if Zacarias Moussaoui was eligible for the death penalty. Unlike other federal death penalty trials, there was to be no "guilt phase," in which guilt or innocence was determined. Moussaoui had already pleaded guilty in April 2005. But Judge Brinkema had ordered that there would be two phases to this sentencing trial. In November 2005, the judge had arranged that the first phase would determine whether Moussaoui

"intentionally participated in an act (lying to agents about his knowledge concerning September 11) contemplating that the life of a person would be taken or intending that lethal force would be used with a person, other than one of the participants in the offense, and the victim died as a direct result of the act," in violation of 18 U.S.C.§ 3591 (a) (2) (C). (Docket No. 1372)

This eligibility phase would focus on testimony and evidence concerning Moussaoui's involvement in the deaths of the victims of 9/11, and the steps the United States could have taken if he had not concealed his real purpose for taking flight lessons.

If the first phase determined that Moussaoui was eligible for the death penalty, the second phase of the trial would determine if the death penalty would be imposed. During the second phase the lawyers for the prosecution would introduce evidence of aggravating factors, showing the horror of the crime, and the reasons why the defendant should receive the death penalty. The defense would introduce evidence of mitigating factors, showing his difficult childhood and the possibility of mental illness. These would be reasons why the defendant should not receive the death penalty.

Congressional legislation had approved access to Moussaoui's trial by closed circuit television for family members of 9/11 victims, for those injured in the attacks, and for those who had responded as fire or emergency personnel. Judge Brinkema decided that federal courthouses in Boston, New York, New Jersey, and Philadelphia would provide this service. At the Alexandria courthouse, two benches were reserved inside the courtroom, and a separate courtroom with closed circuit access was also reserved for family members.

In Alexandria, courthouse officials initiated several systems to cope with the large numbers of reporters, their cameramen, the satellite trucks, and the public at the courthouse itself. Space was reserved across the street from the main entrance to the courthouse. Camera crews set up small tents, and the satellite trucks were allotted space away from the courthouse. Reporters and producers could apply to the courthouse for a seat in the courtroom, but would forfeit that seat if it was not occupied every day. This procedure worked well for groups with large Washington bureaus such as the *Washington Post*, the *New York Times*, and CNN, but not for smaller organizations, such as Al Arabiya, or for organizations without large Washington bureaus, such as some of the French news services. In order to control access to the limited number of seats inside Courtroom 700, each morning Edward Adams, the court information officer, stood at the door leading from the elevators into the courtroom antechamber. He handed out pre-printed stickers with the day's date in black or red. Those who arrived when there was still space in the main courtroom received black-lettered stickers. Those who arrived later were less lucky. They received red-lettered stickers, and went to the overflow courtroom opposite Courtroom 700. Courtroom 701 had three large closed-circuit television screens. The television camera did not show the jury, nor could it catch the emotional drama in the main courtroom, so there was to be increasing pressure to get into the courthouse early in order to get the prized black-lettered stickers for Courtroom 700. The advantage to the overflow courtroom was that one could chat quietly, although there were guards even in that courtroom, and they made everyone stand when the judge entered and left Courtroom 700.

March 6, 2006: Day One, Eligibility Phase

The final jury panel of 18 members was selected on the first day of the trial. One woman appeared upset at the thought of serving on this jury, and was excused from the panel. Of the 17 remaining jury members, seven were women and ten were men. One was black, the rest were white. All 17 members of the panel were expected to sit through the trial. At the end of the eligibility phase, five alternates would be picked out of a hat (MSNBC, 2006a). The jury panel was given instructions. They were not to watch, listen to, or read news of the trial. There was to be no talking with family, friends, or business associates about the trial. The press was not to contact them. If the press tried, jurors were to tell the judge. Judge Brinkema said that, unless she warned them ahead of time, court would not be in session on Fridays. They would be able to work then and over the weekends if they needed to do so.

The judge explained that several types of evidence would be admitted into the trial. There would be witness testimony from witnesses physically present in the courtroom. In some cases, when a witness could not be present, his or her testimony was videotaped elsewhere and played in the courtroom. When witnesses could not be present for security reasons, nor videotaped, their testimony was to be given in the form of summaries of what they had said. She was referring to al-Qaeda detainees, to whom Moussaoui had been denied access except through these controversial summaries. There would also, she said, be physical evidence in the form of photographs, records of wire transfers, and receipts for equipment purchased, inventories of items found, and the like. There would be stipulations, meaning that both the defense and the government had agreed on a fact (tr. March 6, 2006a, page 6, lines 4–25; page 7, 1–10).

Just before the break for lunch, Moussaoui asked through one of his attorneys that the judge reconsider her ruling concerning his self-representation. The request was denied. "It's over and done with," she said (tr. March 6, 2006a, page 17, line 24).

Each side made opening statements on the afternoon of the first day, Robert Spencer for the government, Edward MacMahon for the defense. The judge made sure the jury members had their notebooks, and Spencer began:

September 11th, 2001 dawned clear, crisp and blue in the northeast United States. In lower Manhattan in the Twin Towers of the World Trade Center, workers sat down at their desks tending to e-mail and phone messages from the previous days. In the Pentagon in Arlington, Virginia, military and civilian personnel sat in briefings, were focused on their paperwork. (tr. March 6, 2006b, page 21, lines 11–17)

The day ended, he said, in terror, pain, and clouds of black smoke. Spencer said that Moussaoui was a determined terrorist who prevented the United States from uncovering the September 11 hijacking plot. The United States would prove, Spencer said, that Moussaoui could have prevented the four hijackings and the deaths of nearly 3000 people, if he had not lied.

In his opening statement for the defense, Edward MacMahon said that Moussaoui was clearly not a part of 9/11, and he was inept to boot. Moussaoui

... talked in Oklahoma of wanting to kill infidels, but ... he didn't harm a soul when he was free in our country or even before. That, ladies and gentlemen, is Zacarias Moussaoui in a nutshell, sound and fury, accomplishing nothing.... You will hear evidence that Moussaoui was totally useless to al Qaeda, a headache, obnoxious to everyone he encountered. (tr. March 6, 2006b, page 52, lines 18–21; page 53, lines 1–3)

MacMahon said the defense would show that the United States could have prevented the attacks if those responsible had only paid attention to the numerous threats that had been received over the course of years. The FBI, CIA, and the National Security Agency all had access to numerous threat warnings in the summer of 2001. An FBI agent in Phoenix had sent a memo to headquarters warning that flight schools in the Phoenix area had many students with links to Muslim fundamentalist causes, but agents working on the Moussaoui case did not make the connection. MacMahon said the jury should not judge Moussaoui to get revenge for the victims of 9/11, nor should they make him a scapegoat for the errors made by government officials before 9/11 (tr. March 6, 2006b, page 51, lines 2–6). "Sound and fury," said Moussaoui on his way out of the courtroom.

March 7, 2006: Day Two, Eligibility Phase

FBI agent Michael Anticev was the first to testify on the second day of the trial. He said that the FBI knew that al-Qaeda members were in American flight schools long before September 11. One had trained to be bin Laden's pilot at the Airman flight school later attended by Moussaoui. But, he said, the FBI thought the training could either be for conventional reasons or perhaps for hijacking planes outside of the US. The FBI had no idea that planes would be hijacked and then flown into buildings. Under cross-examination from Edward MacMahon, Anticev did admit that the FBI had known of plans by Algerian rebels to hijack a French plane and fly it into the Eiffel Tower. He also admitted FBI knowledge of another plan to fly a plane into the CIA headquarters in Langley, Virginia.

Next, FBI Agent James Fitzgerald described in detail the work done by the FBI beginning the very day of the hijackings. Called the PENTTBOM investigation, for Pentagon/Twin Towers Bombing, it had involved 7000 of the total of 11,000 FBI agents. Under cross-examination by Edward MacMahon, Fitzgerald admitted that the PENTTBOM investigators found no link between Moussaoui and the 9/11 hijackers. Moussaoui behaved much as the 9/11 hijackers behaved, he said, but there was no evidence linking Moussaoui to them (Markon and Dwyer, 2006a).

Devastating evidence followed. Radio transmissions and cell phone calls from the hijacked planes were read aloud in the courtroom. "We are flying low. We are flying very very low … oh my God, we are way too low," said flight attendant Amy Sweeney, just before her plane hit the tower. As these words were read, the family of Betty Ong, a flight attendant on the same plane, wept. Moussaoui pumped his arm and smiled. Leaving the courtroom for a recess, he said "Allah akhbar! God curse America, bless Osama bin Laden" (Riley, 2006a).

Moussaoui's mother, Aïcha el-Wafi, was in the courtroom. She had flown in from France to attend the beginning of the trial, but her son would not acknowledge her presence. By the time of the lunch break on March 7, the second day, she could take no more. She left the courtroom and ran out of the courthouse. Reporters followed her outside; one was with her when she collapsed in tears and fell on her knees. He shielded her from the cameras, and they walked off.

March 8, 2006: Day Three, Eligibility Phase

The jury viewed videotaped testimony from one of Moussaoui's contacts in Malaysia. This testimony was taken in November 2002, when Moussaoui was still his own lawyer. Unfortunately, the connection between Singapore and the Alexandria courthouse made it difficult on occasion for the two sides to hear each other. Fauzi bin Abu Bakar Bafana, in custody in Singapore, said he was asked to give Moussaoui a place to stay in July 2000. According to Bafana, Moussaoui had traveled to Kuala Lumpur to investigate flight training. Bafana said Moussaoui told him of his dream to fly a plane into the White House. Frank Dunham, who was still on the case in 2002, said to Bafana, "You thought he was cuckoo, right?" Bafana said "yes." Bafana also said that Moussaoui used internet chat rooms to look for a wife. Dunham said this was not the sign of a man who intended to die soon (tr. March 8, 2006, pp. 516–607; Hirschkorn, 2006a).

March 9, 2006: Day Four, Eligibility Phase

Clancy Prevost, the flight instructor with Pan Am International in Minnesota, testified on Thursday, March 9, that Moussaoui could have flown a 747-400 even with his limited knowledge of flying.[3] He described his mounting concern that this quite likeable person had no background similar to the other flight students he had taught. FBI Agent Harry Samit then told of the telephone calls from Pan Am to the Minneapolis FBI that led to Moussaoui's arrest. Samit's testimony was scheduled to continue on Monday. But over the weekend the prosecution notified the judge that Carla Martin, a lawyer for the Transportation Security Administration (TSA), had improperly coached government witnesses (Sniffen, 2006b).

March 13, 2006: The Trial Comes to a Halt

The following Monday, on what was to have been the fifth day of the trial, Judge Brinkema halted the proceedings. She was angry. She said she had expressly ordered that no witnesses were to know of opening statements or testimony during the trial. "An attorney for the TSA ... egregiously breached that order," the judge said, and she sent the jury home (Sniffen, 2006b). The defense moved to throw out the death penalty. The lawyers debated how to continue the trial. The judge said she wanted to think about what to do. Moussaoui's comment on leaving the courtroom was, "The show must go on!"

The judge did not sanction the government by removing the death penalty but on Tuesday, March 14, she ordered that all aviation testimony was prohibited. "I don't think in the annals of criminal law there has ever been a case with this many significant problems," she said (Markon and Dwyer, 2006b). A teleconference was held late that day. Rob Spencer said the government did not think it worth continuing their case against Moussaoui given the judge's ruling barring aviation testimony. They needed aviation witnesses to testify about "no-fly" rules in order to prove that, given enough information, at least some of the hijackers could have been found before boarding the planes. The judge reconsidered and told the prosecution that if they could find untainted aviation witnesses, the trial would continue. In her order, she made clear that any aviation witness would be limited to testifying as to what the US *could* have done to prevent the attacks, not as to what *would* have been done to prevent those attacks. The difference between *could* and *would* became a contentious issue in some of the testimony that followed.

March 20, 2006: The Trial Begins Again, Day Five, Eligibility Phase

The jury returned to hear further evidence on Monday, March 20. FBI Agent Samit returned to be cross-examined by the defense. Edward MacMahon drew from him testimony that described in detail his difficulties in getting FBI headquarters to pay attention to the possible threat Moussaoui represented. The seemingly impenetrable barrier of the "wall" kept Samit from searching Moussaoui's bags and his laptop. Samit had also turned to the FBI legal attaché in Paris for more information on Moussaoui, who, the French reported, was confirmed in his fundamentalist Muslim beliefs. Some lighter moments, at least for the courtroom, came from this testimony as well. When the FBI legal attaché in Paris was told to make sure this Moussaoui was not being confused with any other Moussaoui, the attaché emailed Samit that he had the white pages (residential telephone directory) for Paris and was looking through it. According to one spectator, this reduced the courtroom spectators to giggles. Edward MacMahon asked if the Paris legal attaché didn't know that there were other cities in France. Furthermore, the FBI dithered about the cost of sending him back to France, leading MacMahon to ask if $1500 wasn't less than 3000 lives.

March 21, 2006: Day Six, Eligibility Phase

The following day began with a videotaped interview of a very frightened looking Hussein al-Attas. He had been Moussaoui's roommate in Oklahoma, and he also drove Moussaoui to Minnesota. Hussein al-Attas was a Yemeni living in Norman when he met Moussaoui. Al-Attas was a student, but not a good one, he said. He felt pressure from his family to do well, and he wanted to get away from that pressure. When he met Moussaoui at a mosque in Norman, Moussaoui talked with him about jihad. Moussaoui told al-Attas he could learn more about jihad by talking with scholars in Pakistan.

On the drive up to Minnesota, al-Attas said, Moussaoui warned that for their safety they should not speak in Arabic. Before they left Oklahoma they bought two knives, boots, and boxing gear. During al-Attas's videotaped testimony, it appeared that Edward MacMahon was trying to show that Moussaoui was mentally unstable. "Did he seem to talk to himself?" "No, he was praying." "Were there any other odd things that he did?" He wanted the battery taken out of his cell phone before they could talk together. Al-Attas said it was clear that Moussaoui annoyed people at the Oklahoma mosque. Moussaoui seemed to engage al-Attas in something exciting. Moussaoui told al-Attas that they would go on to New York together as tourists. There they would rent a nice car.

As the spectators in the courtroom watched al-Attas's testimony, Moussaoui rubbed the prayer callus or zabib, on his forehead. It had gotten larger since jury selection in February. He touched it every so often, taking its measure. One reporter said it came from banging his head on the floor. The reporter from Al Arabiya was careful to point out the desirability of such a callus. It was a mark of devotion to prayer. Ayman al-Zawahiri, second in command to bin Laden, has a noticeable prayer callus, she noted, as she worked on filing a story. She was sitting in the back table of the deli with her cameraman, reviewing footage from the morning. The deli had become their office space, as it did for several of the French reporters.

The FBI on Trial
Michael Rolince was called to the witness stand. Now retired, he was an FBI Special Agent in charge of counterterrorism. A section chief at FBI headquarters in Washington, he was in the International Terrorism Operations Section, or, ITOS, from October 4, 1998 through January 1, 2002. According to one reporter, after 9/11 Rolince worked tirelessly with the families of the victims of 9/11, even giving out his

personal telephone number to them when they needed to talk. Unlike other FBI officials, he said, Rolince gave on-the-record interviews to the press.

The day Rolince testified at the Moussaoui trial he wore an American flag tie. He spoke of all the measures the FBI had undertaken, and of the procedures for investigating the plans of radical fundamentalist terrorists. In a 2004 interview he had said that because the hijackers were such professionals, and had made no mistakes, the chances of having caught them before they got on the planes were almost nil (Zeman et al., 2004). Now he was testifying to all the things the FBI could have done to connect the dots leading to 9/11, and did so over the objections of Edward MacMahon. On his way to lunch Moussaoui said, "God curse America." It sounded like, "God course Americaaaaa." Conversations in the cafeteria turned to the morning's testimony. One reporter defended Rolince's character. Others in the FBI were "knuckle-draggers," he said, but not Rolince.

After the lunch break, pulling keys, coins, pens, and other forgotten objects out of pockets, Rolince came back through security. He continued his testimony. Under questioning from David Raskin, he explained the positions and terminology unique to the FBI. He talked of Title IIIs. The judge wanted the term explained to the jury; he said that a Title III is a wiretap. The CSG was the Counter-Terrorism Security Group, which met in the White House Situation Room. It reported to the National Security Council. Members included Richard Clarke, then the counterterrorism advisor on the National Security Council, and "detailees," which, Rolince explained, meant members of other agencies including the CIA, FBI, FAA, the Coast Guard, and Defense who were assigned to the Counter-Terrorism Security Group. Richard Clarke chaired the group. Clarke, in Rolince's opinion, was "strident, combative, but focused as we all were focusing on terrorism." MacMahon objected to the comment, and the judge sustained the objection. Rolince moved on.

He described the Ressam case in order to depict what the FBI could do when it did connect the dots. By December 1999, intelligence agencies, including the FBI, knew that threats concerning the coming millennium had to be taken seriously. Ahmed Ressam, an Algerian living in Canada, was stopped at the Canada–US border in Port Angeles, Washington, when he came into the US on a ferry. Customs agents found explosives and timing devices in a spare tire well of his car. His room in Montreal was found to have traces of chemicals used in bomb-making. Ressam, said Rolince, had a telephone number for "Ghani." Rolince said that 22 FBI centers were "stood up." This meant that annual leave, Christmas, and New Year's holidays were cancelled. Phone numbers were tracked, and other suspects were identified in Seattle, Boston, and New York. "BOLO" ("Be On The

Lookout") was the watchword for information relating to a person or vehicle. John O'Neill, FBI counterterrorism expert – "God rest his soul," said Rolince – found a blue van and Abdel Ghani in New York. (O'Neill left the FBI in August 2001 to become head of security for the World Trade Center. After the attacks his body was found under debris on a stairwell. He had been on his new job for 20 days.)

The testimony turned to Moussaoui. Rolince said that David Frasca, FBI Unit Chief of the Radical Fundamentalist Unit, the RFU, "approached me in a hall conversation, walking to Psy Ops." Frasca told Rolince that Rolince would be getting a phone call from Minnesota about someone held in detention there. The Minnesota FBI wanted to travel to France with this person to get information, especially from his laptop. The conversation lasted approximately 20 seconds, Rolince said. Rolince never got the phone call from Minnesota.

Rolince was asked what the FBI could have done to prevent the attacks. He replied with a list of things: vet the information full on, do a polygraph, request convening Dick Clarke's CSG, visit the flight school, and fan out all agents. MacMahon objected. The judge said Rolince was editorializing. Exhibit 901 was displayed on the courtroom screens. It was titled "Bin Laden Determined to Strike in the US" (see CNN, 2004a). Dated August 6, 2001, some of the information for this Presidential Daily Briefing, or PDB, had come from Ahmed Ressam, the millennium bomber caught in Washington state. Rolince said he didn't receive it.

Edward MacMahon then cross-examined Rolince. Threat reports were buzzing all during that year, MacMahon said. Khalid Sheikh Mohammed was recruiting people to go to the US. "You knew that, didn't you? You knew that [George] Tenet's 'hair was on fire', you knew the term, you knew that the World Trade Center was to be a target. Ramzi Yousef just needed the money to finish the job." MacMahon put up Defense Exhibit 792. It was an April 2001 communication from Dale Watson of the Radical Fundamentalist Unit to then FBI Director Louis Freeh, concerning a threat report on the connection between Ibn Khattab of Chechnya and Osama bin Laden. Rolince's name was on it, as a member of the authorizing chain of command. Rolince said he had not seen it. The judge said: "This communication could be approved by you without you seeing it?" "Absolutely." The spectators, including family members, could not contain their laughter. Things were not going well for Mr. Rolince.

MacMahon questioned him about the attempts by Agent Samit and others in the Minneapolis FBI office to get the attention of FBI headquarters. Rolince said that Samit's hunches and suspicions were one thing, "What we knew was another." He had heard very little about Samit's requests to investigate Moussaoui further. MacMahon then read from an August 18, 2001, document from Agent Samit of the Minneapolis FBI to headquarters. Rolince looked puzzled and asked what document MacMahon was reading from. "Samit's communication to your office." The spectators shifted in their seats and laughed. Rolince was excused.

Flight School Testimony
The afternoon continued with flight school personnel from Florida and Arizona. The office manager for Florida Flight Training Center testified about her problems getting a visa for Ramzi bin al-Shibh to enter the United States as a flight student. Bin-Shibh was from Yemen. The office manager said she had never heard of Yemen before the bombing of the USS *Cole*. Perhaps he had trouble entering the US because of that, she said. He never did receive a visa. The witnesses testified as to their contacts with the hijackers. Mohammed Atta and Marwan al-Shehi, the pilots of the planes that hit the World Trade Center, had been students at Huffman Aviation in Florida for about seven months. Susan Hall, office manager at Huffman, said Atta was cold, steely, and hateful. She called him "the little terrorist." Moussaoui, listening, rubbed his zabib, smiled, and nodded. Al-Shehi was more on the friendly side, she said. Leaving for a break, Moussaoui said "God bless Mohammed Atta."

March 22, 2006: Day Seven, Eligibility Phase

Wednesday, March 22, was cold and windy. There was snow on the ground. The crowd waiting outside the courthouse doors shivered, drank coffee, and chatted. Larry and Arnie were two spectators who had followed the Moussaoui proceedings for a while. Larry, a retired contractor, had been in the Marine Corps. Arnie, a retired dentist, lived in a condominium next to the courthouse. Yamen, tall and smiling, was the cameraman for Al Arabiya. He was a place holder for the reporter, Nadia Bilbassy-Charters. He had to be in line in time to get a sticker that would admit Bilbassy-Charters into the main courtroom. James Gordon Meek, in the Washington bureau of the *New York Daily News*, had covered the war in Afghanistan and was on the terrorism beat in Washington. Phil Hirschkorn of CNN arrived. With slick-backed hair and a long trench coat, he kept up with text-messaged news as he stood in line. Staff members from MacMahon's office slipped to the head of the line.

The Flight Schools, continued
In the courtroom, the Huffman Aviation story continued. The two flight students, Atta and al-Shehi, were memorable. Daniel Pursell, chief flight instructor at Huffman, had taught them both. On December 26, 2000, Pursell was having a post-Christmas dinner when

he received a phone call from Mohammad Atta. Atta and al-Shehi were sitting in a small plane on the runway at Miami International Airport. "The airplane has quit," said Atta. Pursell went through checklists with Atta, talking him through what to do. Nothing worked, so Pursell told Atta to move the plane. Atta called Pursell back. How were the two to get back to Huffman, he asked. Rent a car, said Pursell. Atta wanted Huffman to pay for the car rental. Atta was told that was his problem. A tower chief from Miami International called Huffman the next day. Huffman had some explaining to do.

Early in 2001, Pursell received a call from an airport security guard at Clearwater, Florida. The airport there is small, and there is a curfew on "touch-and-gos," practicing take-offs and landings, after dark. Atta and al-Shehi were at it again. Pursell said Huffman Aviation breathed a "collective sigh of relief" when the two left. Ken Troccoli, on cross-examination, asked if anyone reported the two to the FBI. Pursell said no. A little sigh escaped from the spectators, including the family members in the courtroom. A large man in the row reserved for family members, who brought a rubber donut for a cushion, groaned at the lost opportunity. Troccoli asked Pursell if one can fly into an international airport without a flight plan. Pursell replied, "That's one of the great things about America."

Peggy Chevrette of Jet Tech, a flight school in Phoenix, Arizona, testified that Hani Hanjour, the pilot of the Pentagon flight, had difficulty with just about everything. His English was poor, and he had trouble with understanding the terminology of aviation. This made Chevrette worried that he would kill someone. She said it took him eight hours to finish what was normally a two-hour exam. She said he didn't want to learn how to take off and to land. He just wanted to fly. She called an FAA agent, John Anthony, who was at the flight training center there. They had at least three conversations, she said. She told Anthony that Hanjour was not capable of flying and was having trouble with the exams. Anthony suggested Hanjour get a translator – even though FAA rules state that the pilot must do it himself, in English, the international language of aviation. She said that on September 11 she was driving to work when she heard that the third plane hit the Pentagon. Knowing that her company had been responsible, she cried the rest of the way to work. The FBI came to see her on the next day. She said, "You are here because of Hani Hanjour." They had no name or photo with them. She gave all the flight school records to the FBI. "I knew in my heart" that it was Hani Hanjour, who was on the Pentagon plane, she said. John Anthony, the FAA agent, called her. "Your worst nightmare has been realized."

Western Union and ATT: The Government Connects the Dots
For days the jury and the spectators had heard what mistakes had been made by the FBI, the FAA, and the flight schools. Signals and threats

could have been acted on, if only the clues had been connected. Now the prosecution demonstrated the strengths of the government's investigatory powers after 9/11. Don Rigby, the subpoena compliance officer for Western Union, was called to the witness stand. Western Union, he told the jury, is an instant money transfer company, with 230,000 agents worldwide. By tracking ten-digit transfer control numbers, one can follow both "send money" transfers and "receive money" transfers. This was done for the transfers of money from the United Arab Emirates to an Ahad Sabet, presumably Ramzi bin al-Shibh, in Hamburg. Denied a US visa, bin al-Shibh had become the paymaster for the hijackers and for Moussaoui. Moussaoui received $10,060.53 through a Western Union transfer from "Ahad Sabet," which he picked up at a Buy for Less in Norman, Oklahoma. Later he received a second transfer for $4063.25. The Western Union testimony continued on through the morning. On September 8, 2001, Mohammed Atta had sent money back to the United Arab Emirates, as did Marwan al-Shehi and others of the group on September 9 and 10. Money was going to be of no use to them.

The judge called for a break in the proceedings. "God curse America," said Moussaoui, as he went through the door. A cell door clanked behind him as one of the marshals shut the courtroom door.

Robert Schultz testified after the recess. Schultz provides corporate security for ATT. When the FBI requests information, he provides compliance with subpoenas, which must give a specific telephone number and time period. Telephone calls can be traced through a variety of means, and Schultz demonstrated how. Searches can be made on originating calls and terminating calls (the source and the receiver of the calls). Originating call searches are more common, but can take two to three weeks to trace unless the search is expedited. Prepaid phone card calls go through a center in Ohio which keeps track of all such calls. There was a break for lunch. As he left the courtroom, Moussaoui said: "Victory for Moussaoui." Edward MacMahon listened, and said "That's new." The press huddled. Rumors passed through the courtroom: the eligibility phase of the trial should end next week, Moussaoui wants to testify. Reporters headed off to file their stories. Some went to the deli next door. The reporter and the cameraman for Al Arabiya sat in the back of the deli, editing video footage, other reporters sat over their laptops, too busy to talk with each other.

Aviation Testimony
Robert Cammaroto testified for the government. He was to provide the testimony the prosecution needed, and was almost refused, concerning what the aviation industry *could* have done if it had known of the plans for 9/11. Chief of commercial airports policy

with the Transportation Security Administration (TSA), Cammaroto was with the FAA for 25 years, working with commercial groups and airports on security. This being the United States, he said, public security mandates had to be worked out with privately owned airports and airlines. A juror sneezed; Cammaroto said "Bless you."

How many names were on the "no fly" list that summer? Less than a dozen. Eight or so. None of the hijackers were on the list. Moussaoui scratched his zabib. The last hijacking in the US was in 1991, Cammaroto said. A homesick Cuban wanted to return to Cuba. In August 2001 there were concerns that the main threat was overseas, not inside the United States. Could all planes be secured? Could all knives be stopped from coming on board? "I don't think so. You cannot stop all threats." That, he said, is why there are a number of security systems. One measure may fail, another is there to pick it up. He said that for three of the 9/11 flights, at least one of the hijackers was selected by a part of the system, screened for explosives or because there were no bags checked. But no one was removed from a plane. At the break in the proceedings Moussaoui called out "Victory for Moussaoui, God curse America."

Special Agent Zebley
Robert Spencer called to the witness stand Assistant US Attorney Aaron Zebley. Zebley had been a special agent with the FBI. Unlike the other witnesses, he had been present throughout much of the trial and was privy to what other witnesses had said. The judge had issued an order back in February that Zebley was to testify only as to what the United States government *could* have done to prevent the attacks (Docket No. 1617). When he was with the FBI, he had worked on the East African embassy bombings case, he said. At the mention of the bombings, Moussaoui smiled.

Zebley was in New York at the time the planes struck the Trade Center, and he responded to try to help. He was made part of the PENTTBOM squad. The group, including Zebley, was moved to FBI headquarters in Washington. He had investigated the workings of the Hamburg cell, and knew of the financial arrangements made by Ramzi bin al-Shibh. He also went to Oklahoma to investigate Moussaoui's presence there. In court, Zebley gave a tight presentation on what was known about Ramzi bin al-Shibh's money transactions. The day ended. The court officer said: "All rise; God save these United States and this Honorable Court." Moussaoui said "Victory for al Qaeda."

March 23, 2006: Day Eight, Eligibility Phase

Aaron Zebley took the stand again the following morning and picked up the money trail where he left off the day before. His testimony was well prepared. It connected the information from Western Union with that of ATT. The phone number in Sharjah, United Arab Emirates (UAE) led to Moussaoui through money wired from the UAE to Hamburg, then from Hamburg to Moussaoui. Ahad Sabet, the name on the transfer from Hamburg to the US, actually was an American living in Arizona. In 1998 he was on vacation in Spain, where his passport was stolen. In 2001, he was in Arizona, not in Germany. Sabet's identity was used to wire money to the United States. The true sender, according to Zebley, was Ramzi bin al-Shibh.

Zebley described the process of tracking telephone records. The US Attorney's office issues a subpoena. Call detail records (CDRs) can be provided the same day. Both toll records (calls from a place) and reverse call records (finding the calls to a place) can be determined. This method was used by Zebley and the Kenyan police in searching for a bomber who was supposed to have died in the American embassy bombing in Nairobi. In fact, he survived and made several phone calls to a certain number. Four days later, the Kenyan police got the reverse phone records and tracked down the bomber.

Zebley testified that Moussaoui, using a prepaid calling card, called a telephone number in the United Arab Emirates from the United States. Forty-one calls were made to this phone number by Moussaoui and others. Nine different phone cards were used, including ATT, IDT, MCI, and Telstar. Zebley went on to dazzle the spectators with the apparent efficiency with which the FBI found the hijackers' traces. Rob Spencer asked Zebley that, knowing all this and the connection to Moussaoui, what could one do? "One could notify the Secret Service when a threat to the president is known," Zebley said. MacMahon objected: there was no threat to the president. Zebley countered: there was a threat to the White House. "What investigation could have been done?" Spencer asked. Zebley said that one could look through information on flight schools. The connection between bin al-Shibh and the hijackers at the Florida flight schools could have been made. There was a break. Moussaoui said "Victory for al Qaeda."

Alan Yamamoto, on cross-examination, asked Zebley: "You were here for the whole trial, weren't you?" "Yes." The judge said "Mr. Zebley ... " "Agent' is fine," he said. "Agent Zebley," the judge continued, "the New York field office *could* have been involved, the Washington bureau *would* have listened." She continued: "Take a deep breath, calm down just a titch. You've got to let him [Yamamoto] finish." At the break Moussaoui said "God curse America. God curse you all." Some of the reporters said they felt offended.

After the break, Zebley said it was a daily occurrence that the FBI got information about bin Laden's associates. Zebley testified that there was concern over the information on Moussaoui. The FISA issue and the "wall" were problems. He quoted Steve Bongardt of the FBI as saying in an email, "someday someone will die, wall or not; the public will want to understand why everything was not thrown at it." Zebley was asked if lying can be part of a conspiracy. "Yes, definitely," he said.

The government rested its case in the eligibility trial. Moussaoui looked at the clock. It was 2:40 p.m. The judge said there would be a sealed, or closed, hearing on the sixth floor, at which the defendant could be present. As they all left, Moussaoui said to the defense: "I will testify. You can't stop me."

The Defense Begins its Case
After the hearing the judge, lawyers, and defendant returned to Courtroom 700, and the defense called its first witness, Erik Rigler. Ken Troccoli then asked "The Court's indulgence?" The judge said, "This is a very indulgent court; all right, two more minutes."

Erik Rigler, formerly with the FBI, now was working in aviation forensics. He gave a PowerPoint presentation on the failures of intelligence concerning the presence of Khalid al-Mihdhar and Nawaj al-Hazmi, two of the hijackers, in the United States. This presentation did not have the zip of that of Zebley. Rigler summarized the work of the Senate and House of Representatives' Joint Inquiry Investigative Committee, which made recommendations to various inspectors to investigate the Department of Justice, State Department, CIA, and FBI in their conduct before 9/11. Rigler said that the Inspector General for the Justice Department, Glenn Fine, was critical of the FBI's handling of the threats coming in from overseas. Rigler laid out the evidence that the FBI and CIA had concerning a meeting in Malaysia in January 2000, of al-Mihdhar and al-Hazmi, with Khallad, who planned the attack on the *Cole*. The FBI was never told of that meeting until August 2001, when they started a low priority search for al-Mihdhar and al-Hazmi. The FBI learned that al-Mihdhar had entered the US on July 4, 2001, and there was no record of his departure. This was, for the FBI, an "oh shit" moment. By August 24, 2001, the two were watch listed by the CIA and the FBI. By September 5, 2001, the FBI had run their criminal histories, credit card checks had been done, as well as motor vehicle checks, a Marriott Hotel check, and Choice Point (data mining) searches. The two were not found until too late.

March 27, 2006: Day Nine, Eligibility Phase

Moussaoui Testifies
On Monday morning, March 27, Soledad O'Brien of CNN interviewed Jonathan Turley, a law professor at George Washington University. Turley has taken on high-profile cases, including one that came out of this particular court. Moussaoui was due to testify that day. Turley

said that by testifying Moussaoui would put his head in a noose, and that it was hard to see how he would avoid the death penalty. Moussaoui was, Turley said, a "barking lunatic." Moussaoui had "done everything short of chewing the carpet in the courtroom" (Turley, 2006).

From the point of view of Turley, of other lawyers who were following the case, the press, and the public, Moussaoui's insistence on testifying appeared to be a crazy act. This was the only way Moussaoui could be explained to their satisfaction. Moussaoui was playing a different game from the one that Turley imagined him playing, or thought he should play.

Moussaoui took the stand. Gerald Zerkin began direct examination of his client. Concerning the statement of facts that Moussaoui had signed as part of his guilty plea, Zerkin asked how he signed it. Moussaoui said he took a pen and signed it. Your signature, said Zerkin, what signature did you use? Moussaoui responded that he signed "20th Hijacker." When asked why he signed it "20th Hijacker," Moussaoui answered, "Why not?" He then said it was because everybody used to refer to him as the 20th hijacker, and "it was a bit of fun; that's all" (tr. March 27, 2006, page 2310, lines 6–17). Moussaoui was asked if he was to be the fifth hijacker on Flight 93, the Pennsylvania plane. No, he was not. Were you to be the 20th hijacker? No. He said he was to be a pilot of a fifth plane in the September 11 attacks. He was, he said, supposed to pilot a plane to hit the White House. Richard Reid was to be a member of his crew. As to the others, it was not definite. Asked who Moussaoui thought might be in the crew, he responded "Abu Usama Kaini." He was asked to spell it for the court reporter; Moussaoui said that since English wasn't his first language, you have to spell it for yourself. When asked if there was anyone else he thought might be in the crew, he said "Haythama Kaini" and "Abu Aytha Kaini." More stonewalling was to follow: Zerkin asked if, in his statement of facts, Moussaoui said that he lied to allow the hijackers to go forward. Did you agree that you lied? Yes. And what did you mean by that statement? "I mean I lie. I didn't say the truth. That's what I meant" (tr. March 27, 2006, page 2314, line 12). He said that there are three instances when it is acceptable to lie: in order to bring Muslims together, when your wife asks if she is beautiful, and during jihad.

Rob Spencer on cross-examination asked Moussaoui about his involvement as a pilot of a fifth plane. Moussaoui said:

Basically, I had, I had a dream, and I had more later, but I had a dream, and I went to see Sheikh Usama Bin Laden, and I told him about my dream. He told me, "Good." Maybe, I don't know, a few days later, I have another dream. So I went again, I saw him, and I told him about this. This was after I have declined, I was asked before. Then I had this dream. Then maybe a week, a short time, Sheikh Abu Hafs [Mohammed Atef] came to the guesthouse. He asked me again if I wanted to be part of the suicide operation, me and Richard Reid, and this time I say yes. (tr. March 27, 2006, page 2338, lines 6–15)

Gerald Zerkin, now on re-direct examination, asked Moussaoui: "Mr. Moussaoui, the dream that you had about flying a plane into the White House, did you, as part of that dream, envision who was with you on your crew?" Moussaoui replied: "Yeah, not specific. I knew that I was a pilot because I was in a pilot suit, and there was four other people on the tarmac with me" (tr. March 27, 2006, page 2402, lines 1–9). He went on to describe his reason for wanting to fly a 747:

... but if you want to say the original reason, okay, what I believe, okay, it is I thought I had a dream where I was into the runway of an airport and I actually took a map out, okay, and I open it and it was the White House with a circle with a cross, like you do when you do target.

And next to me, okay, in front of there was the four brother, I couldn't recognize. And next to me there was a 747, the very distinct, you know, like the cockpit, was very distant [sic]. (tr. March 27, 2006, page 2402, lines 18–25)

He said he told his dream of flying a 747 into the White House to bin Laden. Moussaoui went on to describe how dreams are interpreted:

And I say this to Sheikh Usama Bin Laden, and we – talked to him ... I talk to him about this, it was the first time, it was something middle of 2000, it was March or something like that, okay? And when I came back from Malaysia, we talk about it again because there was – I had another dream with more metaphorical. And I used to go see him each time I had dream, okay, to – because people have more knowledge, understand more because you explain the dream by the Qur'an. You don't explain it because you just think like that, okay? You have to incorporate your explanation with statements you find in the Qur'an or statements you find from the Prophet Mohammed. And this book will deal specifically with interpretation of dream. So I refer to Sheikh Usama Bin Laden and some other sheikh there to explain to me the reality, but the dream about the White House, it was very clear to me. (tr. March 27, 2006, page 2403, lines 1–18)

He ended his testimony by saying he was grateful to be an al-Qaeda member (tr. March 27, 2006, page 2416, line 24).

Khalid Sheikh Mohammed's Stipulation
Following Moussaoui's testimony, Khalid Sheikh Mohammed's statement was read into the court record. Mohammed, or "KSM," was captured in Pakistan in March 2003, and since then had been held by the CIA in a secret off-shore location. As with the other statements from the al-Qaeda captives, the jury was told that his statements: "were made under circumstances designed to elicit truthful statements from the witness." Mohammed was in a good position to know about Moussaoui's participation because Mohammed, beginning with bin

Laden's approval in 1999, worked out most of the plans for September 11. Mohammed Atef also played a major role in choosing targets and finding participants. Khalid Sheikh Mohammed denied that Moussaoui was to participate in the attacks. Moussaoui was to take part in a later, follow-up attack. Mohammed denied that Moussaoui ever knew Atta. Moussaoui's arrest did not in any way affect the planning for 9/11, because he was not involved. Mohammed detailed the planning of the operation, which originally had been even more expansive. He said the reason for the attack was to "wake people up" to the atrocities Americans were perpetrating by its support of Israel and through its foreign policies. Moussaoui was chosen for the second wave because he had a European passport and would be able to pass through the heightened security Mohammed anticipated after the first wave of attacks happened. However, there were problems with him, Mohammed said, and he had misgivings about enlisting him. But bin Laden and Mohammed Atef had wanted to use him. When Moussaoui came back to Pakistan from Malaysia in late 2000 he was made to complete additional training in Kandahar. Mohammed thought Moussaoui "did not have any particular personality flaws," but Moussaoui was highly confident. Because of the freedom of his Western upbringing he was not good at taking orders (Defense Exhibit 941).

March 28, 2006: Day Ten, Eligibility Phase

On Tuesday, March 28, the defense read statements from Mustafa al-Hawsawi, Mohammed al-Qahtani, Khallad, and Hambali, all of whom had been captured at various times after 9/11 and were being held in secret prisons.

Mustafa al-Hawsawi
Mustafa Ahmed al-Hawsawi was captured in Pakistan in March 2003. His testimony was also given at a secret location to interrogators. Al-Hawsawi was sent to the United Arab Emirates by Khalid Sheikh Mohammed. He became a financial manager for many of the hijackers, providing them with air tickets and money. Mohammed Atta called him from the US and asked him to make flight arrangements for a number of the "muscle" hijackers. Several of those men were surprised, and delighted, when they learned they were to go to the US. According to al-Hawsawi, both Khalid Sheikh Mohammed and Ramzi bin al-Shibh told him that the "last man," who would "complete the group," was Mohammed Mani' al-Qahtani. Al-Hawsawi bought al-Qahtani a one-way air ticket to Orlando. Al-Qahtani did not speak English, apparently did not know how to fill out the landing card, was detained at customs, and was shipped back to the United Arab

Emirates while Mohammed Atta was waiting for him at the airport. Al-Hawsawi had no financial dealings with Moussaoui, whom he had only seen several times in Afghanistan at a guest-house in Kandahar (Defense Exhibit 943).

Mohammed Mani' al-Qahtani

Mohammed Mani' al-Qahtani's story may have been similar to that of the other "muscle" hijackers. He trained for three months at the al-Farouq training camp in Afghanistan, then was told by bin Laden, to whom he had sworn bayat, to go see "Mukhtar," Khalid Sheikh Mohammed. Bin Laden told al-Qahtani that he, al-Qahtani, was someone who loved his religion and would do things for it. "Mukhtar" would have a way for al-Qahtani to express that love.

Al-Qahtani left Afghanistan for Karachi, Pakistan, where he met with "Mukhtar," who told him to go see "Mustafa," al-Hawsawi, in the United Arab Emirates. First al-Qahtani went back to Saudi Arabia, his home country, to get a new Saudi passport (his original one would show that he had been in Pakistan). In July 2001 he got visas to both the United States and Germany. Al-Qahtani then went to the United Arab Emirates, where he bought Western clothes and stayed with al-Hawsawi. On August 4, 2001, he flew to London and then Orlando. Unable to explain why he had a one-way ticket to Florida, he also did not know who was picking him up. He was returned to the UAE. He later said he knew none of the 19 hijackers, nor did he know Moussaoui. According to al-Hawsawi, it was al-Qahtani who was to be the last of the hijackers (Defense Exhibit 944).

Hambali

According to the statement, Hambali, or Riduan bin Isamuddin, was head of Jemaah Islamiyah (JI). JI's goal is to establish radical Islam in Southeast Asia. He operated in the Malaysia/Singapore/Thailand area, and was a liaison with al-Qaeda. He was captured in August 2003, and was also interrogated at an off-shore location. His statements concerning Moussaoui were the most colorful of the al-Qaeda members. Hambali said that Moussaoui came from Afghanistan via Pakistan to see him without a clear idea of what he was to do. He thought Moussaoui was "very troubled, not right in the head." Moussaoui complained about everything, including the plans which JI was making. Hambali said Moussaoui wanted 40 tons of ammonium nitrate, sometimes used in making explosives. Hambali did not want to pay for it, and instead bought 4 tons. Nothing happened with the explosives and Hambali was stuck with the bill. Moussaoui criticized the JI members for sitting around reading the Koran all the time when they could be out kidnapping Chinese businessmen and robbing motorists. Hambali told Moussaoui if he wanted to do such things he should do it in Europe. Finally, to get rid of Moussaoui, Hambali paid for a plane ticket back to Europe. One of his men in Pakistan went to Khalid Sheikh Mohammed to ask for repayment for the money they spent on Moussaoui. Mohammed paid. Hambali said Moussaoui told him frequently of his dream to fly a plane into the White House, but that Moussaoui seemed to do little to follow through on flight lessons. Flight schools are expensive, Hambali said, and Moussaoui never had any money. Hambali was not going to help him in that regard. They were glad to see Moussaoui go (Defense Exhibit 946).

Tuesday afternoon the defense played videotaped testimony given before the 9/11 Commission by Thomas J. Pickard, acting chief of the FBI until Robert Mueller was sworn in on September 4, 2001. Pickard was asked by the Commission whether, knowing that Moussaoui was an Islamic extremist, and taking into account the Phoenix memo, the FBI would have moved to stop the 9/11 attacks. He said that, given the thousands of leads and threats coming through that summer, it would have been difficult to put those facts together. Videotaped 9/11 Commission testimony by Condoleezza Rice, at the time national security advisor, George Tenet, head of the CIA, and Richard Clarke, head of counterterrorism at the National Security Council, was shown to the jury. Clarke apologized to the 9/11 families, saying: "Your government failed you" (Collinson, 2006).

The defense then read part of the transcript of the hearing when Moussaoui pleaded guilty on April 22, 2005. He had said then: "Everybody know that I'm not 9/11 material" (tr. April 22, 2005, page 33, lines 3–4). The government lawyers, hearing that the transcript had been read, called FBI Agent James Fitzgerald back to the witness stand. Fitzgerald revealed that, in February, four days before jury selection was to begin, Moussaoui met with the prosecution and a defense lawyer. Apparently, he was afraid the defense would not let him testify. Moussaoui had said he would testify for the prosecution, against himself, if he could at least have a better cell before what he thought would be his execution. He did not want to testify against any other al-Qaeda member, but he would talk about his own role. FBI agent James Fitzgerald said Moussaoui thought it better to die in battle than in jail, on a toilet (Riley, 2006b).

March 29, 2006: Day Eleven, Eligibility Phase

The Defense Rests its Case
Wednesday, the defense once again asked that the death penalty be struck. The judge denied the request, saying that the case had changed substantially since Moussaoui's testimony on Monday. The defense rested, and the case went to the jury to decide if Moussaoui was eligible for the death penalty. Over the next days, messages

came back from the jury. The jury wanted to know the definition of "weapons of mass destruction." She told them airplanes flown into buildings could be weapons of mass destruction.

APRIL 3, 2006: THE JURY'S VERDICT

Eligible for the Death Penalty

On Monday, April 3, the jury told the judge that they had reached a verdict. Word went out via the internet that the decision would be announced in an hour. Moussaoui refused to stand and face the jury. The jurors had voted unanimously that Moussaoui was eligible for the death penalty. Each count had four questions. To each they said yes: he was 18 at the time of the offense, he lied to federal agents on August 16–17, 2001, he lied contemplating that a life would be taken or intending that lethal force would be used on a person, and at least one victim died as a result of his lies. He was responsible for at least one death in the September 11 attacks.

And so the next phase of the trial would begin. Now the jury would decide whether Moussaoui would receive life in prison without possibility of release, or death by injection. As he was taken away, Moussaoui said: "You'll never get my blood. God curse you all." The press began to speculate that he would be sentenced to death (Reid, 2006).

THE PENALTY PHASE BEGINS

April 6, 2006: Day One, Penalty Phase

The second phase of the trial began on Thursday, April 6. The prosecution could present evidence as to the aggravating factors that would support the death penalty, and they did so. The horrible evidence of the pain and destruction of the attacks was not held back. Former New York mayor Rudolph Giuliani testified as to what he and his city did that day. He described the chaos, collapse, and confusion of the morning's events, and the toll it took on the victims, those who responded, and the families left behind.

Photographs were then shown of body parts on the streets; stories were told about bereaved wives, one of whom committed suicide after the attacks. A former New York City firefighter told of watching in horror as his good friend was hit by a falling body. James Smith, a New York City policeman, described the loss of his one-time partner, who was also his wife, to the collapsing towers, leaving a young daughter. The wife of a civilian engineer who worked at the Pentagon described her husband's last words to their son. As his son's school bus drove away, her husband called to him: "Say bye bye to daddy one more time." The son called back, for the last time. He now wants to be an astronaut, in order to go look for his daddy, she said. Tamar Rosebrook had videotaped the burning towers. She tried to narrate the video through her tears. The video showed people hesitating at the top floor windows, and then jumping to their deaths as they aimed for a canopy over a doorway. Some were on fire as they fell (Markon and Dwyer, 2006c). Moussaoui, once a Bruce Springsteen fan, said "Burn in the USA" (Hirschkorn, 2006b).

April 10, 2006: Day Two, Penalty Phase

The next day court was held, Monday, April 10, Judge Brinkema told the lawyers to be less heavy-handed with the devastating evidence. But it was hard to stop the tears. Witnesses for the prosecution, one after the other, told of the horror they witnessed that day, and the continuing pain they felt. One grandfather told of the loss of his son and grand-daughter, who never made it to Disneyland. Telephone calls were re-played, one from Kevin Cosgrove of Aon in the World Trade Center. One could hear the collapsing building, his screams, and the phone go dead. Melissa Doi in the Trade Center stayed on the phone as long as she was alive, talking and praying with a dispatcher. Spectators in the courtroom, tough reporters and military people had tears running down their cheeks, and wiped their noses (Beale, 2006).

April 11, 2006: Day Three, Penalty Phase

On Tuesday, April 11, Pentagon survivors told of crawling through debris and smoke to get out of the burning building. Some were incinerated before they could react. A photo showed one person, burned beyond recognition, but still in a sitting position. A Pentagon police officer described trying to pull someone out a window. The victim's burned skin pulled off in the survivor's hands. Photos were shown of another body, hardly looking like a body. Moussaoui said "Burn all the Pentagon next time!"

The jury then heard the phone calls of passengers aboard Flight 93. The passengers knew the World Trade Center had been hit, and were grimly aware that they were not going to survive this flight. A stewardess was boiling water to throw at the hijackers. Another was readying breakfast knives for an attack. Mark Bingham made four phone calls to report that the plane had been hijacked by three men with a bomb. He sent his love to his family. Jeremy Glick called his wife to say that passengers were preparing to storm the cockpit.

Todd Beamer called to say he thought one of the hijackers had a bomb. He then could be heard shouting: "The plane is going down!" Someone says: "Let's roll." In the courtroom, Moussaoui yelled "Let's roll to victory!" (Serrano, 2006). The following day, April 12, the jury heard the cockpit recording from Flight 93. The prosecution rested its case.

April 13, 2006: Day Five, Penalty Phase

Witnesses for the Defense
It was now the defense's turn. They had worked out a strategy, but it would be hard to counter the memories of that day. Moussaoui took the stand again, and scoffed at the witnesses. He said it was disgusting that they cried, including those who worked at the Pentagon. This is war, he said. He had no remorse for the victims or for their families. He was glad he was a member of al-Qaeda, and he would have wished the attacks of 9/11 "could have gone on and on." "We have to be the superpower, we have to be above you, and you have to be subdued," Moussaoui said. "You organize the misery of the world." He said he would have had another strategy for his defense than the one chosen by his lawyers. He thought he could have been offered, at some point in the future, as an exchange for American hostages. He also said to his lawyers: "I thought your idea to portray me as crazy was not going to work" (Hirschkorn, 2006c). Later, the jury would agree with that assessment. The press wrote that he seemed to want to be a martyr by trying to get the death penalty. He certainly did not seem to help himself.

April 17, 2006: Day Six, Penalty Phase

The defense planned to focus on Moussaoui's early family life and his mental state in an effort to present mitigating circumstances. On Monday, April 17, Jan Vogelsang, a clinical social worker, was the first witness for the defense. She testified that Moussaoui's father Omar was abusive and violent. Starved for food and beaten by her husband, Aïcha el-Wafi took her four children to a series of orphanages and children's homes. The two divorced, then reconciled, then separated again. This upheaval took a toll on all the family, but in particular Moussaoui's two sisters. They both testified via videotape that they receive medication for forms of schizophrenia. Their father is in a mental institution in the Paris region, apparently too heavily medicated to be interviewed. Yet Moussaoui was, according to his sister Jamila, "a pretty little baby, always smiling ... he was the little sweetheart of the family" (see Jamila Moussaoui, 2005).

Moussaoui's boyhood friends testified; one of whom had a Jewish parent. The two friends, Arab and Jew, thought that if they could be friends, why couldn't others? Moussaoui appeared to pay little attention to the testimony. When one former friend left the witness stand he looked intently at his old friend as if, one member of the press said, he was looking for the old Zacarias. The old Zacarias was not in the courtroom, but he listened attentively when his French girlfriend, Karine Bocat, was discussed.

Moussaoui's decision to leave France for London appeared to lead to his transition to al-Qaeda. The old friend who loved Martin Luther King Jr., dancing, and hanging out with friends became a regular attendee at London mosques. The chairman, or imam, of the Brixton Mosque described that transition in a videotaped interview (see Baker, 2005). The formerly friendly and eager person who was fun to be with began to change over the course of several years. Moussaoui's friend at South Bank University, Nil Plant, said he regularly went to Friday noontime prayers, and worked hard at his master's degree courses. He did not press Islam on her, although she was a former Muslim trying to learn more about Christianity (see Plant, 2005). But she has not seen him since 1993 and, by the time he finished his degree in 1995, he was creating difficulties for Imam Baker at Brixton Mosque. Moussaoui was recruited to other, more militant mosques and prayer rooms in London. The final straw for Baker occurred when Moussaoui showed up at the Brixton mosque in military clothing and a backpack, asking where the jihad was. Baker asked him to leave (Baker, 2005).

Vikas Ohri, one of the guards at the detention center where Moussaoui was held, testified that Moussaoui frequently told Ohri, as the guard made his rounds, that he dreamed about September 11 and of being released from prison by President Bush. Xavier Amador, a psychologist and expert in schizophrenia, took the stand to testify as to Moussaoui's own mental state. Moussaoui did not think much of the day's mental health testimony. He called it "a lot of America bullshit" as he left for one of the day's recesses.

April 18, 2006: Day Seven, Penalty Phase

Mental Health Testimony: Illness or Culture?
Xavier Amador, in what would be a long day's testimony, said he was asked by Moussaoui's lawyers to speak to Moussaoui in April 2002. Moussaoui was insisting on representing himself. The judge had asked a forensic psychiatrist, Raymond Patterson, to examine Moussaoui in order to determine his mental competence. Patterson met with Moussaoui, and determined he was not mentally ill. Amador read over Moussaoui's numerous pleadings (over 270) and observed him

in court, determining that he was paranoid, possibly schizophrenic. While in court one day, Amador was asked by the judge to go downstairs to talk with Moussaoui, for there was an incident with a difficult "cell extraction." Amador said water was everywhere, and paper towels were covering the floor. The marshals said Moussaoui had been "spitting water all over people all morning." Moussaoui was speaking to himself in a low, distressed tone, in English. Amador asked: "Are you praying?" "I have the right to protect myself. Praise Allah." Amador said: "Good morning. Judge Brinkema is worried about you." Moussaoui replied: "You have seen me, now go." Moussaoui then spat water on Amador, who had turned his back. There were five dowsings, then two more; a guard gave him some cardboard. Ten more dowsings; then Moussaoui became resigned. "You cannot help me, go." "American shit Jew, prostitute. Shit. My job is to kill you so I can enter paradise." "Five jumped me, they beat me, they bloodied my face. They were sent to kill me."

"At quarter to seven they attacked me. You should get a video of the attack; it is in the court record." Moussaoui then asked: "What do you do for work?" Amador replied: "I am a psychologist." Moussaoui said: "I always cooperate; I don't know why they jumped me." His affect changed; he was angry but calm. According to Amador, Judge Brinkema then said, from the courtroom above: "Mr. Moussaoui, it is your right to see this [deposition by his Oklahoma roommate Hussein al-Attas]; here's what you will have to do. I know you can see and hear this; you will have to place … " Amador stopped. The spectators in the courtroom assumed Amador meant that the judge was talking about a stun belt. Zerkin asked if such spitting incidents were common. Amador says it had happened to him more times than he could count.

Amador went on to say that, when Moussaoui heard Amador was at the Alexandria detention center, Moussaoui refused to meet with him because Amador was working with the defense. Moussaoui said that Amador would say he is crazy. In April 2005, Amador wrote a report, based on Moussaoui's writings and Amador's interactions with him, saying that Moussaoui was delusional. For instance, said Amador, Moussaoui would tell his guards, who also thought he was delusional, that Bush will release him, and he will go back to London. He has a dream that he will be released, fly back to Heathrow on a 747, and write a book. Listening to Amador, Moussaoui nodded his head several times, as he did each time witnesses mentioned his dream. Amador said that he himself has read on Islam, but had concluded even earlier, in the fall of 2003, that Moussaoui was psychotic.

Amador went to London and France in order to learn more about Moussaoui's "subculture," but his behavior indicates mental illness, Amador said. Amador spoke to experts on political Islam, including two in France, looked into cultural and subcultural differences, and read al-Qaeda literature. He is not rational, said Amador. Moussaoui's behavior is not from the al-Qaeda subculture. Moussaoui says his lawyers are trying to kill him, a sign of paranoia. He is grandiose, another indicator of irrationality, in that he thinks Bush will release him. He is grandiose and paranoid because he says that if only he can testify, he will "clear up" 9/11 and gain his immediate freedom. He believed he was monitored by the FBI, and during the summer of 2002 kept writing about this belief.[4]

Zerkin asked what evidence Moussaoui might have had that his lawyers, including Zerkin, were trying to kill him. Letters from Frank Dunham to Moussaoui were introduced; Dunham referred frequently to Moussaoui's intellect and insights. Dunham stopped by the detention center on Saturdays to talk with Moussaoui. In one note sent when Moussaoui refused to see him, Dunham wrote: "Zacarias, I came by to see you. I did not come by to argue with you or try to change your mind about anything, but simply to talk. It is Saturday morning and I couldn't imagine not coming by." During this testimony, Moussaoui was slouched in his seat, apparently not paying attention. At one break, Moussaoui said: "Beautiful terrorist mind." At the lunch break, he said: "Crazy or not crazy, that is the question." Indeed, it was. All the reporters wrote it down.

After lunch, Novak questioned Amador about Moussaoui's emphasis on representing himself. Perhaps, Novak suggested, this was so he could spread the horrible words of al-Qaeda. It was a bad idea to refuse his court-appointed lawyers and to rely so heavily on the Koran for guidance, said Novak. Novak then asked Amador, who was born in Cuba. "If you were in Cuba, you would want a Cuban lawyer?" "Yes, it would be the only way," replied Amador. Judge Brinkema said: "Mr. Novak, Cuba is not an issue in this case." The spectators, looking for a light moment in this long day, burst into laughter. The testimony continued, as people shifted in their seats. Moussaoui turned around to the sketch artists behind him, and signaled to one that he would like to see what was being drawn. The artist refused, knowing that he would probably be reprimanded by the marshals.

Amador discussed the signs of disorganized thought. Speech can sound like something he called "word salad," a mixture of concepts and thoughts without a train of thought. Reporters in the overflow courtroom leaned to each other. "Sometimes I sound like that," said one. "I sound like that in the classroom," said a college professor. David Novak asked Amador how Moussaoui has behaved in the courtroom. There have been no outbursts since February 6, Amador replied. "He's giving a sound bite to the press who will report it, right?" said Novak. Moussaoui nodded his head, looking around at the spectators. Novak brought out the fact that Moussaoui actually did think the FBI was surveilling him from the time he arrived in the US, and thought they were capable of putting a bug in the fan he picked up in the street in Oklahoma. He did not know of FISA requirements and the subpoenas necessary to do wiretaps and plant listening devices, and testified that he had since learned about the American laws of search and seizure.

By 4:45 even the judge was rubbing her eyes. The jury members looked a little weary, jiggling legs and hands. At the end of the day Moussaoui said to Amador: "I think you should fly back to Cuba."

April 19, 2006: Day Eight, Penalty Phase

The trial was coming to an end. Spectators and the press were now lined up outside the courthouse by 6 a.m., when the streetlights were still on. A protocol developed concerning the line. People gave themselves numbers in the order in which they arrived. Someone was detailed to go get coffee and bagels. After the number 8, chances of getting into Courtroom 700 were slim. A reporter from Roanoke would throw down her change purse, indicating her presence, and then leave to have a cigarette. The French ran from their cars to get into place. As one of the French reporters said, the French could smell blood, and they wanted to cover the final events of the trial. Guillemette of *Le Figaro* sat on the ground to work on her blog. Phil Hirschkorn from CNN followed the Duke lacrosse scandal with his Blackberry. As the crowd pressed into line, a reporter mentioned that Moussaoui had a pair of Scooby Doo briefs in his possession when the FBI took an inventory. The guards up on the roof above watched. One behind the other, the group entered the building through the revolving door, pulling out IDs, taking off coats, preparing to go through security. The cameramen waited outside under their little tents, hoping the morning would go fast.

Cults and Culture
Inside, Dr. Paul Martin, an expert on cults, was the first witness of the day. He had testified in the Lee Malvo, Washington, DC, sniper case. He had testified as well in the Ohio trial of a leader of a breakaway Mormon group. In that case, a family was murdered because they did not approve of the leader's practices of "blood cleansing." Martin himself had belonged to a Jesus band in the 1970s that traveled around the country in a VW bus. It seemed like the thing to do at the time, he said.

Martin laid out the reasons why recruitment to al-Qaeda worked for Moussaoui. It provided him a support group when he had economic, housing, and occupational problems. It provided social assistance and a sense of community. For this large favor, one owes a large debt.

He probably thinks he owes them his life, Martin said. Moussaoui smiled, hitting his palms together. Most al-Qaeda members were well educated, said Martin. Quoting from Marc Sageman's *Understanding Terror Networks*, Martin said that, of 400 al-Qaeda members, 75 percent were from the middle class, 90 percent came from intact families, 63 percent had gone to college. Seventy-five percent were engineers and scientists, 73 percent were married, and most had children. The groups in London provided Moussaoui and people similar to him with support, Martin said. During this discussion, Moussaoui shook his head no, laughed, and on occasion talked quietly to himself. Martin was excused.

Mental Competence and Moussaoui's Dreams
Michael First is a psychiatrist at Columbia University. Zerkin established his credentials as a diagnostician of mental illness. First was involved with a case involving a prison inmate; he had been asked to determine whether the inmate was mentally competent to be executed. Moussaoui listened and smiled. First went on to explain what in his opinion was delusional about Moussaoui's behavior. First had traveled with Amador to England and France, where he interviewed Imam Baker and Moussaoui's mother. He talked with Moussaoui's guards at the detention center. Through those interviews, and by reading Moussaoui's pleadings and the transcripts of the court hearings, he determined that Moussaoui's actions were not part of his subculture. A delusion, he said, was a false belief based on an incorrect inference about external reality. This belief is held with delusional conviction. The belief is not ordinarily accepted by other members of the person's culture or subculture. First said that Moussaoui's refusal to agree to a mental health assessment was problematic; that his suspicion over orders to have cell-side access by mental health experts was indicative of mental issues. At the break Moussaoui said: "Moussaoui fly over the cuckoo nest."

First returned to the witness stand to further describe delusions. With Santeria, he said, the belief that the Virgin Mary could appear is not delusional, because other people share that belief. It may be part of a cultural belief that Mary appears during the night. It is delusional when one individual believes he or she is doing the tango with Mary. Zerkin asked if First had determined whether Moussaoui had delusions. First said he had. Moussaoui smiled to himself. First continued: Moussaoui believes that Bush will free him. Moussaoui nodded. First said the idea first appeared in a pleading by Moussaoui posted on April 22, 2003. "No doubt Dunham will go crazy when I will leave on a 747/400 first class, no smoking, no drink, no women" (Docket No. 853). Moussaoui reportedly said in jail that: "You will know Allah is the true God when George W. Bush sets me free to go to

JFK." He has told everyone in jail he talks with that this will happen, and he tries to convert them. A female guard said: "If George Bush does do that I'm going to convert to Islam." Moussaoui nodded and laughed and looked at the spectators.

First continued, saying that it is Moussaoui's testimony and conviction that this will happen. He is 100 percent sure. Moussaoui nodded. First did agree that dreams and their interpretation are important in Islam and in the Judaeo-Christian tradition. Dreams require interpretation, as they are typically allegorical. However, First said, they are proven to be true retrospectively. They are not to be believed with 100 percent certainty prior to the occurrence of the event. For the interpretation of dreams, one must go to a scholar of Islam.

In his testimony, First said, Richard Reid described a dream that was important to him. Zerkin and Novak then argued over whether Reid's testimony was admissible. Judge Brinkema ruled that it was. In Reid's Yahoo account there were three files. One was a letter to his mother explaining why he had gone on jihad. Another was a description of a dream he had a year before, in December 2000. In his dream, he wrote, he was waiting for a ride. A pickup truck full of people came along. Reid couldn't get in because it was too crowded. He was upset. A smaller truck came along. "I now believe the pickup truck was 9/11. I was upset at not being sent." This was an allegory, First said, which only made sense after the events had occurred. Thinking a dream will become reality in the future with 100 percent certainty is very different. Moussaoui nodded. Moussaoui has had a dream, First said, of Joseph from the Old Testament. The dream involved Joseph and Zachariah, the Old Testament prophet. Joseph could interpret dreams. There were six different dreams which foretold what would happen to the people of Israel.

Moussaoui, First said, insisted that the charges against him will be instantly dismissed if only he can tell his story. Moussaoui nodded and smiled. This has been a common theme in his pleadings, First continued. He refused to accept government documents from his defense team. He refused to sit with the defense lawyers at their table. Zerkin asked if this was part of al-Qaeda subculture. No, First said. One of the al-Qaeda training manuals says to get a lawyer, whether retained by the brother's family or court-appointed. There are no other known examples of this behavior from other imprisoned terrorists. Moussaoui blew air and smiled. He pointed to himself and shook his head no. He does not follow that training manual. He then smiled and talked to himself. At the break for lunch Moussaoui said: "God bless crazy Moussaoui."

During cross-examination Novak pointed out that the guards at the detention center are not of Moussaoui's subculture. Therefore, how can they assess his behavior? Novak said that Moussaoui knew he was communicating to the world through his pleadings. Moussaoui smiled. That was his primary reason, to communicate, right? Moussaoui nodded. Novak proceeded, using the arcane language of psychiatry. "Tangentiality" caught his tongue, making the jargon seem a bit silly. Let me ask you this, said Novak. Some turn to religion in times of dire stress, to give one hope. Moussaoui is in a tough spot. There is not a lot of hope for him. Moussaoui smiled. Novak said that religion is a factor in how he has acted. It is not delusional to turn to religion to give him hope, isn't that right? First agreed. Novak was finished.

Family Members Testify for the Defense
The afternoon moved on. While a number of family members of the victims had testified for the government, some family members had contacted the defense lawyers and asked to testify regarding the mitigating factors in Moussaoui's case. Although they could not talk about what they thought should happen to Moussaoui, they did talk about how they coped with their losses. Marilynn Rosenthal's son Josh was killed in the World Trade Center. The family has established a lecture series at the University of Michigan in his honor. "John Alan Rosenthal," she said, sadly. "JAR.... He was fond of those cookies. I should have brought some," she said. Reporters wiped their noses.

Alan Yamamoto called Robin Therkauf. Therkauf's husband Tom died in the World Trade Center. They had been married 14 years. He did most of the cooking. He had been through the 1993 bombing of the World Trade Center and always talked about moving the office. He had arranged for office space in Stanford, Connecticut. The move was delayed, and was rescheduled for September 18, 2001. Robin Therkauf was a political scientist, teaching as a lecturer. "How is it for you?" Yamamoto asked gently. She replied slowly, "It is a hard thing to come to accept." She kept very busy. By the second year, she took time off from teaching. She became a student at Yale Divinity School. Moussaoui listened without expression, stroking and pulling on his beard. People are flawed and broken, she said. "The Bible attempts to explain the fallen nature of humanity. We are all broken, broken people. On the other hand, we are all the children of God and loved by God." At the break Moussaoui said: "God curse America."

The stories of heartbreak continued through the afternoon. Patricia Perry's son John was a New York City policeman. On the morning of September 11 he went to police headquarters, signed his resignation papers, and turned in his badge. He was starting a job in medical malpractice as a lawyer. As soon as he heard of the attacks at the Trade Center, he walked back into the Police Department. "Give me back my badge," he said. He bought an NY Police polo shirt, and went to the Trade Center. Eleven hundred people came to his service, his mother said. Both Stony Brook University and New York University Law School have honored his name with memorials.

Orlando Rodriguez, a sociologist at Fordham University, spoke of his son Greg, who worked as associate vice-president for email security at Cantor Fitzgerald. Two days after 9/11 the head of Cantor Fitzgerald told the families that if the victims' names were not in a hospital directory that they had died. Greg's name was in no hospital directory. "What did you learn from him?" Alan Yamamoto asked. "How to make contact with people," Dr. Rodriguez replied. He said his son had an extraordinary capacity to look at people as human beings regardless of their culture. A photo of the two of them taken in New Hampshire's White Mountains was flashed on the screen. They were both smiling, happy to be together. Rodriquez said now he honors Greg's memory by teaching his students about terrorism and state response to violence.

Donald Bane's son Michael Andrew worked on the 100th floor of the North Tower of the World Trade Center. Michael was an assistant vice-president for Marsh McLennan. Bane's wife said just after 9/11 she had a vision of Michael in a tennis shirt and khakis, reassuring her. He said he would be all right. He was walking down the stairs, looking back at her. Bane has tried to think of ways to understand people who could do this sort of thing. His wife has started a music scholarship at Stony Brook University, Michael's alma mater. This is one way to try to keep the music going, he said.

Alan Yamamoto called Anthony Aversano. He recounted a period of his life when he was not talking with his dad, who worked at Aon in the Trade Center. Anthony finally called his father and reconnected, for which he felt extremely grateful. "How do you cope with your loss?" Yamamoto asked. Aversano replied that this act of terrorism was doing something inside him. He felt fear and anger. Then he thought that he had a choice here, and that he needed to decide how to focus his energy and use his life. Otherwise he would be hijacked as well. To build bridges, one needs to get life back, he said. There is nothing else to do in life but to live the path of love and compassion for other people.

It was the end of the day. Moussaoui said: "Moussaoui dream or American dream. One or the other."

April 20, 2006: Day Nine, Penalty Phase

The following morning the courthouse door crowd was there before 6 a.m. Coffee and bagels helped keep people awake. Before 8 a.m. the sirens wailed. Moussaoui's convoy sped into the underground garage. A courthouse guard called to one of the spectators in line. He had been heard the day before asking which vehicle was Moussaoui's. Word had spread through the security detail. It was not exactly a problem, but notice had been taken.

Court began promptly at 9:30 a.m. Anne Chapman called Jennifer Glick. Her brother, Jeremy Glick, was killed on Flight 93, in Pennsylvania. He was scheduled to fly out the day before, but there was a small fire in the airport, so he waited and flew out the following day, September 11. Jennifer, an attorney, was on her way to court when she received a call from Jeremy's wife. Jeremy had called to say he was on board a plane that had been hijacked. Glick said that Jeremy had been a national collegiate judo champion. He and his wife had a newborn baby, Emmy. Chapman asked what Jennifer Glick sees in Emmy. "A happy, blond, force of life," Glick said. "How would you like Jeremy to be remembered?" "I would like us to celebrate his life." She cried. "His goodness," she said.

Adele Welty's son was a New York City firefighter. Timothy had a newborn baby daughter, born in August 2001. He had been on duty all night and was about to head home. He responded to the Trade Center with Hazmat 1. Welty works downtown at Lafayette and Chambers. She watched the towers fall. On December 11, 2001 – the day Moussaoui was indicted – the medical examiner called to say they had found Timothy. "Or a body part." She could not speak through the tears.

Andrea LeBlanc's husband Bob was an emeritus professor of geography at the University of New Hampshire. He was on Flight 175, headed out of Boston on a business trip. Bob always took the other perspective, she said. He wanted to better understand the cultures of the human family. How ironic that the man who had spent an entire life trying to understand the tribes and nations of the world should die this way.

Paula Shapiro's son Eric is, she said, in the spirit world now. He was in Tower 2 of the World Trade Center, working for Aon. That morning he called to tell her not to worry. A plane hit the other tower and his group was evacuating. Eric and another co-worker helped get people out. Shortly afterward, she went to New York. There were posters everywhere with photographs on them; one was a poster with Eric's photo on it. She saw a picture of the Trade Center being held in two hands. The spirits of people were depicted as rising up. She now gives time to organizations concerned with retribution and violence. It works, she said, "but I miss my kid." What should we remember? She answered: the values of this country, and, being in this court, fairness, understanding, compassion. To know they have not died in vain.

Alan Yamamoto called Alice Hoagland. Her son was Mark Bingham. He had been captain of the Berkeley rugby team. Moussaoui was paying attention now. The team won 21 straight championships, she said proudly. Mark had saved her brother's life when rafting. He told his mother he was gay when he was a junior. He was on Flight 93 because he was going to the wedding of a fraternity brother. The brother was an Egyptian Muslim. Mark called from the plane to say the plane had been hijacked, that there were three guys on board. He said they had a bomb. Five or six people have been murdered. Yamamoto asked her reaction to his death. "Well," she said, "it takes a while." She was proud of those on the plane, proud of Todd Beamer, of Tom Burnett, of Jeremy Glick, and of Mark. Their sports ability helped them on Flight 93, she said. She has tried to become the sort of person her son was. He reached out, as she tries to now. In the past she had not understood being gay, but is now a spokesperson for gay and transgendered sports. At the break, Moussaoui said: "America will be destroyed like Sodom and Gomorrah." The spectators hoped Alice Hoagland did not hear.

Richard Reid

The defense introduced a statement from Richard Reid. He and Moussaoui had been associates in training in Afghanistan. Reid bequeathed his belongings to Moussaoui. It would be highly unlikely for someone to do so knowing Moussaoui was to go to his death. Reid stated that he was involved in an ongoing war between truth and falsehood. This is a war between Islam and democracy. Democratic countries are ruled contrary to God's will. Moussaoui rubbed his hands together. America should keep its nose out of our business. Moussaoui laughed quietly. Reid was, he said of himself, ready to be a martyr and be rewarded in heaven. Moussaoui nodded slightly. At the break Moussaoui said: "God curse America."

The Defense Rests: Dr. Patterson Takes the Stand

The defense rested its case, and Novak called Dr. Raymond Patterson for rebuttal testimony. Patterson's field is general and forensic psychiatry. He had been appointed by Judge Brinkema to assess Moussaoui's competence to represent himself. He tried to meet with Moussaoui on four occasions in May 2002. Twice Moussaoui refused to come out of the cell, but on May 18 the door was opened and Patterson stepped in. Moussaoui had been lying down but he sat up. The cell was clean and orderly. There were books and a prayer rug. The books included the Koran, a little prayer book, the Bible, and his own brother's book about Zacarias's life in France and London. Besides Moussaoui's own cell he had an area outside it where he kept papers, and there was space for an exercise machine. There was no real conversation, for Moussaoui didn't want to speak to Patterson, he wanted to speak to the judge. There was not enough information to provide an opinion on his mental state.

On June 6, 2002, Patterson went back to see him. Moussaoui gave him an interview of about two hours. Moussaoui wanted to make it clear that he wasn't mentally ill, and he did not want his own attorneys to use mental health factors as a defense. He was at war with Americans, and wanted to kill all Americans, even Patterson. Primarily, he wanted to testify, he wanted to be heard. Patterson went on to describe the spitting incident. He said that Moussaoui did not want to come into court. He was not psychotic at the time; instead, said Patterson, Moussaoui was pissed off. At this, Moussaoui smiled and raised his eyes to Amador, who was in the courtroom. In fact, said Patterson, Moussaoui returned to the courtroom the same day to view a video deposition.

Patterson's diagnosis was that Moussaoui has a personality disorder. There are various traits that form personality disorders, Patterson said. Some people become obsessive-compulsive; some are narcissistic. This does not mean they cannot function, because some become actors, doctors, or attorneys. "Let's let that slide by," said Novak. Patterson determined that Moussaoui was competent to represent himself. Similarly, Judge Brinkema determined that he was competent. Cultural differences may appear irrational, said Patterson. Moussaoui's decision to represent himself was unwise, but rational. Prior testimony from others that Moussaoui couldn't learn to fly in a short time wasn't necessarily evidence for a diagnosis of failure to function. His own daughter had flown for 50 hours and could not solo.

Furthermore, Moussaoui had become an expert on explosives, and he did not blow himself up. Moussaoui laughed. Novak asked why Moussaoui's pleadings seemed so odd. Well, Patterson said, remember James Joyce's writings. And there is Moussaoui's context. He had been in a cell for a long period of time. His pleadings became a tool. Patterson didn't know if he was using code, but as the al-Qaeda training manual said, it is important to get the word out "by pen and bullet, by tongue and teeth." Furthermore, the deputies at the detention center did not observe schizophrenia and mental illness, although they were on 12-hour shifts. Moussaoui continues to fight his war, Patterson said, through his writings and interactions with people, by any means necessary. His pleadings were his way of poking fun and taunting Americans.

Moussaoui's Dream

Patterson continued by discussing Moussaoui's dream. The dream is not delusional, Patterson said. If one's belief is based in a religion or a culture, that is not a delusion. His dream is based in his faith, in the Koran. If we try to evaluate such a belief without taking religion into account, there would be many diagnoses floating around. Moussaoui's belief that he will be released is not that odd, said Patterson. For instance, after an Air India hijacking, the hostages and the hijackers were swapped. As to Moussaoui's distrust of his own lawyers, he has always wanted to represent himself. And those attorneys kept sending Amador and First to see him. As to his delusion that he could clear up 9/11 if he only had a few minutes: Moussaoui, said Patterson, thinks that is a way of getting time in court. That, and his pleadings, allow Moussaoui communication with the outside world that he is continuing his war. Also, said Patterson, he thought that the FBI knew more than they did. He thought they knew of the plans for 9/11. The fan he thought was bugged was a mistake on his part. He did not know that the FBI could not, and did not, use wiretaps and bugs except through legal procedures.

Gerald Zerkin pressed Patterson concerning dream interpretation. He asked where in the Koran does it say that one can have dreams of a predictive nature. The judge said: "Mr. Zerkin, I think we are WAY beyond, this is not about theology." Zerkin replied: "I think Mr. Patterson was talking about theology." The judge replied: "That's enough. Move on." At the last break Moussaoui said: "Crazy about those 72 virgins."

APRIL 24, 2006: THE CASE GOES TO THE JURY

The defense and the prosecution had both finished presenting their cases. On Monday, April 24, the two sides gave their closing arguments. David Raskin said that Moussaoui had come to the United States to kill as many people as he could. It is time, he said, to put an end to Moussaoui's hatred, venom, and evil. He reminded the jury that Moussaoui welcomed the pain brought to America and the victims on 9/11. Do not hesitate to give him the death sentence even if you think he is goading you into it, he said. Gerald Zerkin countered that the jury should indeed be concerned about just that fact. He is baiting you to do it. Moussaoui came to America to die in jihad and the jury's decision to put him to death would be his last chance to do so. Do not give him the death of a jihadist; give him the long slow death of a common criminal (Stein, 2006). David Novak countered the defense's argument that Moussaoui had a violent childhood and, like much of the rest of his family, is mentally ill. "Just because we can't comprehend this kind of evil, doesn't mean he suffers a mental illness," he said. "We will never understand evil like this" (Associated Press, 2006a).

Moussaoui left the courtroom clapping his hands, as though this trial had been a theater performance. The jury received the case that afternoon. The verdict form was 42 pages long, full of questions concerning aggravating and mitigating factors. The jurors would have to unanimously agree on finding the aggravating factors to impose the death penalty, and those factors would have to be proven beyond a reasonable doubt. The mitigating factors did not need unanimous agreement in order to be taken into consideration. Nor did they need to be proven beyond a reasonable doubt. During their deliberations, one juror was reported to have used a dictionary to define "aggravating." The jury was reprimanded by the judge. If they want to know the meaning of a word, they should ask, she said, and not look it up in a dictionary. "Aggravating," she said, means to make something worse. On the way out of the courtroom, Moussaoui said: "Moussaoui, aggravating curse on America" (Hirschkorn, 2006e).

MAY 3, 2006: THE VERDICT

In the afternoon of Wednesday, May 3, 2006, after seven days of deliberation, the press and the spectators were alerted that the jury had a verdict. It was a month since they had decided that Moussaoui qualified for death penalty consideration. The jury's final verdict was delivered by the judge inside Courtroom 700 at the same time that Edward Adams, the court information officer, read the verdict to the press and spectators assembled outside the courthouse. Adams introduced himself, and then said:

In the case of *United States* vs. *Zacarias Moussaoui*, as to count one, conspiracy to commit acts of terrorism transcending national boundaries, and count three, conspiracy to destroy aircraft, and count four, conspiracy to use weapons of mass destruction, the jury has found the defendant should be sentenced to life in prison, without the possibility of release.

He went on to read the rest of the statement. Inside the courtroom, the judge read the verdict to the family members, spectators, and Zacarias Moussaoui, who refused to stand for the verdict. The aggravating and mitigating factors were the same for each count. The prosecution had presented ten aggravating factors on count one, conspiracy to commit acts of terrorism transcending national boundaries. The jury had to unanimously agree to three statutory aggravating factors for the death penalty to be imposed. They agreed on two. The jury unanimously agreed that Moussaoui knowingly created a grave risk of death to one or more persons, that he committed the offense after careful planning and premeditation. They did not all agree that he committed an offense in "an especially heinous, cruel, or depraved manner" involving torture or serious physical abuse. They did find that he entered the United States to kill as many people as possible. The jury was not unanimous in finding that Moussaoui's actions led to the deaths of close to 3000 people. As to the 23 mitigating factors, they were not unanimous in finding Moussaoui's family's mental problems a mitigating factor. No juror found that Moussaoui was schizophrenic or psychotic. Jurors were allowed to write in mitigating factors that they were not asked about on the verdict form. Three jurors wrote that Moussaoui had limited knowledge of 9/11.

According to one reporter, Moussaoui stood up and said something unintelligible. The reporters turned to Edward MacMahon, who said: "Who the hell cares?" On his way out, Moussaoui yelled: "America, you lost."

The White House issued a prepared statement by President Bush. It said:

... this represents the end of this case but not an end to the fight against terror.... Our cause is right, and the outcome is certain: Justice will be served. Evil will not have the final say. This great Nation will prevail. (Bush, 2006a)

MAY 4, 2006: THE SENTENCING

Moussaoui was formally sentenced by Judge Brinkema the following morning, Thursday, May 4. The press and spectators were in line outside the courthouse by 3 in the morning, standing and sitting in the dark. As court began, family members made sure they had seats, knowing they would have a chance to speak. Abraham Scott, Lisa Dolan, and Rosemary Dillard had been present in the courtroom for days. Scott's wife died in the plane that crashed into the Pentagon. Dolan's husband had died in the building. Rosemary Dillard spoke of her husband and the loss she feels. She said: "You have wrecked my life." Lisa Dolan said: "There is still one final judgment day." Moussaoui was then allowed to make a statement. "You wasted an opportunity for this country to understand why people like me, like Mohamed Atta and the rest have so much hatred of you," he said (Al Jazeera, 2006a). "I am *mujahedin*," he said. "America, you lost, I won," he said. The judge disagreed. "You will spend the rest of your life in a supermax prison," she said. She told him: "It's absolutely clear who won." "Mr. Moussaoui, you came here to be a martyr in a great big bang of glory," she continued, "but to paraphrase the poet T.S. Eliot, instead you will die with a whimper." It was appropriate, the judge said, that he would never get a chance to speak again (Associated Press, 2006b). She informed him that he had the right to file an appeal. His attorneys would not be relieved until that notice had been filed. "God curse America and save Osama bin Laden. You will never get him," said Moussaoui (Al Jazeera, 2006a). "My liberation will be the proof that we are the soldiers of God and you are the army of Satan" (Johnson, 2006).

Reactions to the Verdict

Both the defense attorneys and the government attorneys made statements outside the courthouse. Edward MacMahon said the case revealed the deep divisions in the US concerning the death penalty. Paul McNulty, who had been involved with the case since 2001, and was now Deputy United States Attorney General, made the statement for the government. He said it was a victory for the families, that their bravery was inspiring, and he thanked the many lawyers and investigators with the case, including the judge and the jury. The jury has spoken, he said, and we accept its decision. Outside the courthouse some family members and observers were angry, others were relieved. Some cried. One said it would be better to pay 28 cents and put a bullet through Moussaoui's head. Others spoke of their own loss. Back home in France, Moussaoui's mother said:

I feel there is a part of me that is dead, buried with my son who will be buried for the rest of his life at the age of 37 for things he hasn't done.... The whole world knows it now. France knows it too but France prefers to please the Americans anyway. (Al Jazeera, 2006b)

The French press reported that France may, at some point, ask for him back, to complete his life sentence there. Members of the French administration were cautious in their statements. The human rights lawyers were relieved that he had not received the death penalty.

One juror contacted the *Washington Post* the day of the formal sentencing to say that he had not voted for the death penalty because he and others on the jury thought that Moussaoui had little to do with 9/11. This juror said he thought Moussaoui was a "despicable character," who was capable of taunting the victims, but he did not deserve to die. The juror said he was haunted by nightmares. He hears not only Moussaoui's voice but also the family members' testimony, he said. He hoped he never had to sit on another jury again, ever (Markon and Dwyer, 2006d). A CNN poll taken the day the verdict came back from the jury asked if online readers agreed with the jury's decision to give Moussaoui life in prison: 65 percent said yes (99,502 votes), 35 percent said no (54,487 votes) (see Hirschkorn, 2006f).

After the formal sentencing, Moussaoui told his lawyers that he wanted to change his guilty plea of April 2005. He did not realize, he said, that he could get a fair trial in the United States. His lawyers submitted a motion to withdraw his guilty plea on Monday, May 8; the judge denied the motion the same day. She did say he could appeal within ten days; he did so, through his lawyers, to the Fourth Circuit Court, on Friday, May 12.

On that day the *Washington Post* revealed that there was one anonymous holdout against the death penalty on the jury. The foreman of the jury had called the paper to say that the person never did reveal himself to the other jurors. Only one person, presumably the juror who had contacted the *Washington Post* the day of the sentencing, had kept Moussaoui from death. The vote on the death penalty had been 11–1 on count one, 10–2 on count three, 10–2 on count four, for the three counts that carried the death penalty (Dwyer, 2006).

News arrived on Saturday, May 13, that Moussaoui had been flown overnight by small jet from Virginia to Florence, Colorado. He is incarcerated there, at the "Supermax" federal penitentiary, officially known as the Administrative Maximum Facility. He is alone in his cell 23 hours a day. One hour a day he goes to a recreation area.

On May 23 Osama bin Laden said in an audiotape titled in English "A Testimony to the Truth" that:

This is a brief message whose topic is my testimony on behalf of the Muslim prisoners you are holding, and in it I will talk about the truth concerning them.... I begin by talking about the honorable brother Zacarias Moussaoui. The truth is that he has no connection whatsoever with the events of September 11th, and I am certain of what I say, because I was responsible for entrusting the 19 brothers – Allah have mercy upon them – with those raids, and I did not assign brother Zacarias to be with them on that mission. And his confession that he was assigned to participate in those raids is a false confession which no intelligent person doubts is a result of the pressure put upon him for the past four and a half years. And were this pressure lifted from him for him to return to his normal state, he would state the fact I mentioned. (MSNBC, 2006b)

"Since Zacarias Moussaoui was still learning how to fly, he wasn't No. 20 in the group, as your government has claimed," bin Laden said. This statement came as no surprise. According to Fox News, the government was monitoring jihadi websites, expecting some reaction from al-Qaeda to the verdict (Fox News, 2006).

By summer 2006, the lawyers had moved on. David Novak went back down to Richmond, David Raskin back to New York. Rob Spencer left the US Attorney's office to work as counsel for Lockheed Martin. The US Attorney's Office for the Eastern District of Virginia posted the following on its website:

The Eastern District of Virginia-based Moussaoui prosecution team handled the most complex and cumbersome criminal case ever brought in an Article III court with grace and dignity, in the finest traditions of this District and of the Department of Justice. (USDOJ, 2006a)

On the defense side, Frank Dunham was ill, Gerald Zerkin was back in Richmond. In Alexandria, Ken Troccoli moved on to other cases. People were interviewing to be Dunham's replacement. Alan Yamamoto returned to pick up his solo practice in Alexandria. Ed MacMahon went back to Middleburg with his staff. The Washington press corps moved on as well. They had other things to cover. There would be other cases, but none quite like this one.

4 ZACARIAS, MY BROTHER: THE MAKING OF A TERRORIST[1]

He had all these dreams and ambitions, and thoughts, mapped out, roaring to go, nothing to channel his intelligence and his dreams and all the things he had in his head ... (Nil Plant, 2005)

ZACARIAS MOUSSAOUI'S EARLY LIFE

Zacarias Moussaoui's parents were born in Morocco. Moussaoui's father, Omar, was from Arfoud, southern Morocco. Close to the Sahara desert, the town was once a staging point for caravans heading south into Algeria and on to Mauritania and Mali. The French officially took much of Morocco as a "protectorate" in 1912, and Arfoud became a French colonial post. Zacarias drew one of his names, al-Sahrawi, from his father's origins near the Sahara. Sahrawi was "the name of my tribe in Morocco" he said in court (tr. March 27, 2006, page 2309, lines 12–13). The word has several meanings; "of the Sahara" the most obvious. But it can also have a political connotation, for refugees from a dispute over contested land in the territory of Western Sahara, to the south and west of Morocco, also are Sahrawi.

According to court documents, Omar spent much of his childhood to the north of Arfoud, in Fez and Azrou, Morocco. His father worked for the railroad, his mother sold gold (Defense Exhibit JV002.17T). Moussaoui's mother, Aïcha el-Wafi, was born to middle-class parents in 1946 in Azrou, in the Middle Atlas mountains. Omar became a skilled mason, and Aïcha had learned to sew and embroider. She was a bride at age 14. She married against her will, she has said (el-Wafi, 2006). Zacarias is the youngest of four children. He has two older sisters, Nadia and Jamila, both born in Morocco, and an older brother, Abd Samad, who was born in France. Zacarias was born on May 30, 1968, in St. Jean-de-Luz, in south-western France, on the Atlantic coast.

Omar Moussaoui had heard there were jobs in France, and the family moved there in 1967, the year before Zacarias was born. The 1960s were a period of economic growth in France, and North and West Africans were sought for their labor. Some spoke French as a result of French control over territories ranging from Algeria and Morocco across the Sahara to Mali and Senegal. France offered economic security to these workers when their home countries could not. The Moussaoui family was not unusual in choosing to leave North Africa for France, nor were they unusual in later experiencing social and racial discrimination in France.

During the trial, the press tended to sensationalize the chaotic upbringing of the Moussaoui children, saying that the children, especially Zacarias, spent years in orphanages, or that he was in and out of orphanages for the first six years of his life (Malkin, 2006; see also Lewis, 2006). Judging from court testimony and interviews with friends of family members, there is no question that things were difficult. Moussaoui's two sisters, Nadia and Jamila, were interviewed on videotape in France, and the videos were shown at the trial. Testimony from Jan Vogelsang, a clinical social worker, and legal documents admitted into evidence during the trial indicate that there were some troubled times in the Moussaoui household. The children were indeed placed in orphanages for the first years of their lives. However, their mother was actually with them for much of that time. She managed to find jobs at the institutions where the children were placed, and Jamila Moussaoui remembers being a tightly knit family (Jamila Moussaoui, 2005).

At the age of one month, Zacarias was admitted to a public nursery for very small children, a *pouponnière*. He was there for two months. The children were all temporarily placed in the custody of Childhood Welfare Services, as Aïcha was at the time living at a women's center (JV002.1T). According to a hearing in front of the Children's Court Judge, and later court testimony, Omar Moussaoui did not give the family enough money to feed them. In November 1970, the children were placed in St. Vincent de Paul Children's Home, Biarritz, also in south-western France (JV002.5T). Their mother lived with them and worked there as an assistant laundry supervisor (JV002.17T).

Omar and Aïcha separated in May 1971, after eleven years of marriage, and their divorce was granted in June 1971 (JV002.12T). All four children were released from St. Vincent de Paul in February 1972 (JV002.7T). They then moved with their mother to the Dordogne, a region to the north. She found an apartment in Périgueux, and the children went to a daycare center while their mother worked. In March 1972, she found work doing laundry at a children's home in St. Amand de Vergt, to the south of the city of Périgueux. Again, she lived there with the children. Jamila remembered that difficult period as part of her mother's battle to keep the children with her. They were *un vrai cocon*, a real cocoon, Jamila said, a very tight, strong family, until after their later move to Narbonne, when the children were in their teens (Jamila Moussaoui, 2005). Nadia Moussaoui remembered this period in a videotaped interview.

We loved each other, we four children. Father was a bad father, a bad husband. He beat his wife and children, starved them, spent at the café the money he earned, we were unhappy with him. He threw a glass at Jamila which split her skull, when she was three or four years old. (Nadia Moussaoui, 2005)

The children were terrorized, Nadia said. They didn't dare say anything during those episodes. For their mother to have four children with a man she did not love, "it was very very very difficult for her" (Nadia Moussaoui, 2005).

Jamila also recounted her own memories of the violence. Jamila said that their father was very violent, alcoholic, and that he traumatized all of them, but more her and Abd Samad than the others. "He had us in his grip," she said. In her opinion, he should never have had children. Jamila remembered Zacarias as *très joyeux, gentil*, often smiling. He loved kisses, and he loved his mother. He was the "little sweetheart of the family" (Jamila Moussaoui, 2005).

Nadia said that "Zacarias suffered from not having the love of his father or his mother. *Zacarias a beaucoup suffert.*" When asked of her memories of Zacarias she smiled with joy. Yes, his *embonpointment*, she said. He was quite chubby and stout. He was cute, handsome, and affectionate. She remembered that one day at the orphanage in Dordogne, St. Amand de Vergt, Aïcha had made sardines Moroccan style. They all loved them. After the meal, Zacarias went outside to say, in singsong fashion, "we ate sardines, we ate sardines" to other children playing outdoors. Aïcha hushed Zacarias, saying perhaps the other children had not eaten. Nadia laughed and said he then began to sing: "We didn't eat sardines, we didn't eat sardines" (Nadia Moussaoui, 2005).

Life in Mulhouse

In mid-summer 1972, when Zacarias was four, Aïcha left the children to rejoin Omar Moussaoui, who was now living in Mulhouse, in north-eastern France. The children were placed in a home in the Dordogne, Temniac Foyer de Bonté, near Sarlat. The following month the Moussaoui parents, according to court documents, asked to have their children back before the start of the school year. According to M.J. Burckard, a social worker, the Moussaouis were "intelligent," "well dressed," and "spoke good French." Omar Moussaoui was taking a class at night to improve his French. Burckard said the children were also intelligent and well behaved (JV002.17T).

The children were released to their parents by September of that year. However, domestic problems started again in December 1972.

Burckard wrote on April 12, 1973, that Mrs. Moussaoui was requesting a place to live as she was in a shelter at a women's assistance center in Mulhouse (JV002.18T). By April 14, 1973, the children were separated. The two girls went to a shelter in Mulhouse, Zacarias and his brother to a placement in the region, at Le Chalet in Rimbach, Guebwiller (JV002.20T). The children were subsequently released to their mother who had moved to a large apartment on the rue des Châtaigners, Mulhouse (JV002.21T). She had found a job cleaning in the central post office of Mulhouse. According to Abd Samad Moussaoui's memoir, titled in English *Zacarias, My Brother: The Making of a Terrorist*, she obtained French citizenship, and received a permanent post office position, working a second job at night (Moussaoui, 2003: 16). The family later moved to the Bourtzwiller project in Mulhouse. Many of the families living there were North African immigrants, some were not. Life there was sometimes difficult. Abd Samad reported that the Kol family, who lived in their building, called both Zacarias and Abd Samad "dirty niggers" (2003: 17), a refrain which was repeated later in their lives. Abd Samad made clear his own feelings about his mother at the time:

For us real life happened outdoors. In the apartment was not much; my mother didn't have a lot of time for us. She always had other things to do. It would have been misguided to expect the slightest tender word from her, or the merest gesture of affection. She didn't know how to do that. (2003: 18)

Their father tried to see them in Bourtzwiller, but they had been told to avoid him. Aïcha then bought a house in Mulhouse and, according to Abd Samad, "Saïd" moved in with the family. Also a Moroccan, he worked for Peugeot, the automobile company, and tended a vegetable plot nearby (2003: 19). Abd Samad reported that the family went to Morocco in 1974. It was, he said, the family's first summer trip together. Zacarias would have been six years old, Abd Samad was seven. For the first time, they went with cousins to a Koranic school there:

... though Zacarias and I hardly knew what the Koran was. We liked it, and found it very unusual at the same time: all those children in a large room, repeating after the teacher the verses of that mysterious, holy book.... That's where we first heard the chant, *"Bismillah ar-Rahman ar-Rahim"* (In the name of God the compassionate, the merciful), which we memorized quickly and repeated with great vigor. Those were lovely times. (2003: 23)

DIFFICULT MOVE TO THE SOUTH OF FRANCE

In 1980 the family experienced a major upheaval when their mother decided to look for a position in the south of France. Zacarias was 12. He protested that he wanted to stay in Mulhouse, where he had friends and where he had discovered handball, at which he excelled. But the family moved to Narbonne, close to the Mediterranean. His brother wrote: "From that moment on, something in Zacarias changed. There was a sort of uncertainty about him, an edge of bitterness and rancor. Like a very fine scar, hardly visible, which never heals" (2003: 27). Zacarias enrolled in the sixth level at the middle school, the Collège Montesquieu. According to his report cards, his teachers thought he was "lazy and absent-minded" (JV002.37T). He was there for one year, and then moved to the Collège Jules Ferry, in a middle-class neighborhood, where he remained from 1981 through 1984. The boys had dreams of doing well, and of going on to university. However, after his third year in high school, Abd Samad was transferred, without his permission, to a vocational training school (Moussaoui, 2003: 33).

Zacarias made friends at his school. He was 15, in the *troisième*. But, in 1984, he chose to move from the middle school, the Collège Jules Ferry, to a technical high school, Jean Moulin, where he was unhappy. He would have gone on to the Lycée Dr. Lacroix, where his middle-class friends would go, but he was not encouraged to do so by the school administration. In fact, his report cards that year, 1983–84, said that he was "overall very inadequate, making promotion to the '*seconde* class' very unlikely" (JV002.45T) and he was told: "You are facing very serious difficulties" (JV002.46T). According to the report card for the school year 1988–90, he was "earnest but problems" (JV002.29T).

During that period, their father had also moved to Narbonne, where he had a construction company. They decided to see more of him. Contrary to the testimony during the trial concerning Omar's violence toward the family, Abd Samad said that "he'd never been mean. He'd never hit us…. But it seemed never to occur to him to give our mother the slightest allowance" (2003: 39).

According to Abd Samad, the relationship between Zacarias and their mother deteriorated from the time of the move to Narbonne. A low point came when she said she was too tired to get up and take him to his exam for the vocational school diploma. He arrived late, without her help, and ran out of time on the exam. Zacarias did get the diploma, but, according to Abd Samad, he said: "I knew she wouldn't do a thing to help me, but I didn't know she was capable of doing something to hurt me" (2003: 47).

MIDDLE CLASS

Aïcha had struggled to keep her family together. With a great deal of work, some savings, and a savvy business deal, she built a house in Narbonne's middle-class Roche Grise neighborhood. The house has a view towards the Mediterranean. There is an underground two-car garage. Zacarias's bedroom had a door out to a yard planted with pear and plum trees (Willing, 2002). Zacarias met a French girl, Karine Bocat, whose family lived close by the Moussaoui family. Her brother was a friend of Abd Samad. "Fanny" as she is called in Abd Samad's book, was blonde. Her family was middle class; the father drove a sports car, they had a pool, the mother was a civil servant (2003: 45). Abd Samad said:

It was the start of a real love story, a story that lasted ten years. What Zacarias could not find in his own home he tried to construct it elsewhere. He was looking for harmony, gentleness, affection, honesty, loyalty, integrity – in short, emotional security. He found it with Fanny. (2003: 43)

During the trial Jan Vogelsang, the social worker, said that Karine told her Moussaoui was "a very generous, kind, and funny person," who showed no signs of mental illness while she knew him (Arthur and Elsibai, 2006). Unfortunately for Zacarias, Karine's parents did not think him an appropriate choice for their daughter. However, their close relationship continued past high school, and they lived together during the years before he left for London.

Moussaoui graduated from high school in 1986. About the same time he left home over a fight about the electricity bill. Aïcha had asked each of the boys for 500 francs. According to Jamila, Abd Samad was willing to pay, but Zacarias was not, and so he left. He stayed for several months with Gilles Cohen, a recent friend. During the trial, Cohen described their relationship, which continued for some years, as very close. Cohen has a Jewish parent and Moussaoui came from a Muslim family, yet they felt their friendship could overcome those differences.

During those years, Moussaoui and his sister Nadia talked often of Martin Luther King Jr., and the work King did for social and racial justice. According to Nadia, Moussaoui hated injustice. He had much compassion, conviction; he was for non-violence and the rights of black people, she said. "Since we are mixed race, *métis*, neither black nor white, at the time we identified with black people. We were going to vanquish through the force of love.... It's funny how things get turned around," she said (Nadia Moussaoui, 2005).

FRENCH INTOLERANCE

Abd Samad described the brothers' increasing awareness of racism, and illustrated its damage through an incident that happened to him personally. It was the night of July 14, 1989. This was the bicentennial of the beginning of the French Revolution, marked by celebrations throughout France. In Narbonne, Abd Samad had left some friends and was to meet Zacarias and other friends before the fireworks started. Abd Samad was walking through an area filled with many people when he felt a tap on his shoulder. Someone asked him to turn around, but he kept walking. He felt another tap, turned, and was hit in the face. Abd Samad ran to a group of policemen and asked for their help. Instead of stopping the other man, a policeman sprayed tear gas into Abd Samad's face. He ended up in the hospital. The next day, when he and his mother tried to file a complaint with the police, both of them were told to leave the police station. Later, with the help of the social justice group SOS Racisme, the man who hit Abd Samad was identified and charged with assault. He was given a suspended seven-day prison sentence and a fine. Abd Samad did not learn if anything happened to the policeman (Moussaoui, 2003: 67–68).

Unfortunately, this was not an isolated incident. Zacarias Moussaoui had similar fights, some at a nightclub not far from where they lived. The boys were frequently called *sale arabe* and *sale nègre* (dirty Arab, dirty nigger). At this time Jean-Marie Le Pen's *Front National* political party became particularly vehement about the "problem" of immigrants in France, many of whom were from North and West Africa. As his party grew in strength, so did attacks on immigrants, and the two fed on each other. The attacks on the Moussaoui boys were both emblematic and symptomatic of the racial discord in France, which grew through the late 1980s and early 1990s.

Despite this treatment, Zacarias worked and went to school at the same time. After he received his vocational diploma, he passed the entrance exams for the technical and commercial advanced vocational diploma in Perpignan, not far away, where he studied mechanical and electrical engineering. In 1988–89, he was able to live in a dorm at Perpignan. Fanny/Karine was there as well, studying business (2003: 75).

Abd Samad joined him the next year. "That academic year ... would be a year dedicated to partying," said Abd Samad (2003: 76). In June 1990, Zacarias passed the exam for his technological and commercial license. By the end of the year Fanny/Karine had her diploma in sales and marketing and began to study law. Zacarias enrolled at the university in Montpellier in Economic and Social Administration, but he needed more credits than the advanced vocational diploma had given him. His friends were moving on, either to business school, which was too expensive for him, or to jobs. Zacarias realized that he would not be able to work as a sales technician with the advanced vocational diploma (2003: 78). He would have to find another route to education.

Religion and Politics

During the summer of 1990, Abd Samad and Zacarias met a Moroccan first cousin, Fouzia, who was staying with their mother (2003: 76). Aïcha, according to the press, places some of the blame for her sons' turn to Islam on Fouzia. Things had been fine in the family until Fouzia came along, Aïcha is reported to have said. Fouzia introduced them to codes of Muslim conduct they had not experienced before (Barte, 2002). Abd Samad and Fouzia married several years later, and they attend a mosque in Montpellier which is affiliated with the Lebanese Muslim Habashite group in France known as the Association des projets bienfaisance islamiques en France, or APBIF. Abd Samad credits that group with deterring him from adopting the Wahhabism preached in mosques financed by the Saudis.[2]

This was the time of the Gulf War (1990–91), which began with the Iraqi invasion of Kuwait and ended after the American and coalition forces' intervention early in 1991. Bosnia and Algeria were also in the news. In Bosnia, Serbs were attacking Muslims, attacks that included the rape of women, during conflicts that resulted from the break-up of the former Yugoslavia. The imam from the APBIF mosque in Montpellier preached against these attacks on Muslims, as did other leaders of mosques. In Algeria, university students demonstrated over election reform and other issues. Elections to end one-party rule were to be held in 1991. An Islamic political party, the Front Islamique du Salut, or FIS, was gathering support there. Students in France were following the news in Kuwait, Bosnia, and Algeria, and were organizing their own protests. Zacarias increasingly spent time with the North and West African university students, and those from the Middle East. His political sympathies, framed by a concern for civil rights, were not unlike those of many people of his age in the early 1990s. Judging from the testimony of his sisters and friends, he cared deeply about these causes and the political events all the students were following at the time.

Omar Moussaoui

In October 1991, Fouzia returned to Morocco. The boys decided to find their father in Toulouse, and they did. They spent one night together in their father's apartment. But at dawn the police entered the apartment and took Omar away. He had been arrested because he had been in a fight (Moussaoui, 2003: 83–84). This was not the first time Omar had been in difficulties with the law. In January 1983 the *tribunal de grand instance* had sentenced him to three years of probation and alimony payments to his ex-wife. Another ruling from the *tribunal* in December 1984 convicted Omar of the theft of work tools and sentenced him to four months in prison, sentence suspended, and a fine (JV002.28T). This was while Zacarias was trying to make a go of it at the middle-class school in Narbonne, the Collège Jules Ferry.

In Toulouse, according to court documents, Omar worked in construction for the aerospace industry. In December 1993, he moved temporarily to a hotel from his apartment in Toulouse, because, he said, worms were climbing up the stairs. Asked how he would pay for the hotel room, he said he was not ready to pay. An altercation ensued and the police were called in. In January 1994, a hearing was held and he was sentenced to four months in prison, but Mr. Moussaoui was absent from the hearing (JV002.61T).

The psychiatric information that was developed in his son's case is revealing. The day of the assault, December 7, 1993, he was seen by a psychiatrist in Toulouse. He told the psychiatrist he was educated in Morocco to the level of law school, and that his mother was a law professor. He said that in 1970, when he was working hard, his wife left him. He said he was a dance professor who likes karate and construction. The report, presumably written by the psychiatrist, said: "All that is quite incoherent and not very likely." There had apparently been previous mental breakdowns, when Aïcha left him in 1970, in 1990, in 1992, and in 1993. He told the psychiatrist he not only had problems with worms in his apartment but also with bugs in the hotel he had checked into. His glasses, he said, are treated against lasers. The psychiatrist noted "psychotic organization" and "particular thoughts of persecution almost systematic" (JV002.67T). Moussaoui said his "ex-wife's team" was putting drugs in his coffee. He thought a downstairs neighbor was making a hole in the ceiling. "A sorcerer who came over from Morocco" was performing witchcraft. The hotel had germs which he could see. The psychiatrist noted that Mr. Moussaoui had "serious personality disorders evocative of a psychotic personality" (JV002.67T).

He later wandered to Paris, and is now in a residential home there.

THE MOVE TO LONDON

During the year 1990–91, Zacarias was at Montpellier but not attending class. He felt "stuck," his brother said. He needed more credits but he was not working on them (Moussaoui, 2003: 87). According to the French newspaper *Midi Libre*, he enrolled in a language program at Perpignan. He wrote:

Je voudrais acquérir l'anglais commercial pour pouvoir travailler dans des entreprises internationales. De plus, j'ai l'opportunité de me rendre en Angleterre. [I would like to learn business English in order to work for international companies. Furthermore, I have the opportunity to go to England.] (Sabouraud, 2001)

He never arrived at the university. By the end of 1991 he decided to leave for England. He sold his car, saved some money, and flew to London in February 1992 (Moussaoui, 2003: 88–89). For the first nights after his arrival, Moussaoui had nowhere to sleep. He found the 'New to London' program, which provided short-stay housing at St. Mark's House, on Old Marylebone Road. In June 1992, he moved to Nevern Mansions, Earl's Court, run by English Churches Housing.

The following year he applied to the Presentation Housing Association for a place to live. Nevern Mansions was a short-stay hostel and was due to close in 1994. He asked for "self-accommodation" for his study. The form asked "Do you have furniture?" He checked "No." "Do you have savings to buy furniture?" He checked "No," then wrote "but I will." A letter of reference from them said that he had not given them any problems. On the form he was asked to check one of several boxes. He checked "African" instead of "British/European." He checked "black" instead of "white," or "other," which he had checked and then crossed out. He was to move to 66 Christchurch Road in Streatham, London, an address he would keep for five years.

London: South Bank University

Moussaoui took, and passed, an entrance exam to a master's program in international business at South Bank University. He entered in the fall of 1992. The program required two semesters and a 20,000 word dissertation. His courses included international trade, marketing, and finance. According to *The Guardian*, Colin Knapp, who was Moussaoui's course director, said: "He was reasonably hard working, reasonably committed, quite quiet. At first, he had a problem with some of the language but there is nothing which stood out." Considering the fact that he did not know much English when he arrived the winter before he entered, he learned quickly. Knapp said that Moussaoui was a practicing Muslim but did not profess extreme views and generally wore Western-style clothes. "He had no major political convictions at all" (Woodward, 2001).

Dina Newman, an acquaintance at South Bank, said in a BBC interview that he was very quiet, even inconspicuous. He had a slight speech impediment, she said. She found him interesting because of his views. She was from the Soviet Union. Zac, as she called him, had a lot of very angry questions, great doubts about the market economy, about globalization, about the West's effect on the Third World. She said he talked often about France's policies in North Africa. He didn't seem to have broad knowledge, she said, but he was very emotional about these issues. He wanted to know if socialism was an alternative to capitalism. He seemed to have an open mind and was searching for answers. He wanted to know about racism in the Soviet Union. She thought he must have had a problem with racism in France because he mentioned it several times. He never mentioned Islamic militancy. In fact, they did not discuss religion at all (Newman, 2001).

Nil Plant, another friend of Moussaoui at South Bank University, was interviewed by Anne Chapman, assistant federal public defender in Alexandria. The interview was videotaped for the court proceedings for the defense. Plant said she and "Zac" spent time together, had a few drinks at a student pub, met in the university at the canteen, and worked on a few essays together. She remembered him as nice and very friendly. He ate a lot of Mars Bars; he kept an extra stock in his bag in case he ran out. She said he had a very strong faith and attended Friday midday prayer at a mosque in central London. She had grown up as a Muslim in Turkey, but by then was attending Bible study as she had Christian stepchildren. They talked a lot about the Bible study and Islam. He was not judgmental of her learning about Christianity, she said. He did not try to bring her back to Islam. Plant did say that some of Moussaoui's classmates found him difficult to work with. There were groups that worked together on projects, and she remembered that Moussaoui and a Russian usually argued with each other. Plant said it was because Moussaoui wanted to get the work done, and to do it well. The Russian's command of English was not good, and for that reason Moussaoui did not like working with him. Moussaoui wanted to finish his degree and get on with his life. Plant was envious of him. He did not have the family obligations she had, and so he spent more time in the library than she could. "On a few occasions, he said he had been in the library for six hours; I thought it was a bit unjust as I knew he was going to pass and I was going to struggle" (Plant, 2005).

Plant spoke of their dreams:

We thought once we finished we all would start running big multinational companies right away. He wanted a nice respectable title to go with a big salary and he mentioned a girlfriend back in France. I wasn't sure if she was the one he talked about when he talked about getting married. He said he wanted to marry a Muslim girl, have a nice and clean and faithful life, big house, big car. (Plant, 2005)

She last saw him in June 1993. She never handed in her dissertation. "He would have done" (finished his dissertation), she said. "He wanted to get the best mark that he could. He was a very clever and intelligent person." Attorney Chapman asked why the two were so close. Plant replied:

I suppose because we were both Muslim, even though I wasn't up to scratch with it to Zacarias's standards. He was a little eccentric. He was very smart and a quick thinker. A bit of a misfit ... he wasn't a proper Arab, not a proper French boy. I wasn't a proper Turk and felt like a misfit. I didn't fit in England either. We were in a foreign country, not knowing which country we wanted to live in, nor what we wanted to do with our lives. His life hadn't started yet. He had a lot going for him but nowhere to go. He had all these dreams and ambitions, and thoughts, mapped out, roaring to go, nothing to channel his intelligence and his dreams and all the things he had in his head.... I doubt that he had any guidance or anything like that. Sometimes you finish a degree, you go on to a job, meet the right people at the right time. I suppose that didn't happen for Zac. (Plant, 2005)

At the time, Moussaoui was still in touch with his family. He returned home in the summers, and he telephoned. When he came home to France in 1994, Abd Samad said he invited Zacarias to go to the mosque with him, but Zacarias preferred to go to town (Moussaoui, 2003: 93). He returned to France in 1995 and told his brother that he had to go back to London to receive his diploma. Abd Samad took him to the airport at Montpellier. His mother has a photo of Zacarias in a cap and gown, wearing a suit with a blue tie, smiling happily, holding his diploma (Downey, 2001; Woodward, 2001). An October 30, 1995, psychiatric report for Jamila Moussaoui said that she was "happy with a call from her favorite brother who lives in England" (JV002.68T). Abd Samad has not seen Zacarias since 1995, but Zacarias did return to France in 1996, and again to see Jamila and Aïcha in 1997, for what was to be the last time until Aïcha saw him in Alexandria, Virginia (McKenna, 2004a; Moussaoui, 2003: 133).

CONVERSION

According to Abd Samad Moussaoui, the family was brought up knowing little about Islam. At one point, when they were living in Narbonne, their mother decided to celebrate Christmas. Muslim food prohibitions seem to have been observed; at least, Abd Samad says that at school pork and ham were pushed on them by school cafeteria workers, something the Moussaoui boys did not appreciate. The children occasionally returned to Morocco for summer vacations, where Abd Samad reported that they enjoyed attending the Koranic school. He says that it was not until their cousin Fouzia arrived in France to live for a while with their mother, that the family began to learn more about their Moroccan family and Islam. The boys apparently knew little Arabic. The girls, however, spent more time in Morocco with their relatives and knew the language better than their brothers.

According to Nil Plant, by the time she knew him in 1993 Moussaoui was a committed Muslim. Craig Smith of the *New York Times* reported

(Smith, 2005) that Moussaoui was a member of a Muslim teaching group, Tablighi Jamaat, when he was still in France, although other sources do not confirm this and claim that his conversion happened in London. He did attend a moderate mosque when he was first in London. However, in the early to mid 1990s there were many groups in London preaching a militant Muslim message. These messages stressed the importance of jihad.

At the trial, the defense presented a videotaped interview with Imam Baker, chairman of the Brixton mosque that Moussaoui attended when first in London (Baker, 2005). Baker was not specific as to the time when Moussaoui arrived there, but it was in early to middle 1990s. He was specific, however, about Moussaoui's transition from a person eager to learn and pleasant to be with to a more distant, brash, even defiant member of the mosque. Baker blamed the "young soldiers" of more militant Muslim groups in London at the time, who would stand outside the Brixton mosque passing out leaflets designed to attract people to groups such as al-Muhajiroun, "the Emigrants." According to Imam Baker, Moussaoui was targeted for proselytizing. Baker said that bright, questioning young people like Moussaoui were particularly sought after. Some who were approached sampled the preaching of a militant Islam but then returned to the more moderate Brixton mosque. Others, like Moussaoui, were attracted to the message of groups such as those that met in the Brixton town hall. There an imam presided who had been asked to leave the Brixton mosque for being too radical. Moussaoui also went to gatherings at the Four Feathers Youth Centre, where Abu Qatada preached sermons which later landed him in detention. Moussaoui is thought to have attended the Finsbury Park mosque where Abu Hamza al-Masri preached. Dubbed "Captain Hook" by the press, Abu Hamza had lost both hands and an eye to explosives. The Finsbury Park mosque, located in a richly diverse neighborhood of north London, where the shops and markets are West Indian, Middle Eastern, African, and Asian, was raided by the police in 2003.

Moussaoui's attendance at these mosques and his friendships did not go unnoticed. In 1994, a French investigating magistrate was in London following leads on the assassination of three French consular officials in Algeria. He had a lead on a "Zacarias." He wanted to search Zacarias Moussaoui's apartment, but the British authorities told the magistrate there was not sufficient evidence to interview Moussaoui or to search his apartment (Burrell et al., 2001; Chambon et al., 2001). The French continued to keep a dossier on Moussaoui. By October 1995, Jean-Louis Bruguière, an anti-terrorist judge, was following his case. The French later told the FBI they knew that Moussaoui had not only left France, but they knew his addresses in London, and surveilled him as a member of a group of young Islamists who had trained in Afghanistan. For instance, some sources claim that Moussaoui was in Afghanistan by 1995, and that he subsequently traveled to Chechnya. They knew that he had recruited for Ibn Khattab, the Chechen rebel leader.

According to Imam Baker of the Brixton mosque, Moussaoui's clothing and appearance began to change, although this is not unusual for young converts. He grew a beard and sometimes wore a *thobe*, a long white robe commonly worn by Saudi men. By the time Moussaoui was working on his dissertation for the master's degree, Imam Baker felt Moussaoui was burning his bridges with the Brixton mosque. Although Moussaoui sought out Baker for help on the dissertation, Baker was already concerned about him. Baker noted that, earlier, Moussaoui would chat with the other members of the mosque. As time went on he came into the mosque alone and sat by himself. There was no more discussion and no more learning. Moussaoui became curt. He spoke with one-word answers. Baker said that one summer, when Moussaoui was returning to Britain from vacation in France, the customs officials questioned him about the Brixton mosque. This apparently was a source of pleasure to Moussaoui, who reported it to Baker. Baker became uneasy. He didn't want the mosque to be an object of attention. He thought Moussaoui somewhat childish for taking pleasure in being part of something that made the authorities suspicious. The final straw for Imam Baker was when Moussaoui arrived in the mosque dressed in military fatigues, with a knapsack on his back, demanding to know where the next jihad was. Baker asked him to leave. Baker said that he saw him at some later time. This time he was clean-shaven and was wearing civilian clothes. The imam said that, with other people, this meant that they had rejected militant Islam and were coming back to more moderate ways. With Moussaoui, the interpretation was that "he was trying to blend into the civilian world without having changed his militancy" (Baker, 2005). The Islamic group Takfir wal Hijra advocates this form of deception when living in the West. Shaving one's head, wearing Western clothes, and blending in with the civilian non-Muslim, or *kafir*, population, are all recommended behaviors. The appearance may be Western, but the ideology is troubling (Gleis, 2005).

Finsbury Park has been considered a center for the group Takfir wal Hijra. Sometimes translated as "excommunication and exile," the word *takfiri* has taken on a bloody connotation in Iraq and is seen as a menacing presence in Europe. *Takfir* philosophy approves not only the killing of unbelievers such as Jews and Christians but also Muslims who are not sufficiently observant. Accusations of adherence to takfiri beliefs are widely flung, and the truth is hard to determine. Anyone who espouses the concept of killing even Muslims has been called a takfir. The attacks by Sunnis on Shiites, and vice versa in

Iraq has led to the use of the term takfiri for all sectarian fighters.[3] In London, Djamel Beghal, a French citizen, worshipped at Finsbury Park and is said to have recruited for Takfir at the Finsbury Park mosque and the Four Feathers Youth Centre. Testimony at a French trial revealed that Osama bin Laden agreed to help finance Takfir wal Hijra in Europe if the group, in turn, "joined the global jihad and targeted the U.S." (Bright et al., 2001; Livesey, 2005). According to Gleis, Takfir was too much even for Hamza al-Masri, imam at the Finsbury Park mosque, who is quoted as saying they "create nothing and destroy everything" (Gleis, 2005: 1).

Takfir wal Hijra has done well in Europe. Part of its appeal is the concept of hijra, or exile, which is central to its name. Just as the Prophet went into exile from Mecca to Medina, just as bin Laden went into exile in Afghanistan, so too do many Muslims feel that they are in exile in other countries, some because of the political situation in their original homes in Egypt, or Algeria, or Pakistan, others because their families were economic refugees, metaphorically exiled from their homes in the Middle East or Africa. Even in exile, one can be part of the Muslim ummah, or community.

SOCIAL NETWORKS IN LONDON

Xavier Tchilao Djaffo

Moussaoui had no difficulty making friends in France. One friend also went to London. Xavier Djaffo was born in Bordeaux, France, in 1971, and grew up in Montpellier. His brother excelled at soccer there, and went on to play professionally in the UK. Abd Samad met Xavier in Perpignan, when Abd Samad was 23 and Xavier was 20. Xavier was tall and handsome. He had a ready smile (Moussaoui, 2003: 121–23). Zacarias and Djaffo soon became friends as well. Zacarias told Djaffo of South Bank University's program in international business. Djaffo moved to London, took the entry exams, and became a student. In 1995, Djaffo told Abd Samad that he converted to Islam and had met the musician Cat Stevens, now known as Yusuf Islam, at the Regent's Park mosque (Moussaoui, 2003: 124). Djaffo received his degree, but found the call to jihad too great to resist. Foreign fighters were being recruited to fight the Soviet Union in both Afghanistan and in Chechnya. He went to Chechnya. According to his obituary, shortly before going he and his friends chose war names, or *kunya*. He was already using the name Yusuf. Now a new name was chosen. The natural choice for Djaffo, his friends decided, was "Masood," or "happy." He had previously been given the names "al-Britani" or "al-Francee," since he was living in Great Britain, and he was French by birth. He did not like either name because they were too Western.

Instead he chose the name of the "tribe" of his father, "al-Benin." He became Masood al-Benin. In Chechnya he joined Ibn Khattab, a charismatic leader and financier of the foreign rebel forces there. Khattab had apparently fought in Afghanistan together with bin Laden. Moussaoui said in court that he and Djaffo had flown from Turkey to Dagestan to fight the Russians (tr. March 27, 2006, page 2408, lines 14–17). Moussaoui may have worked there as a combat photographer or computer specialist with Djaffo. Djaffo stayed on in Chechnya for some years, working on information technology and filming combat scenes for release on the internet. According to some reports, Djaffo was a commentator for Azzam.com, an al-Qaeda internet news source, and Qoqaz.com, a Chechen internet source.

Djaffo died on April 12, 2000, in Chechnya, when the truck he was riding in tried to break through a Russian blockade. The internet obituary for Djaffo called him a martyred brother, a *shaheed*. The French police were alerted and, in September 2000, they interviewed Djaffo's own family and the Moussaouis. An email communication of August 30, 2001, from the FBI legal attaché in Paris went to Harry Samit, Michael Maltbie, and others, detailing the connections between Moussaoui and Xavier Djaffo. This information presumably came from the French Direction de la Surveillance du Territoire, the DST. On September 28, 2000, French security interviewed an unnamed source concerning the death of Djaffo in April 2000. According to this source, "it was well known" that Moussaoui had converted Djaffo to radical fundamentalism while they were in school together in Perpignan. The source of this information was a "habachi" (meaning a member of the French Association des projects de bienfaisance islamiques en France, or APBIF). This particular group, the DST said, had as its "intellectual guide" Imam Khaled el Zant. This person was for moderation, which Zacarias Moussaoui rejected. The FBI memo went on to say that Moussaoui had been arrested by the Moroccan police upon his arrival in Morocco in 1997, and thrown out of a mosque in Narbonne. Moussaoui was said to be cold and cynical. He would be a danger should he return to France. The source of this information was not to be revealed (Defense Exhibit 59B). Zacarias Moussaoui was blamed by Djaffo's family for radicalizing him and recruiting him for jihad in Chechnya. Khattab would be killed in Chechnya in March 2002. The Chechens allege that the Russians sent him a poisoned letter (BBC, 2002). He remains a hero of the Chechen revolt against the Russians.

The Courtailler Brothers

Moussaoui had other associates and friends in London who were connected to jihadi organizations. According to Marc Sageman, the

author of *Understanding Terror Networks* (2004), David Courtailler
lived with Moussaoui in 1997. David Courtailler and his brother
Jérôme had both converted to Islam in London (CNN, 2004b). David
Courtailler denied publicly that he ever knew Moussaoui. However,
his testimony provides information on how the al-Qaeda recruiters
in London worked. Troubled with drugs, the brothers were told
they could help themselves by going to England. David attended
the Four Feathers Youth Centre on Baker Street. He said someone
there gave him $2000, a visa to Pakistan, and a contact number in
Peshawar, Pakistan. He went to Pakistan, and crossed the border into
Afghanistan where he attended an al-Qaeda training camp. This put
him on a CIA watch list. He was arrested when he shoplifted some
shoes in France. His brother Jérôme was picked up in Rotterdam
and accused of conspiracy to attack the American Embassy in Paris.
The source of the information of Courtailler's complicity in the
plan was Djamel Beghal, the French Algerian who worshipped at
Finsbury Park and Four Feathers. Beghal was arrested in the United
Arab Emirates for using a false passport. He was extradited to France
and charged with complicity in the plot to attack the US Embassy in
Paris (Rotella and Zucchino, 2001). In March 2005, he was sentenced
to ten years in prison.

Richard Reid

Richard Reid, the "shoebomber," was another associate of Moussaoui.
Reid converted to Islam in prison. He got out in 1994. He attended
the Brixton mosque at the same time as Moussaoui, and then moved
on to other more radical mosques. Imam Baker did not have personal
knowledge of whether the two knew each other, but he assumed they
did. British intelligence monitored phone calls between Moussaoui
and Reid in late 2000. Moussaoui has said they were friends. Reid
had made Moussaoui a beneficiary in his will, something the defense
argued Reid would not have done if Moussaoui was to die before him,
or with him in an attack on the White House.

AFGHANISTAN AND BEYOND

According to Moussaoui's testimony on March 27, 2006, he was in
Afghanistan from January 1997 until "March, 1999 or May, 1999" (tr.
March 27, 2006, page 2394, line 25). However, he had applied for a
French passport, presumably a replacement, at the French consulate
in London in July 1997. The last time he saw his family, he stayed
in the summer of 1997 with Jamila. His head was shaved, he had
a long beard, and short pants. Jamila testified that she thought he

was planning to reconcile with his mother but didn't know how to go about it. Aïcha confirmed to Abd Samad that this was the case (Moussaoui, 2003: 48). Jamila said that Zacarias prayed while there, and he was learning Arabic. Jamila was at their mother's house the day Zacarias arrived by bus. He spoke with his mother; and continued to meet with her after that. Jamila found him very reserved, calm, turned inward on himself. He was not sad, but he was not the smiling Zacarias they knew. She missed their discussions of the past. He talked at length of religion. *Il m'a fatigué*; he was tiresome, she said. He was thrown out of the Narbonne mosque that summer, for arguing with the imam (2003: 113–14).

In a hand-written pleading, Moussaoui said that while in London he placed a telephone call to Ibn Khattab. "[I]n December 1997 I personally phone from a phone box outside the train station in Croydon (on left) the commander of Mujahideen in Chechnya Khattab" (Docket No. 241). Croydon is in south London. He said his address at 5 Hubert Road in London was raided by Special Branch Police that same year. That address was used, he said, "when the British Court in 1999 engaged in proceedings against me for a bus infraction" (Docket No. 241).

By April 1998, Moussaoui was in a training camp in Afghanistan. Ahmed Ressam was also at the camp. Ressam, the "millennium bomber," who was caught while coming into Port Angeles, Washington, by ferry from Canada, claimed he recognized Moussaoui when shown a photo of him (McKenna, 2004b).

Moussaoui's claim that he returned to London in "March or May of 1999" was correct. On March 18, 1999, he applied at the French consulate there for a replacement of his French passport, and on March 30, 1999, Moussaoui applied for and got a replacement of his French national identity card. The photos show him with a shaved head, with no beard, and smiling. He wrote that his address was 66 Christchurch Road, Streatham, London SW2, the address he had for almost five years, though he was not there much of the time.

By the spring of 2000, Moussaoui was back in Kandahar, Afghanistan. In court pleadings he said he made two satellite telephone calls from the Kandahar post and communications office to Azerbaijan asking for information on Xavier Djaffo's family, after Djaffo's death in April. He also said that there was a satellite call between Khattab and "a third party" in Kandahar about Djaffo's family (Docket No. 243).

Statements from al-Qaeda Witnesses

Statements made by men captured after 9/11 provide more information about Moussaoui's activities after he left London. Khalid Sheikh Mohammed, Khallad, and Hambali were all captured and were interrogated in "undisclosed locations." Later, Moussaoui and his defense counsel wanted to have access to them. The proposal that they be videotaped from the "undisclosed location" was rejected, and statements were crafted from the interrogations. These were not necessarily designed with Moussaoui's potential questions in mind, and the judge thought the statements not adequate. The Fourth Circuit told the district court that summaries could be crafted with the cooperation of lawyers on both sides, and the judge. The truthfulness of the statements is hard to determine, but the information can be pieced together to understand better Moussaoui's travels and connections.

Khalid Sheikh Mohammed described his initial reservations about Moussaoui. By 1999, Moussaoui had the support of Osama bin Laden and Mohammed Atef. Moussaoui apparently had told bin Laden of his dream to fly a plane into the White House, and bin Laden told him to follow that dream. Moussaoui's Western confidence, and passport, would be of use to them. Khalid Sheikh Mohammed agreed to involve Moussaoui in the plan for a second wave of attacks (Defense Exhibit 941).

Khallad, also known as Walid Mohammed Salih bin Attash, was captured in 2003 and interrogated while being held at a secret CIA prison. His statement was read during the trial by a federal defender. He is accused of planning the October 2000 attack on the USS *Cole*. He was also involved in planning some aspects of the 9/11 attacks. He told his interrogators that he had seen Moussaoui several times in 2000 in Afghanistan at the al-Matar complex and at the Islamic Law Institute in Kandahar. Khallad said Moussaoui went to the al-Matar complex to have lunch on Fridays. These lunches were, Khallad said, attended by most members of al-Qaeda in Afghanistan. Khallad said that Abu Hafs al-Masri, or Mohammed Atef, had told Khallad to take Moussaoui to Karachi, Pakistan, where Moussaoui would take a flight to Malaysia to investigate flight training. He was to meet Hambali, a leader of Jemaah Islamiya, which was affiliated with al-Qaeda. Khallad gave Moussaoui his own phone number, email address, and money. He purchased Moussaoui's air ticket. Although the phone number was given for emergencies only, Moussaoui called Khallad daily from Malaysia. Khallad turned off his phone. Khallad reported Moussaoui's behavior to Khalid Sheikh Mohammed, who instructed Khallad to break off all contact. Khallad did so. Moussaoui returned to Afghanistan shortly afterward, and Mohammed Atef sent Moussaoui out again, somewhere. It wasn't until after 9/11, Khallad said, that he learned where Moussaoui had gone (Defense Exhibit 945).

Hambali was the operational leader for Jemaah Islamiya (JI) in the Malaysia/Singapore region, and a "key coordinator" between JI and al-Qaeda. Moussaoui arrived in Malaysia in July 2000, supposedly sent either by Mohammed Atef, an Egyptian also known as Abu Hafs al-Masri, or by Khalid Sheikh Mohammed. It was Hambali who described the purchase of 40 tons of ammonium nitrate, something Moussaoui claimed he did not suggest. Hambali said that Moussaoui "managed to annoy everyone he came into contact with." Moussaoui criticized members of JI for sitting around and reading the Koran when they should be out kidnapping local Chinese businessmen and demanding ransom, or robbing motorists. "Hambali told him if he wanted to do such things, he should do it in Europe, and not cause trouble in JI's neighborhood." Hambali said that Yazid Sufat wrote a letter of reference for Moussaoui, saying that he was a representative of InFocus Tech, Yazid's own company, and they all hoped he would go off to Europe to flight school "and become someone else's problem." Moussaoui had no money to leave, so Hambali gave him money for a flight back to Europe. Hambali said he "willingly paid the ticket, as he was happy to be rid of Moussaoui." A JI operative later went to Khalid Sheikh Mohammed in Pakistan. This opportunity was used to complain about Moussaoui. Khalid Sheikh Mohammed "agreed that there was something wrong with ZM," and repaid them for Moussaoui's ticket and the ammonium nitrate (Defense Exhibit No. 946).[4]

Fauzi bin Abu Bakar Bafana's videotaped testimony, taken in a detention center in Singapore in November 2002, confirmed Moussaoui's presence in Malaysia in late summer and early fall of 2000. Bafana had given him a place to stay. Moussaoui also told Bafana of his dream of flying a plane into the White House. Moussaoui said he had told bin Laden of this dream, and bin Laden told Moussaoui to follow his dream. It was too expensive to follow that dream in Malaysia, Moussaoui learned, so he asked JI for money to go elsewhere to flight school. Bafana said Moussaoui needed $10,000. They gave him far less, and were happy that he left (tr. March 8, 2006, pp. 516–99).

While in Malaysia, Moussaoui emailed American flight schools asking about lessons. On September 29, 2000, he emailed the Airman Flight School in Norman, Oklahoma. This was the school he chose to attend (*United States v. Moussaoui*, Indictment, 2001).

Return to London

According to court testimony, Moussaoui left Malaysia October 5, 2000, bound for London. He said he waited there for a call from Khallad concerning his next move, but after the bombing of the USS *Cole* on October 12, 2000, he realized he would not hear from his contacts. He had been trained that planners and potential suspects should go under ground after an event. He finally got in touch with his South Asian contacts, and began planning his move to the United States (tr. March 27, 2006, page 2397, lines 13–23).

As a supplementary form of identity he got his UK driving license, dated October 24, 2000. His address by then was 23A Lambert Road in Brixton. There was no beard; he had a shaved head and a smile for the photo. This particular address was of concern to him in court; when he was arguing to undertake his own defense he talked several times about this address and the fact that it had been raided by the police after the embassy bombings. This fact was important to him. On October 31, he received a replacement French passport, though by now the French consulate was reluctant to make it good for more than two years. He then got a visa for Pakistan on December 4, 2000. According to the US government, Ramzi bin al-Shibh, who later sent money to Moussaoui in the US, visited him in London in late 2000. Moussaoui then made a trip to Pakistan and returned to London in February 2001. According to his testimony, he made the trip to "clear up some problems," and to meet with bin Laden and Khalid Sheikh Mohammed.

ALTERNATIVE EXPLANATION:
HOW EFFECTIVE WAS MOUSSAOUI?

Edward MacMahon's opening statement in the trial laid out the defense team's strategy. They were going to demonstrate Moussaoui's ineffectiveness as a terrorist. Evidence would show, he said, that some members of the leadership of al-Qaeda and its affiliate Jemaah Islamiya distrusted him. He was not linked to the other hijackers, he was not discreet, and he got caught. Indeed, during the trial, the statements of Khalid Sheikh Mohammed, Hambali, and Bafana all made clear they thought Moussaoui was a problem. However, Osama bin Laden and Mohammed Atef both trusted him enough to encourage him to move ahead with flight training. Through use of these summaries, the FBI's information from the French intelligence agency, the DST; British surveillance information, as well as the detainees' statements and Moussaoui's own testimony, one can learn his activities after he moved from the moderate Brixton mosque. Moussaoui did travel to Afghanistan several times, and was trained there in the military camps. He went to Chechnya, according to court documents, where he took part in actions against Russian troops. He ran a guest-house in Afghanistan, transporting guests there to bin Laden's quarters. He was close enough to bin Laden to describe his own dream to him, and to be told to pursue that dream. He was close enough to al-Qaeda leadership to travel with Khallad from Afghanistan to Pakistan, and then receive funds to go to Malaysia, where he again met with Jemaah Islamiya leaders. Moussaoui's behavior may have been annoying to some, and it is clear from the testimony of his friends and relatives that he took a strong position on issues. But he was a bright, competent, person who managed to make his way through a French society that was not always sympathetic to him as a North African, to learn English well enough to enroll in a graduate business program seven months after he arrived in London, and to take on a mission that led him from Afghanistan to Malaysia to London. He was ready to go.

MOUSSAOUI FLIES TO THE UNITED STATES

Moussaoui bought a ticket for the United States, and left Heathrow on February 23, 2001, bound for Oklahoma by way of Chicago. He had a return ticket for June 23, 2001. He enrolled at Airman Flight School in Norman. He found a mosque, and roommates. He joined a gym; he bought flight manuals. He talked with his new roommate, Hussein al-Attas, about religion, and about jihad. He wasn't very good at flying, as he later admitted to one of his lawyers. After trying with little success to fly a single-engine Cessna, he emailed the Pan Am International Flight School, telling them of his dream to fly. He wrote in his notebook: "The importance of the concept of hijra (exile)." He packed his belongings and left his car. His roommate drove him north to Eagan, Minnesota, to learn to fly a 747-400 on a simulator.

5 WHY CAN'T THEY BE MORE FRENCH?

I stand here as a French citizen. I want to make clear that I am not French and have no relation. I'm a sworn enemy of France. So I want to make this in the record that I'm not French, okay? I tell you I am a Muslim, and I have nothing to do with a nation of homosexual Crusaders. And I am not a frog. That's the first thing. (Zacarias Moussaoui, tr. February 14, 2006, page 4, lines 20–25)

INCLUSION AND EXCLUSION

July 14, 1989, marked the bicentennial of the French Revolution. This was the same national celebration that Abd Samad Moussaoui was celebrating when he was assaulted in Narbonne. I was in France at the same time, doing research in Montbéliard, a town in eastern France near the Swiss and the German borders. The town is south of Mulhouse, where the Moussaoui family lived until 1980. The region is home to several large industrial companies, including Peugeot, which has plants in both Mulhouse and next to Montbéliard, in Sochaux. I was interested in the transition the region made from agricultural to industrial production during the nineteenth and twentieth centuries, and the effects that transition had on households.

The 1980s and 1990s were years of economic and social transition for France. The "*trente glorieuses*," the "thirty glorious years" of the post-war boom were over. Immigrant workers, formerly invisible, were now considered a problem. Family members were allowed to join them. This too was seen as a problem. By 1989, anti-immigrant rhetoric was heating up, and the press was reporting on it. The social issues which the Moussaoui children first discovered in Mulhouse, and later experienced in Narbonne, were not unique to them. The long-term inhabitants of Montbéliard noticed these issues, and discussed them among themselves and with me. The discussions reminded me of similar ones in the US during the contentious period of integration of schools in the 1970s. In the US, race and class were discussed in the news, at dinner tables, and fought over out on sidewalks and streets of Boston, Philadelphia, and the south. There had of course been unrest in France in the 1960s. Then, there were demonstrations by students and workers in May 1968, the same time that Zacarias Moussaoui was born. Massive strikes and walkouts brought the country to a halt. A strike at the Peugeot automobile plant near Montbéliard resulted in the death of two workers. Those demonstrations were over social and economic issues connected to education, pay, and the Vietnam War. The new issues reflected concerns over immigration and foreigners which have still not been resolved. The conversations I had in eastern France reflected those issues.

In Montbéliard, the celebration of Bastille Day began the day before, on July 13. In 1989, the events began in the center of the town. The town office, or *mairie*, faces a seventeenth-century stone Lutheran church. The area in between, usually filled with cars, was closed off. This was a welcome holiday for many of the workers at the Peugeot automobile plant nearby at Sochaux. Long rows of tables were set up in between the trees. Couples and families wandered in, and food was served. A van filled with members of a band pulled in and set up microphones. The keyboardist began to play. Accordions were taken out of cases. The band was an "Accordionorama." They lit into a jaunty two-step, leading wives and girlfriends to coax their partners to dance with them. The crowd was predominantly white and French.

As dusk fell, town employees handed out little Japanese paper lanterns, each with a small candle inside. A new band entered the square, this time with brass instruments. They moved to the head of a line that was slowly forming in front of the *mairie*. Behind the band was the mayor. Behind the mayor were the members of the town council, well dressed, each with a sash across her or his chest. Behind them were the firemen, the *sapeurs-pompiers*, wearing intimidating helmets. Some of the firemen, looking huge in their coats and boots, carefully lit the candles each of us was holding, and then got into line. Behind the firemen were parents and small children, each with their own softly glowing Japanese lantern.

The band members tested themselves on a march, and off we all went, winding through town as though we were moving through a snail. The words of the "Marseillaise" were attempted, but people had difficulty with the second verse. It didn't matter, everyone was in high spirits. The parade moved past crowds of people standing on the sidewalks. As we marched past one group, a tipsy North African, with no shirt but somehow wearing a sash, marched alongside the town council members. He stuck out his chest as he marched, in imitation of them, then turned and gave them a raspberry, rubbing his ear as he did so. The council members ignored him, and marched on. At the next block a band was playing a keyboard and electric guitars on a narrow sidewalk. The musicians were West African, and the music was irresistible for the teenagers in the crowd, who dropped out of the parade to dance in the street. We marched on. The use of space in the town of Montbéliard on the eve of Bastille Day reflected the way in which the inhabitants of the region thought of themselves, either as owners and controllers of certain spaces, or as occupiers of more marginal spaces. The French danced to accordion music in the center town square. The West and North Africans stayed on the side streets, finding their own borrowed space.

Two months later, in September 1989, the workers of Peugeot-Mulhouse, to the north, and then Peugeot-Sochaux, went on strike. Modernization of the plants meant that some workers would lose their jobs. The directors of the company said it was time to cut the "fat," particularly as they brought in robotized assembly lines. The strikes would affect everyone in the area, including workers, their families, and businesses in Montbéliard. Some workers left, others elected to stay on if they could.

The following summer of 1990 I was back in Montbéliard for more research. During the week, in the central shopping district, the busy streets thinned out towards noon. The woman who managed the house wares store ran next door to buy some bread for the noon meal. Office workers and store employees hurried home as steel gates came rumbling down over shop entrances. By 12:15 the streets were almost empty except for four North Africans and me. They had no agenda, for this was no workday for them. They didn't want to stop for expensive lunches. Nearby, I ate a piece of bread and read a newspaper. The North Africans wandered around the empty streets, or sat on the steps near the fountain, smoking and talking together quietly. We were all strangers there. We had no apartment or house close by, where we could go home for lunch.

The newspaper I was reading was a regional one. It carried news about local events, of gatherings of the elderly, and of fundraisers for the firemen, and of some event for school children. An article about permanent residents from North Africa caught my eye, and a conversation over lunch with some French friends came back to me. A few years ago, said one, you never saw men with prayer rugs over their shoulders in the streets. Now you see them more and more. Now the towns in the outskirts of Montbéliard have many such men, he continued. It is the Peugeot plant that attracts them here. But, he asked rhetorically, why can't they be more French?

This was in 1990, several months after the Peugeot strike had ended. The debate over foreign-born workers was becoming contentious. My friend's statement was a quiet reflection of the shared pool of attitudes toward workers from North and West Africa and their families. By 1990, the appeal of Jean-Marie Le Pen and the Front National, as well as the perceived increase in immigration into France, were the topics of conversation. *How* to talk about this perceived problem was an issue as well. Were these issues of ethnicity? Of race? Of class? Of cultural difference? These categories were not ones that were easily discussed by the French (see Donahue, 1997). Statistical numbers based on religion and ethnic affiliation were difficult to come by, unlike in the US or the UK. In the 1990s, ethnicity as an academic study was still new in France (Lorcerie, n.d.). Multiculturalism was accepted as a concept more readily in the US and the UK than in France. What was one to call ethnic affiliation? It became *"communautarisme."* Still to come were the conflict and misunderstandings over the wearing of scarves by young Muslim schoolgirls, the beatings of North Africans in various cities in France, the death of a young North African while in police custody, the desecration of Jewish cemeteries, the riots of 2005, the torture and murder in 2006 of a young man for being Jewish. But the perception of a problem with "integration" was growing.

ETHNICITY, RACE, RELIGION, CLASS, AND CULTURE

In January 1992, French television focused on the news coming out of Algeria. This was the same time that Zacarias Moussaoui was planning to move to London. I was in Montbéliard to finish some research on the region's industrial history, staying in the apartment of a Peugeot retiree. We watched the evening news together and discussed our interpretations of the events in Algeria. My hostess thought it a good thing that France no longer had to take responsibility for Algeria, but problems were going to arise because of France's colonial relationship to Algeria. During the month of January, the Algerian president was forced to resign and a second round of elections cancelled because it appeared the political party of the Islamic Salvation Front, or FIS, was strongly favored to win. There were demonstrations in the streets of Algiers. The following month a state of emergency was declared, and in March 1992, the FIS was legally banned.

One January afternoon that year a group of us was eating lunch at a restaurant in the center of Montbéliard. Several were retired Peugeot employees. One woman had lived in Morocco while her military husband was stationed there after World War II. The conversation turned to relations between the French and the North Africans. One woman said:

There are more North Africans in the area than there used to be. They seem to be different from the Lebanese. They are perhaps less intelligent than the Lebanese. It is economic reasons that create the problems; there are not enough jobs. They have a different religion and habits, which make them different from the Poles, Italians, and former Yugoslavs, who are Europeans. The people of the Maghreb of North Africa have not risen as much as the Lebanese or American blacks. (V.A., personal communication, January 1992)

My informant embellished her point with an example. An acquaintance of hers had a daughter – a French citizen – who lives with a North

African. The North African is all right, she said, but *his* mother is impossible. My informant thought the North African was living with her friend's daughter in order to get better benefits than he otherwise would have been entitled to. The informant also thought he was trying to use the relationship to obtain French citizenship.

Late one afternoon that January I went to visit an acquaintance in Belfort, to the north of Montbéliard, and to the south of Mulhouse. We sat over a long dinner with some of her friends. She was celebrating Three Kings Day, or Epiphany. She had baked a cake with a dried bean inside. Whoever got the bean was to have good luck. I got the bean. Fortified by home-made fruit liqueur, the conversation turned again to North Africa, as it would all that January. It appeared, one person said, that the racial situation in France was now somewhat similar to the way it had been in the United States in the 1950s and 1960s. "Race" had not been considered a problem in France, now it was. A retired worker from Peugeot spoke up. He was living on his retirement pension and he also owned a vacation house in the south of France. He was direct about his feelings. "The North Africans, I don't like them," he said. "They all come here just for the benefits" (C.A., personal communication, January 1992).

His comment revealed the changing economics of the Mulhouse–Sochaux–Montbéliard area. In the post-World War II era, North Africans had helped rebuild France's automobile and rail industry. Automobile assembly lines were manned by North Africans, Poles, and the French themselves. Now, in the 1990s, the strike was over and the assembly lines at Peugeot-Sochaux were automated. I went on a tour with a group of Japanese engineers who were curious to see how the French had adapted some of their own ideas. The skilled workers who remained employed were primarily French natives, yet the high-rise apartment blocks in the new sections of Montbéliard had many North and West African residents.

During a return trip to Montbéliard in 1999, a friend who taught high school noted that North and West Africans were moving out to find jobs elsewhere. Where do they move to, I asked. To Paris, he said. In a sense, my friend was correct. The region that included Mulhouse and Sochaux–Montbéliard, where industry had expanded during the post-World War II era, was facing cutbacks, strikes, and acquisition by even larger corporations. The growth and job opportunities that drew Omar Moussaoui to Mulhouse in the 1970s declined not long after he arrived. The region had depended on jobs with Peugeot and with Alstom, a manufacturer of heavy engines. Zacarias's mother's friend Saïd worked for Peugeot-Mulhouse (JV002.24T; Moussaoui, 2003). The oil embargoes of the 1970s and Peugeot's acquisition of Citroën in 1976, together with their acquisition of Chrysler-Talbot, led to a difficult financial period for the Peugeot company in the 1980s

(Peugeot, 2006). Peugeot's later automation of its Sochaux plant meant that fewer workers were to be employed in the Montbéliard–Sochaux region. The number of workers was halved, from 40,000 in the 1970s to 18,000 by the end of the 1990s (see Pialoux and Beaud, 2000). Peugeot also took over what was formerly Ford, and then Talbot, plants near Paris, at Poissy (Yvelines). Now, nearly 20 years later, 8000 workers come into Peugeot-Poissy by shuttle bus, by train, and by car from a wide area around Paris. A large number of these workers were originally Turks, Pakistanis, Algerians, and Moroccans (Khedimellah, 2005). According to INSEE, the French National Institute for Statistics and Economic Studies, these workers live in an area in which one of every six residents is an immigrant. As of 2005, 40 percent of all immigrants in France live in the Ile de France, the area around Paris. The other areas with a high number of immigrants are the south (about 10 percent), southeast (10 percent), and the Alsace region (about 10 percent) (Borrel, 2006).

The informants in Montbéliard wove together French attitudes toward people they considered to be foreigners. These attitudes included their observations of differences in skin color and their assumptions about geographic origins. People from Algeria and Morocco, particularly the *magrhébins*, were of a different race to the Montbéliardais. There were, they observed, also differences in culture, in particular because of their Arab dress and language, and because of their practice of Islam. These observations came from middle-class people, several of them well subsidized by their retirement pensions from Peugeot. The North African residents of Montbéliard were not an economic threat to them, and their reactions to the North Africans in their community were not angry. They did think North Africans were taking a part of the economic pie that wasn't rightly theirs. They thought it inappropriate that foreigners should lay claim to French social security benefits. Their reactions were mild compared to those of Jean-Marie Le Pen's followers in the streets of southern France. But they shared the same perceptions, that there were more immigrants than in the past, and that more were taking advantage of the social security system.

MIGRATION TO FRANCE

A great deal is learnt about a country through its treatment of foreigners. The census, its definitions, the handling of the figures are also the image of a society and its moods. (Singer-Kerel, 1991: 281–82)

Migration statistics, although they usually represent official numbers and may undercount the number of actual immigrants, do allow for some understanding of trends and flows of migration. According to Jeanne Singer-Kerel, since the early nineteenth century, France has been the second largest importer of foreign labor after the United States. The declining birth rate, the need for agricultural workers and

labor in heavy industry, as well as the use of colonial subjects for the
military brought many North and West Africans into France (Singer-
Kerel, 1991: 279). In the 1990s, the popular press and the rhetoric
of right-wing parties gave one the impression that migration into
France, both legal and illegal, was at higher levels than ever before.
One elderly French woman told me that she and her friends were
ras le bol, fed up, with all the immigrants living there. She was born
in Vietnam to French parents, and lived in Morocco during World
War II. Yet her sympathies were not with immigrants to France. She
was not one of them.

Accurate migration statistics are difficult to come by. By law,
French censuses and surveys cannot collect information on ethnic
background or religion. Statistics are collected on place of birth and
nationality. There are several categories of persons used in French
statistics, indicating a problematic relationship to nationality. The
category of "foreigner" indicates a person residing in France who is
not of French nationality. In 1990, INSEE adopted a new category
of "immigrant." This category is constructed from data for people
residing in France whose place of birth was outside of France, and
from data on nationality (Brinbaum, 2005). It was probably no
coincidence that this statistical category was created just as French
society was discussing the immigration matter. Many immigrants are
those people who enter France hoping to "regularize" their stay there.
Some are *sans papiers*, people with no documents. The government
claims there are approximately 250,000 *sans papiers*, although the
number may be far higher (Engler, 2005: 2). The term *sans papiers* can
include a number of categories of people, including the *clandestins*, or
illegal immigrants who enter France, in particular from West Africa,
to live in crowded rooms and hotels in areas around Marseille and
the Ile de France. Occasionally, the children of residents in France,
with documents or not, are considered *sans papiers* if they cannot
acquire the proper documents of residence. However the numbers
are counted, according to INSEE, there were 4.3 million immigrants
in 1999, 7.4 percent of the population. The portrayal of a rising
tide of immigration is a somewhat suspect construct of reporting
by the popular press, among members of the Front National and its
adherents, and in the general consciousness of the French. Again,
according to INSEE, the percentage of immigrants has stayed about
the same for the last 25 years (Boëldieu and Borrel, 2000).

In the case of North Africans, close to a million repatriates, i.e.
French who had lived in Algeria, came to France as a result of the
1960s Algerian war for independence. Another half-million *harkis*,
Algerians who had fought side by side with the French, also entered
France during the early 1960s (Husbands, 1991: 172–73). Many of these
repatriates and immigrants are now part of the general population, and

are therefore not counted as immigrants. The 1999 census reported that there were 574,208 Algerian immigrants living in France, similarly, there were 522,504 Moroccans, and 210,561 Tunisians for a total of 1,307,273 people from North Africa (Engler, 2005: 2).

Who Has the Right to Be French? The National Construction of Rights

French citizenship has become increasingly restricted, raising the question of who has the right to be French. In 1990 Harlem Désir, at the time leader of the group SOS Racisme, held an interview with the French journal *Le Débat*. SOS Racisme was the group to which Abd Samad Moussaoui and his mother turned for help after he was attacked while waiting for Zacarias and his friends in Narbonne in July 1989. Concerning integration into French norms, Désir quoted Napoleon as saying:

The children of foreigners who are established in France have the French spirit, French habits, the attachment which each one bears naturally to the country where [he] was born. (1990: 53; my translation)

This somewhat generous spirit evaporated by the mid nineteenth century. Napoleon's expansionist vision of a French empire in Europe and Africa contracted with the retreats from Egypt and Russia. The Napoleonic code emphasized citizenship by blood (*jus sanguinis*), as well as birth on French soil (*jus soli*). The national census of 1851 was the first to ask specifically about the presence of foreigners in France (Silverman, 1991). In the 1880s, a legislative debate centered on whether a tax should be imposed on foreigners in order to protect the jobs of French workers. In 1889, a Nationality Code was established and, by the end of the nineteenth century, the French educational system had established its own unique way of ensuring that all children attending school, either on the French mainland or in colonial outposts, would be instilled with a French identity. Although control of education has been somewhat decentralized, the system has tended to be reproduced to this day (Citron, 1987; Silverman, 1991: 335–36).

The Evian Agreement, in 1962, gave rights of citizenship to Algerians in France, except political rights. Children of these Algerians, born on French soil, were considered to be French citizens, under the concept of *jus soli*, even if they were not French under the concept of *jus sanguinis*, French by "blood" inheritance. Immigration law since the 1960s has gradually tightened. By 1974, immigration was declared to be at an end. But families had a right to join resident workers, and the right to asylum continued.

By 1983, Jean-Marie Le Pen's party, the Front National, was making an impression. The anti-immigration speeches of Le Pen, a former military man, resonated with French voters. During the spring and summer municipal elections of 1983, members of Le Pen's Front National won seats on the Dreux municipal council, and one member became the deputy mayor. Dreux is outside Paris, and news of this success heartened many French citizens. Young North Africans, or *beurs*, however, marched in the streets of Paris. Villages and towns in the south of France experienced increasing unrest between native and immigrant youths (see Silverstein, 2004).

By Bastille Day 1989, anti-immigrant feeling was rising, fueled by the success of Le Pen's nationalist message. This was the situation when Abd Samad was attacked by a stranger, and when Abd Samad and his mother turned to SOS Racisme. But the 1990s did not turn out to be any more welcoming to the children of immigrants than were the 1980s. The state that had extended its borders during the colonial period and had declared many of those subject peoples to be French, helped to create the situation now in hand. By 1993, politicians in the Balladur government made increasing attempts to restrict immigration into France, to restrict visas, and to empower the police to search for and demand identity papers of persons on the street. In the early 1990s, about the time that Zacarias Moussaoui left France for London, Charles Pasqua claimed that his goal was "zero immigration." During that time, the waiting period for family reunification was lengthened, and foreigners who graduated from French universities were barred from finding jobs in France (Engler, 2005). The "Pasqua Law" became a flashpoint for controversy.

Sans Papiers

To get to Paris's eighteenth *arrondissement* from the Gare de Nord, one walks up the Boulevard de Magenta to the Boulevard de Barbés. It is necessary to pass under a rail line which follows the Boulevard de Rochechouart. In doing so, one also passes into another world from the Paris of sidewalk cafés and white-shirted, black-vested waiters. The crowds are larger, the street sales more intense, and young men press small slips of paper into one's hand, advertising Professeur or Marabout Hakim, who can solve your problems, divine your future, help assure success with your exams or driver's license test, payment after success. The eighteenth arrondissement has markets on Saturday and other days of the week, much like the rest of Paris. But these markets sell not only French and European produce but also African escargots the size of a softball, strange fruits and vegetables unobtainable elsewhere in Paris. Across the street, shops sell cloth with "African" patterns made in Holland and England, and suitcases the size of trunks. North African men stand around outside *halal* butcher shops in the middle of the day. With no jobs, there is not much to do except enjoy one's friends.

In 1996, a group of *sans papiers* who had been threatened with deportation occupied several churches in this area. The police broke into one church and removed the protesters. They moved to St. Bernard church. Hunger strikes and street demonstrations drew attention to their plight. The police broke into St. Bernard church, deporting some of the protesters, many of whom were from Mali. During the spring and summer of 1999, I was in Paris researching the attitudes of West African musicians toward life in France. Interviews with these musicians, from Mali, Guinea, Côte d'Ivoire, and Senegal revealed the economic necessity for immigration, as well as the feeling of marginalization some of them experienced. Some said they lived on the meager tips they received in the restaurants where they played. Some had not seen their families in years (Donahue, 2005). That spring and summer there were marches in the Paris streets, still in support of the *sans papiers*. The marches were peaceful. The police presence was obvious. The marches did not succeed in changing immigration policy. School-age children were allowed to finish their school year, but, if their documents were not correct, they were then deported. In August of 2006, Jeff, a young Nigerian, was brought onto a plane bound for Lagos, Nigeria. He was being deported, and passengers on the plane, in support of him, refused to sit down to allow the flight to take off. Two passengers were arrested. The plane took off with Jeff, amid protests at Charles de Gaulle airport (BBC, 2006).

Liberté, Egalité, Fraternité?
On October 27, 2005, two teenaged boys were electrocuted in the Paris suburb of Clichy-sous-Bois. Bouna Traoré, 15, and Ziad Benna, 17, climbed over a fence into an electrical substation, apparently trying to escape an identity check by the police. Bouna was Mauritanian, Ziad, of Tunisian descent. Their deaths touched off three weeks of riots in 300 French towns, as well as unrest in Guadeloupe, Belgium, Germany, and the Netherlands (*L'Est Républicain*, 2005a). Montbéliard and the region around it experienced on a smaller scale the unrest that occurred in the larger cities. According to *L'Est Républicain* (2005b), in that area 61 vehicles were burned and, a less damaging favorite of the young, there were 66 fires in trash bins. There were 39 arrests. Much as elsewhere, property owners were on watch through the nights of unrest, trying to prevent fires on private property and in schools.

The riots were not a surprise. Car-burnings in the French suburbs have been common practice for a number of years. The fact that the torched cars were often Renaults and Peugeots was not lost on French journalists and politicians; nor was the fact that other objects of attack were schools and hospitals. These are all symbols of the state or of privately owned industries which represent the failure of national policies. Journalists who interviewed the rioters of 2005 were occasionally chilled by what they heard: one said he wanted to return to Morocco, because he hated the Jews; another reportedly displayed, on his cell phone, a video of a Chechen beheading a Russian soldier. The widespread unrest at the time, and the continuing discussion in the press, was an indicator of the problematic response of the French republic, and its citizens, to the second- and third-generation descendants of the workers who were originally invited to help rebuild France.

The fact that the protesters are called "third-generation immigrants" is noteworthy. In the United States, third-generation, even second-generation immigrants are most often thought of as Americans. They may be labeled with an ethnic appellation, as in "Italo-American"; nevertheless, they are American. Not so in France. The suburbs and high-rises in which North and West Africans live are home to "the Other." They are seen as being "crime-ridden," "dirty," and "smelly." The telling phrase used by Minister of the Interior Nicolas Sarkozy in reference to the protesters, "*racaille*," often translated as "scum," indicates how the French think about their unwanted neighbors.

The grandfathers of many protesters had come to work in the automobile factories and heavy industries of post-World War II France on the assumption that they would then return to North and West Africa, to Algeria, Morocco, Mali, and Senegal. But to what were they to return? Many stayed in France. French policies aimed at integration allowed their spouses and families to join them. The French educational system would integrate their children into French values and norms. In 1991 I was told by a Parisian architect of Lebanese origin that he thought the French educational system was indeed the genius of the French creation of identity. Through the education system all school children, of whatever origin, became French. He laughed about the saying that all school children in French schools, whether in Paris or in Senegal, learned on the same day at the same time about the rivers of France. Still, he said, something about it worked (G.J., personal communication, May 1991).

Thanks in part to this educational system, and to a successful economy, second-generation children succeeded to a degree. But their children often have not been able to find jobs, even after receiving university degrees. Underemployment is obvious. Hotel desk clerks in Paris who are originally from Tunisia or Morocco may well have advanced degrees. I talked with one Tunisian with an advanced degree in literature from the Sorbonne who worked at a hotel in the upscale seventh arrondissement. He is not happy about his lack of ability to find a teaching position. People who did less well than he at the university now have better jobs, he said.

Economic and Cultural Issues

According to one report (Ghannoushi, 2005), 26.5 percent of "immigrant" students with university degrees are jobless, as compared to 5 percent of non-immigrant university degree holders.

Unemployment in some of the French suburbs, or *banlieues*, is edging over 20 percent (*Le Monde*, 2005). Such figures lend credence to the argument that young men in difficult economic situations find themselves drawn to groups like al-Qaeda. Some have been. But the group of French al-Qaeda and Takfir members with whom Moussaoui was affiliated were, on the whole, educated and employable, as was Moussaoui. Moussaoui's dreams were not necessarily being met, and he did feel blocked in his ambitions, but Zacarias Moussaoui's decision to leave France and join al-Qaeda cannot be directly attributed to a lack of education or a dreary life in the banlieues. He was not a disadvantaged youth. He did want to enhance his possibilities, and moving to London could make that possible. He had options, which he created for himself. Furthermore, he was not, when living in France, a good example of Samuel Huntington's clash-of-civilizations youth. He fully participated in French life, going out with friends, playing pool, dancing in discos, and listening to Bruce Springsteen. Sensitive to the racial issue, he fought back with anger, because he had experience of the powers of exclusion and inclusion.

Zacarias Moussaoui's experience of exclusion and alienation were particular to him. He had worked and had managed to live on his own from the time he was in high school. Granted, his brother Abd Samad reported that occasionally he did not have enough to eat, and the two brothers would rely on friends for meals (Moussaoui, 2003: 73–74). But he had acquired a technical education and had received state funding to move from high school to university. In London, though living for a while in a shelter for the homeless, he was able to overcome a language barrier, take exams, and acquire funding to receive a master's degree from South Bank University. Moussaoui turned to Islamic fundamentalism because it offered more than insurance against unemployment. It offered a sense of belonging, a sense of purpose, and a mission. It offered an Islam without borders.

6 ISLAM WITHOUT BORDERS

RELIGION AND THE STATE

Zacarias Moussaoui has disavowed his French citizenship. He has said in court: "I am al Qaeda." He has said he is a slave of Allah. He has sworn bayat to Osama bin Laden. His tenacious adherence to an extra-state religious belief system, in particular one that endorses forms of resistance at once symbolically and physically violent, is indicative of the issues that face nation-states world-wide. What is the appeal of such resistance? Jonah Goldberg, a commentator for the conservative *National Review* has said that: "Radical Islam is globalization for losers. It appeals to those left out of modernization, industrialization, and prosperity – particularly to young men desperate for order, meaning, and pride amid the chaos of globalization" (Goldberg, 2006).

Goldberg is correct in the sense that the Islam which attracted Zacarias Moussaoui is part of a globalized Islam, and that it offered a sense of meaning and pride. But Christianity and Judaism are also religions that cross nation-state boundaries, and they offer meaning and pride as well. Goldberg shares with others the belief that those who slip off across national borders, on their way to jihad, are primarily the *racaille* of the slums. This is not necessarily the case, and Moussaoui was not one of those "left out of modernization, industrialization, and prosperity." He and his friend Xavier Djaffo were well educated. Both Moussaoui and Djaffo had graduate degrees in international business, the engine of globalization.

Since 9/11, American national security experts have trained their sights on European countries such as France and the UK because men like Moussaoui originated there. An expert on the US visa waiver program, the program used by Moussaoui to enter the US, said that:

Radical Islam is spreading across Europe among descendants of Muslim immigrants. Disenfranchised and disillusioned by the failure of integration, some European Muslims have taken up jihad against the West. They are dangerous and committed – and can enter the United States without a visa. (Leiken, 2005)

The politics of a transnational Islam have been widely discussed (for example, see Karam et al., 2004). Bowen (2004a) has asked if French

Islam has borders. The question of the power of the Church in the emerging sovereign nations of Europe was settled during the early modern era. The bloody wars of religion ended with accommodations between the Catholic Church and the emerging nation-states which themselves were establishing national borders. France, the country of Moussaoui's birth, offers an interesting example of the complicated mix of national policies toward religion, the power of the French nation-state, and the rights of individuals.

The borders of nations are more fluid than one might think. France's own national boundaries have been disputed into the twentieth century. Alsace and other regions along France's eastern border, including Mulhouse and Montbéliard, had political ties to Germany. Those ties were dissolved as a result of the French Revolution. Then Germany annexed Alsace, including Mulhouse, after the Franco-Prussian War of 1870–71. France reclaimed the region after World War I, then Germany re-annexed it during World War II. The creation of a larger union, the European Community and the later European Union, to which France belongs, has led to easier movement across those borders for individuals from other members of the European Union. But France, drawing on its own traditions in relation to religion and individual rights, has struggled to cope with changing social issues. Today, those issues involve not only its own immigrant population but also Islam.

At stake for Muslims in France is the conflict between two universalizing principles, those of the French Republic, and those of Islam (see Bowen, 2004a; Kepel, 1997). Not only are the French, both the government and the people, in dispute over policies toward foreigners and immigrants, but they are also in dispute over policies concerning the relationship between religion and the state. On the one hand, the French government pursues its right to maintain control over the doctrine of separation of Church and state; on the other, individuals and groups pursue their right to declare affiliation to symbolic constructs of religion beyond the state.

Islam, in some interpretations, offers a vision of a community reaching across state borders – an Islam without borders. This vision, much as the ones offered by Christianity and Judaism, is attractive to those who seek connection to a power beyond the apparent reach of any secular authority. But, in the current context of politico-religious conflict, such a connection is viewed as a problem by those state officials in charge of administering internal state security and controlling problematic symbols of religious adherence such as female headscarves. These headscarves, or *foulards*, have been an issue in France since the 1980s (Beriss, 1990), and French policies of control over wearing the headscarf even became an issue in the war in Iraq.

Problematic Headwear

On August 20, 2004, two French journalists and their driver were kidnapped near the Iraqi city of Najaf. On August 28, Al Jazeera television announced that the Islamic Army of Iraq was holding them hostage, and had issued a demand that France renounce its impending ban on wearing religious symbols in French schools within 48 hours. The deadline was then extended another 24 hours. Crowds began to form in Paris, some wearing headscarves and some bare-headed, to demand the release of the hostages. The French Republic refused to annul the ban on religious symbols, and on September 2, 2004, the beginning of the French school year, the ban was in effect. The Islamic Army of Iraq gave in, and the two hostages were released, unharmed, on December 21, 2004. As *Le Monde* reported on December 23, 2004, "for 124 days, France held its breath" (see Hopquin, 2004).

For those four months, France was united in its opposition to the demands of the kidnappers. Women who were opposed to the ban walked together with women who were for it. But the collective sigh of relief presaged a return to the controversies inside French borders. The relationship between Church and state, and the concept of *laïcité*, separation of the Church from the state, was under scrutiny, and the French Republic had firmly come down on the side of secularism.

This is not exactly a new inquiry. Every hundred years or so, beginning in 1801, again in 1905, and recently from 2003 to 2005, the French closely examine this relationship between religion and its national body. The 1801 Concordat, an agreement between Napoleon and the Vatican, recognized the Catholic Church as the faith of the majority of the French citizens, but did not make Catholicism a state religion. In 1905, Aristide Briand ensured the passage of a bill separating Church from state. Article 1 of the bill held that the French Republic was to observe freedom of conscience and freedom of worship, and Article 2 held that the Republic will not recognize, pay salary to, or subsidize any religion. France quietly celebrated the centenary of that bill during the year 2005. That centenary was subdued for several reasons, one having to do with post 9/11 fears of Muslim unrest, the other because of the 2003 Stasi Commission Report.

On December 11, 2003, the Stasi Commission submitted to President Jacques Chirac a report supporting a ban on wearing conspicuous religious objects in French schools. The wearing of the headscarf by Muslim girls was not to be permitted, nor were Christian crosses, nor Jewish skullcaps, nor Sikh turbans. Six days later, Chirac released his own "*discours*" on the principle of laïcité in support of the report. He wrote: "*La laïcité est inscrite dans nos traditions. Elle est au coeur de notre identité républicaine*" [Laïcité is inscribed in our traditions. It is at the heart of our republican identity] (Chirac, 2003). Shortly thereafter the French National Assembly approved the ban, and on March 3, 2004, the French Senate approved the French National Assembly's majority vote. Students returning to French schools[1] in September, 2004, were not to wear conspicuous religious objects.[2] The ban on the headscarf was the most problematic, and the focus of intense media coverage. Students who arrived at school wearing a headscarf were stopped at the door to the school. Some were convinced to remove their headscarf, others went home. Lawyers promptly began debating whether such a ban would hold up in the European courts (Riley, 2004).

Resistance

The power of the French state to deny the wearer the right to an expression of religious identity in public places exerts a form of power over symbolic expression akin to that of Pierre Bourdieu's concept of symbolic violence: the power of domination and control of language and expression by one individual or group over another (Bourdieu, 1991). This particular power underlies national policies and bubbles up over certain issues. In the US, debates over flag-burning, and whether or not English should be designated as the national language, inflame legislators and their constituents. In France, the French Academy is a final arbiter of proper French grammar and spelling. The French Senate and Assembly exercise control over the particular clothing allowed in French schools. But the people are left to work out how to cope with these symbolic items of language and dress. Members of the state occasionally resist symbolically. One example was provided by Cennet Dogonay, a French Muslim schoolgirl who shaved her head as an alternative to removing her headscarf, or *hijab*, in Arabic. Her reasoning was as follows:

Hijab for me is a religious obligation; it's a dress of honor and dignity. If I have shaved my head as I did, that was I do not have any other solution to go to my school. I prefer to shave my head than to commit a sin (by not being covered). According to my knowledge, there are no other girls who have done the same.... Generally, my teachers have taken very bad reactions against my protest; they treated me badly and ignore my questions and my existence. Despite that, a teacher told me that what I have done has eradicated at one hour her 37 years of discrimination against the Muslims. (Dogonay, 2004)

The headscarf issue is only the most conspicuous of the issues that confront, and appear to threaten, the French Republic today. If the headscarf, a length of cloth, symbolizes adherence to a belief system that extends beyond borders, then the Muslim bearers of those headscarves, and their families, also bear that belief system.

Control

Recent attempts by the French state to control not only the use of religious symbols such as headscarves, but also the messages of Islam coming from French mosques have led to inquiries into whether it is possible to create an Islam "of" France as opposed to an Islam "in" France (Bowen 2004a; Kepel, 1997: 152). An Islam "of" France would be constituted using French democratic and republican principles of equality; an Islam "in" France would be part of the larger Muslim ummah, or community, without reference to the republican principles of the French state. The fears of international terrorism, and French concepts of equality and fraternity, have loaded the meaning of religious identity symbols, such as the Muslim headscarf, with more weight than they frequently deserve.

The fear of terrorism is not without merit. During the 1950s and 1960s, the war for the independence of Algeria from French control led to attacks aimed at French nationals in France. During the 1970s and 1980s the group Action Directe carried out assassinations and attacks aimed at governmental and military installations. In the 1990s France experienced bombings on the Paris Metro and railroads, as well as an aborted hijacking of a French plane by the Algerian Groupe Islamique Armé (GIA) in December 1994. (The aim had been to fly it into the Eiffel Tower.) More recently, in 2000 and 2001, several plans for attacks on French targets were uncovered, including the one on the American Embassy in Paris in which Djamel Beghal and Jérôme Courtailler were implicated. Beghal, who was in London at the same time as Moussaoui, and was reportedly an associate of his, was sentenced to ten years in prison. France has not been the only target for terrorist acts, for French citizens have also left to join the jihad in Afghanistan, Iraq, and the United States. This is the form of global Islam which creates fear in nation-states, not the moderate Islam of French, British, and American mosques and prayer halls.

ISLAM OF FRANCE OR ISLAM IN FRANCE?

Bowen (2004b) described the practice of Islam as transnational space, and argued that the mapping of that transnational space onto French republican values is difficult if not impossible. On this issue, there appears to be little agreement among Muslim groups in France. Some leaders are confident that an Islam *of* France is slowly developing. A leader of Muslims in Versailles said in a BBC interview: "There should be no (foreign) nationalism. We are all French here" (Astier, 2005). Rachid Hamoudi of the mosque in Lille said: "We must be patient. Things will change with the emergence of new generations" (in Astier, 2005). These Muslims are viewed as appropriately sympathetic to the cause of creating and maintaining control over the French Muslim population. The head of the mosque of Paris, Dalil Boubakeur, said of a proposed march in protest of the ban on headscarves: "Demonstrations in the name of religion are very dangerous.... I ask everyone to be wary of the sirens of political Islam" (Heneghan, 2004).

Two French journalists, Christoph Deloire and Christophe Dubois (2004), in their book *Les islamistes sont déjà là* (The Islamists are Already Here), claim that an Islam of France is impossible, and that foreign interests finance and support French mosques and their adherents. They are not alone in this view. Saudi, Algerian, and Moroccan funds do support mosques. Saudi imams recruit students to Saudi universities. The suspicion of control from outside forces extends to the Habashites, Abd Samad Moussaoui's group, which is connected to the teachings of a Lebanese scholar, and to Syria. It is the case that the networks of support for mosques and prayer halls extend beyond borders, and a number of Muslim mosques and committees openly acknowledge these connections.

The concern over adherence to a religion which reaches beyond state boundaries would not be an issue except for the fact that Islam is linked to two slightly different categories of being: one, a group of people; the other, a particular part of a religious belief system. On the one hand, there are France's immigrants, many of whom come from North Africa and the Middle East, and on the other, a branch of Islamist thought, the global jihad encouraged by al-Qaeda and its associated groups. These two categories are not necessarily the same and the groups do not necessarily overlap because, of course, not all French immigrants are jihadis, nor are all jihadis immigrants. Nor do all jihadis grow up Muslim. Creating a profile of present and potential members of the jihad bedevils members of French, American, and British intelligence communities because there is so little fixity to that profile. Islam is not the only religion of France's immigrant population, and there are, in France as elsewhere, converts to Islam from non-immigrant backgrounds. Some of these converts have joined jihadi causes, but most do not. The Courtailler brothers, David and Jérôme, French boys from a town near the French Alps, are an example, but they were not singular in their attraction to Islam and their transition to jihadi causes.

The connection between immigration and Islam is at once one of perception, and one of reality. There is a general perception that the number of immigrants is increasing when in fact the percentage of immigrants has remained nearly constant. This perception is similar, and related to, the general perception that the number of Muslims in France is increasing. These perceptions are due to several factors. Immigrants were not seen to be a problem while France experienced economic growth through to the 1970s. Once the economic situation became less expansive, the guest worker had no place in France. However, even though official immigration came to an end in 1974, reunification of family members with workers led to an introduction not only of wives but also of children. Wives in the markets and children in the schools and on the streets were more visible than men who went to work and lived in hostels and *bidonvilles*, or shanty towns. (A *bidon* is a tin petrol or gas can – roofing and walls for impromptu housing on occasion came from these cans.) The growth of these bidonvilles on the outskirts of cities such as Paris led to a demand for better housing for its immigrant and lower-income population. Large high-rise, low-income apartment blocks were built to accommodate workers and their families. Fifty years later, these apartment blocks, or *cités*, have become housing for many of the second and third generation of immigrants to France. It is these cités, situated in the suburbs, or banlieues, of France's cities that have seen the unrest associated with the riots of the fall of 2005. The banlieues on occasion have the reputation of no-go zones for non-residents. While walking through one North and West African neighborhood in the north of Paris, I was cautioned by a well-meaning man to watch myself and to not wander too far "in" to the neighborhood.

The riots of November, 2005, have elicited commentaries from all parts of the political spectrum. The causes are thought to range from racism (the left) to indolence and thuggery (the right). The conservative American group Campus Watch reported (disapprovingly) in its "Quote of the Month" that Olivier Roy, a French commentator on social issues, said of the unrest: "It is nothing to do with radical Islam or even Muslims ... these guys are building a new idea of themselves based on American street culture." Roy went on to say: "It's a youth riot – they are protesting against the fact that they are supposed to be full French citizens and they are not" (Button, 2005).

The number of Muslims in France is difficult to determine, since French statistics based on religion are not gathered, but reports indicate that there are 5 million Muslims, or close to 8 percent of the total population of 60 million. There are said to be 15 million Muslims in Western Europe (Denécé, 2005). If these figures are accurate, then France is home to one-third of the European Muslim population, and has the largest Muslim population in Europe. The UK is reported to have 1.5 million Muslims, representing about 3 percent of its population, which was close to 60 million in 2001 (National Statistics, 2001). Germany's Muslim population is also about 3 percent of its total population of 80 million. In the US, there are more that 7 million Muslims, but they represent only 2.5 percent of the total population of 300 million (Muslim Population Statistics, 2006).

Under the aegis of the Interior Ministry, a French council on mosques was created in April, 2003. The government sought a way to gain control over the growing number of mosques, and, by taking the initiative, could participate in determining the composition of the council and by that means exert some influence over France's Muslim population. As the author of one French government report put it: "Due to the organizational chaos of Islam in France, the authorities find that they have a responsibility towards decision and control" (de Galembert, 2006). There were, according to one report, 4000 delegates from close to 1000 mosques who participated in the elections (Camus, 2004). The Conseil français du culte musulman, the CFCM, included several of the largest Muslim groups in France: the Union des organisations islamiques de France (UOIF), reported to have ties to the Muslim Brotherhood of Egypt; the Grande mosquée de Paris (GMP, Dalil Boubakeur's mosque) with ties to Algeria; and the Fédération nationale des musulmans de France (FNMF), with ties to Morocco (Coroller et al., 2006). Later, in 2005 and 2006, the FNMF was riven with conflict, creating a stalemate, since resolved, in electing new officers in the CFCM. There are many other Muslim groups in France, some organized regionally, some representing particular traditions within Islam, such as the Habashites.

The policies of the French administration, the police, and their intelligence branches, are served up by American commentators as an example of how to take the measure of the population considered most at risk for joining the global jihad (DST, 2003; Guitta, 2005; Leiken, 2005). The French mosques, particularly the ones considered radical or fundamentalist, are highly monitored by French intelligence. Deloire and Dubois (2004) reported that by 6 p.m. on each Friday, the Minister of the Interior gets a report on the sermons delivered at prayers in certain mosques of interest (see also Guitta, 2005; Matthies, 2006). Surveillance of mosques, and surveillance of the immigrant Muslim population generally, is done by the Renseignements Généraux, an intelligence arm of the Police Nationale, as well as by the Direction de la Surveillance du Territoire, or DST, also an arm of the Police Nationale. The latter concerns itself not only with security within France but with threats from abroad. The DST's approach to monitoring activities of presumed terrorists has a long reach. For instance, they had a dossier not only on Zacarias Moussaoui's activities in London and Chechnya, they also knew about Ahmed Ressam, the "millennium bomber." They knew about his cell in Montreal. They knew about Djamel Beghal's activities in London. They knew about the Courtailler brothers, Jérôme and David, among many others. The DST had gathered that information not only in France but also in the UK, Eurasia, and Canada. French law permits such seemingly intrusive investigations, and allows suspects to be held in ways that were not legal under British and American law until after 9/11. If Moussaoui had been deported to France, he would have been held under a provision that permits detention for association with terrorist organizations. French law also permits detention of suspects without an attorney for up to three days, and detention without charge for up to four days (see Guitta, 2005; Matthies, 2006; Pontaut and Pelletier, 2002).

CONVERSION

In France, converts to Islam are known to the police. According to Guitta (2005), the Renseignements Généraux (RG) estimates there are 50,000 Muslim converts in France, of whom 1500 are considered "potentially dangerous." The French prison population also experiences conversions, and the RG watches French prisons closely (Guitta, 2005). Farhad Khosrokhavar (2003, 2004) has interviewed Muslims in French prison. He has said that the 15 self-identified radical Muslims in French prisons with whom he spoke did not necessarily feel victimized. Rather, if they did feel they were victims, that they acted as they did to have free agency. Khosrokhavar argued that these people were not schizophrenic or paranoid. Furthermore, most were not lower class – they were primarily from the middle or lower middle class. All spoke at least three languages, some even more. He argued that, in France, there is concern that if a person belongs to a particular ethnic or religious community, taking part in communautarisme, feelings of nationalism and citizenship could not be properly created. However, the men whom he interviewed did not belong to a particular community. Another factor which seemed to affect radicalization was membership in a formerly colonized group of people; this, Khosrokhavar has found, holds true for both English and the French prisoners. Germany has not had this form of radicalization in the Turkish community, he said, because Turkey was not a former colony of Germany (Khosrokhavar, 2003).

Abd Samad Moussaoui reported that his brother's transition to jihad was gradual. There was no epiphany, no overnight conversion. The origins of Zacarias's religious awakening were in his childhood, during those summer visits to Morocco when he and his brother went to the Koranic school. Even if he did not know the meaning of the Arabic words he recited, the community of like-minded young people with whom he recited them made a strong impression. The political ferment of the early 1990s, when Moussaoui was in his early 20s, would open him to the plight of Muslims in Bosnia. After all, the wrongs to the community of Muslims were perpetrated in Bosnia, Chechnya, Afghanistan; and the coming Algerian elections opened up debate about whether there should be an Islamic or a secular state. By 1992, when Moussaoui arrived in London, he was a practicing Muslim. His brother Abd Samad says that by the same year he, Abd Samad, was attending the APBIF, Habashite mosque in Montpellier. Nil Plant, Zacarias's South Bank University friend, said that Zacarias was attending Friday noontime prayers at a central London mosque.

As to Moussaoui's motivation for joining this cause, one can ask what it provided him. There is no question that Moussaoui's childhood was not ideal. But he and his brother Abd Samad both managed to get through school and get jobs. Abd Samad is bitter about his mother's seeming lack of support. However, she had no role models for knowing what to do, or how to help. She had married very young. She had not grown up in middle-class French surroundings, yet her children, through her own hard work were, by the time they were adolescents and young adults, living in a middle-class neighborhood and had middle-class friends. What, then, might lead to such a conversion?

Ali Köse interviewed 70 native British converts to Islam, 23 of whom had become Sufi. Köse (1996: 88 ff.) argues that conversion followed on a difficult childhood or a problematic break in a relationship or a death. He also says that these converts were not necessarily turning away from Christianity as much as they were turning away from British society (1996: 122). They criticized Western culture more than their former Christian beliefs. The transition they sought was from the secular to the sacred (1996: 191). Köse notes that members of his sample "believed that the cognitive problems that used to bother them had been met by conversion to Islam because it had offered them a complete philosophy in life ..." (1996: 193). This conversion led to a different way of being as a person:

Along both structural and subjective dimensions of the religious change, the interviewees reported an identity change. They all experienced a profound change not only in beliefs but also in practices and life-style, though the extent of the latter varied. (1996: 193)

Conversion leads one to a unique and transitory place in which the convert can acquire a new identity. In fact, this happened with Moussaoui. His family reported that he was becoming a different person when they saw him on his summer visits to France from London. Conversion states are reported in the anthropological literature as states which are both emotional and physical (see Buckser and Glazier, 2003). Diane Austin-Broos (2003: 2) notes that conversion includes incorporation into the body of social practice and belief. This is Pierre Bourdieu's habitus, in which belief and customs are incorporated into one's physical being:

Conversion is a type of passage that negotiates a place in the world. Conversion as passage is also quest, a quest to be at home in a world experienced as turbulent or constraining or, in some particular way, as wanting in value. The passage of conversion is a passage to some place rather than no place. It is not a quest for utopia but rather for habitus. It involves a process of continual embedding in forms of social practice and belief, in ritual dispositions and somatic experience. (Austin-Broos, 2003: 2)

If this is so, then it is possible that concepts of jihad, both as an internal and as a physical struggle, fulfill a deep human need. It in some sense provides a passage, symbolically, and for some, somatically, to another state. When Zacarias Moussaoui arrived in the Brixton mosque dressed in military fatigues and demanding to know where the jihad was, was this not the somatic version of jihad at work? Do young people, particularly men, need this somatic working out of a state of being? Is this why the military, or paintball war games, appeal so to groups of young men and women?

The so-called "muscular Christianity" of the mid to late nineteenth century worked out a connection between manly sports and religion. Physical fitness rather than bookish qualities were considered the hallmarks of a good Christian. Religious groups to this day hold summer camps and outings for the children and families of their members. Muslim groups are not unusual in doing so. Press accounts of the outdoor bonding experiences of the 2005 London bombers pointed out this connection, but there are many such outdoor experiences offered to church and mosque groups worldwide.

Moussaoui encountered the attraction of conversion, and the transition to the jihad, when he lived in London in the early 1990s. He had not heard, or at least had not found this message in France. London in the early 1990s was known for its free speech. Muslim groups were recruiting outside mosques, and imams were preaching messages inside mosques that were heard by Moussaoui and his friends. The imam of the Brixton mosque, Abdul Haqq Baker, described some of the competing Muslim groups present in London at the time. The imams preaching in London offered a vision of a global Islam different from the one Moussaoui found at the Brixton mosque.

Abu Qatada arrived in England in 1993, asking for asylum from Jordan. According to a report from the Special Immigration Appeals Tribunal, he was granted refugee status in 1994. In 1998 Jordanian authorities tried and convicted him *in absentia* of a millennium bombing plot in Jordan. In February, 2001, he was arrested by anti-terrorism police officers on suspicion of a connection to a terror cell in Frankfurt which was planning the bombing of a Christmas market in Strasbourg, France. There was "insufficient admissible evidence" against him, and he was released. He had in his possession a large amount of cash, £170,000, in envelopes. One of these, containing £805, was marked "for the mujahidin in Chechnya." In 1999 he was said to have given a sermon at the Four Feathers Youth Centre, which Moussaoui had attended, saying there is no difference between Jews, the English, and Americans, and that they could be killed. The report of the Special Immigration Appeals Tribunal concluded that Qatada was at the center of al-Qaeda operations in the United Kingdom, that he was a "truly dangerous individual" and that his appeals to remain in the UK should be dismissed. Qatada was to remain in detention in Belmarsh prison. Much as Moussaoui refused to submit to the American court, the judgment reveals that Qatada refused to meet with the tribunal. "He had chosen not to attend the hearing or participate in it in any way." He "felt certain that the result of his appeal was a foregone conclusion." "He had chosen not to play any part precisely because he has no faith in the ability of the system to get at the truth" (Special Immigration Appeals Tribunal, 2004: 4; see Israel, 2004).

Hamza al-Masri achieved control over the Finsbury Park mosque in 1998. In April, 2002, the British Charity Commission notified him that he was suspended from the mosque. Next, they told him they proposed to remove him from its Trust by January 20, 2003. That same day the police raided the mosque. They found "hundreds of suspected forged or stolen passports, identity and credit cards" as well as a stun gun, a gas canister, and a firearm which shot blanks (Steele et al., 2003). Following the raid, and until his detention by the police, al-Masri preached outside the mosque, on the street.

The activities of Moussaoui and his associates had caught the eye of the French DST by 1994. The DST was frustrated by its inability to search Moussaoui's London apartment. The DST nicknamed London "Londonistan" during that period, and the British government was criticized for not taking seriously the jihadist threat under its nose. As with the American FBI, the British Security Service, or MI5, thought that jihad and hijackings would occur outside British national borders, not inside them. The 2005 London bombings changed that. And following those bombings Britain engaged in debate over how best to work with an ethnically diverse population, including immigrants from Britain's own former colonies in South Asia, Africa, and the Caribbean that was almost as loud as the one in France. Some of the British immigrants and their descendants were and are Muslim, and some have converted to Islam, as in France.

Immigration, Multiculturalism, and Communautarisme

During the 2005 riots in France, Tariq Ramadan, the Swiss scholar of Islam, weighed in from St. Antony's College at Oxford. Comparing

the unrest in England with that of France, Ramadan said that
the two countries have dealt with immigration in different ways.
Great Britain attempted to use the multicultural model, France
to encourage integration (Ramadan, 2005). Neither one worked
smoothly; perhaps nothing can. Despite France's desire to integrate
the social and economic inequalities apparent in French suburbs are
increasingly seen by the French politicians as a problem. The French
Prime Minister, Dominique de Villepin, proposed tough solutions,
and received President Chirac's support. Nicolas Sarkozy, the Interior
Minister, jockeyed for support and media attention by taking a firm
hand. UPI reported that, as of the fall of 2006, over 12,000 illegal
immigrants had been deported, including "foreign" protesters from
the fall, 2005, riots. Such deportations received public support from
a population suspicious of the foreigners in its midst (UPI, 2006)

Thierry Desjardins (1996, 1999), has specialized in turning
journalistic letters to the President of France into books. His point in
Lettre au Président à propos de l'immigration was to break the "taboo" on
discussion of the difficulties posed by *"un trop grand nombre d'étrangers
de civilisations totalement différentes de la nôtre... "* ["too many foreigners
from civilizations totally different from ours"] (back cover). He joined
a long line of quite public critics of immigration in France. This
line includes Jean-Marie Le Pen who has said: "Massive immigration
has only just begun. It is the biggest problem facing France, Europe
and probably the world. We risk being submerged" (Le Pen, 2002).
Christian Jelen (1996) has written of a French Republic "shattered"
by the influx of immigration. In a similar vein, an online discussion
about immigrants to France led to the following comment:

*Le probleme c'est que bcp de jeune Arabes, ils se disent Francais pour la sécu [securité
sociale] et le smig mais ca crache sur le Francais. Il n'y a aucun effort d'insertion
dans la communauté Francaise. La faute à qui? Tout le monde. Les parents, les
ecoles, etc.* [The problem is that many young Arabs call themselves French
for the social security and the minimum wage, but they spit on the French.
There is no effort to integrate into the French community. Whose fault is
this? Everyone's. Parents, schools, etc.] ("fzer0," n.d.)

French historians, literary critics, sociologists, and anthropologists
have examined the particular concepts inherent in what it means
to be French. Todorov (1989/1993), in *Nous et les autres*, explored
views on human diversity in French intellectual thought and pulled
apart the delicate relationship among universalism, humanism, and
ethnocentrism which exists at the heart of French Republic political
theory. The long-standing conceptual frameworks of equality and
fraternity have led to the construction of a French Republic seen as
antithetical to communautarisme and multiculturalism. In France,
multiculturalism is seen as an ideological pandemic that is running
rampant in Great Britain and the United States. Kepel (1997) and

Wieviorka (1997) discuss the attitudes towards such concepts in France, where there is concern that multiculturalism would lead to a breaking apart of the French citizenry into communities which would set themselves aside from others. Fadela Amara, the president of the French women's activist group Ni putes ni soumises (Neither whores nor submissive) has argued in the journal *Libération* (2005) that the rise in communautarisme is caused by Islam, and that French Muslim women will bear the burden of isolation from social services caused by such separation into communities. Yet the separation is there. On one British blog, titled "blogistan," "CNCZ," presumably female, said:

I think another contributing factor to the hostility against Muslims in France is not so much the communist tradition, but the legacy of the French Revolution, or at least how the French Revolution is imagined, i.e. as a backlash against the Catholic Church. One interesting tidbit I like to share with people is that when you look at unemployment data, Algerians and those of Algerian descent have a significantly higher unemployment rate than that of Moroccans or Tunisians, who should look pretty much the same and have reasonably similar names. I think it speaks volumes for the legacy of the Algerian war. And if you think it is bad in schools, try being sick, going to the hospital, and being told you won't get treated by the doctor unless you take your headscarf off because "France is a secular, free country." Yup. Lived it. (CNCZ, 2005)

The Hijab and Music: An Islam des jeunes

While the scholars of Islam discuss whether it is possible to have an Islam *of* France or an Islam *in* France, the second- and third-generation descendants of immigrants from North and West Africa, the Comoros and the Middle East, are forming an Islam not only of faith but also of culture – a culture which reflects deep difference. Increasingly, in France and elsewhere, there are new arbiters of an Islam *des jeunes*, an Islam of the young which has consequences for the development of an Islam existing in transnational space in the form of music, fashion, art, and media networks (see cooke and Lawrence, 2005; Khosrokhavar, 1997). Jean-Marie Le Pen has been known to say that hip-hop is dangerous music, and that it originated in Algeria. Rapper Boss One (Mohammed) of the French group 3eme Oeil said:

For Le Pen, everything bad – rap, crime, AIDS – comes from Algeria or Islam.... The more Bush and Chirac attack Islam and say it's bad, the more young people will think it's good, and the more the oppressed will go to Islam and radical preachers. (Aidi, 2003)

Hip-hop groups such as 3eme Oeil, Zebda, IAM, NAP are from a variety of backgrounds (e.g. Franco-Italian) and countries including Tunisia, Morocco, Comoros Islands, and Congo. Many of them explore Islamic themes, or discuss in music the growth of their personal interest in Islam. This, says Alim (2005), is creating a "transglobal hip-hop ummah." The multi-ethnic group IAM, from Marseille, is an example of this movement. Ted Swedenburg says of IAM's Akhenaton:

... while he stresses its "spirituality," Akhenaton's Islam is in fact neither quietist nor apolitical. Promoting "Islam" in fact is part of IAM's general effort to widen the space of tolerance for Arabo-Islamic culture in France, through its lyrical subject matter, its deployment of Arabic words and expressions, and its musical mixes which are splattered with Middle Eastern rhythms and samples of Arabic songs.... Here again, Akhenaton demonstrates his creativity in putting forward a vision of a pan-Mediterranean Black-Islamic culture, a position that resonates with the reality of polyethnic Marseille. (Swedenburg, 2002)

Since 9/11, Muslim hip-hop culture has received more attention than in the past. Its transnational appeal assures a global market to its musicians, crossing the boundaries that used to exist between French, African, American, and British music. This is a different phenomenon than the "British invasion" of the 1960s, when British musicians took American blues and American rock and roll to a new level, changed it, and reintroduced it to the world. Muslim hip-hop is not a reinvention of American 1990s hip-hop. It is a reinvention of Islam, speaking for the Muslim communities of the young (Banjoko 2005).

Sky Radio has created an internet blog site which now has well over 3 million blogs. The music available through Sky Radio, and the blog advertisements, is both diverse and creative. Criticized by commentators such as David Brooks of the *New York Times*, who professed expertise on gangsta rap after the 2005 riots (Brooks, 2005), such expressions of culture deserve greater attention. Brooks claimed that the culture of the banlieues was heavily influenced by American hip-hop gangsta rap. He noted that French hip-hop is now finding its own voice, with the same proportions of "violent hypermacho male" imagery. Brooks has a point, but the situation is more complicated.

French hip-hop is not new; in fact, some was indigenous, some came in through West Africa (Alpha Blondy, for instance). The Franco-Algerian rapper Médine is, according to *Time* magazine, against "radicalism." His CDs are "September 11" and "Jihad" (Power, 2005). Abd al Malik is a rapper whose group "New African Poets" comes from Strasbourg in north-eastern France, an area with a large immigrant population. Of Congolese descent, he has also written "Qu'Allah bénisse la France," or "Allah Bless France," apparently in response to a pamphlet titled "Allah Curse France." Profiled by the *Los Angeles Times*, he said:

I realized that my Islam of the ghetto was just a ghetto of Islam.... There's a disconnect, a kind of phantasmagoria of Islam. The so-called reformers are trying to invent something in reaction to the West.... We have to put things in another context. Otherwise, we would be in the Middle Ages. (Rotella, 2005)

Reportedly once a member of Tablighi Jamaat, the Muslim teaching group of South Asian origin, Malik has turned to Sufism which, according to one site, allows him to express his own personal sense of French citizenship (http://www.grainesdecitoyens). The appeal of Sufism has not gone unnoticed by Youssou N'Dour, a Senegalese musician with a large European following. N'Dour specifically sent a musical message to the young people of France who read the work of Senegalese Sufi mystics. His 2004 CD, *Egypt*, contains the following ode to Amadou Bamba, perhaps the most famous Senegalese mystic of them all: "So many disciples in France/They cannot be counted/ Wherever you go they are sharing in/The study of Bamba" (N'Dour, 2004).

Far from the thuggish qualities of unthinking brutality described by commentators such as Brooks or members of Le Pen's political persuasion, the hip hop of the banlieues is, as I have argued elsewhere (Donahue, 2005), commentary that politicians avoid only at their peril.

This is a cultural movement whose practitioners are conveyers of a new vision of a contemporary Islam. What will this new version mean for Muslim scholars who teach courses on *fiqh*, Qur'anic exegesis, Islamic civilization, or Islam and modernity? Will this new knowledge transform our view about the impact of popular culture, particularly hip-hop culture, in constructing an Islam appropriate to the needs of contemporary society? Further, will imams revise their pedagogies in efforts to engage Muslim youth who are living in this postmodern hip-hop world (Alim, 2005)?

ALTERNATIVE EXPLANATIONS:

Clash of Civilizations or Economic Causes?

The vision of a vibrant Islam *des jeunes* bears little resemblance to the Islam learned by Zacarias Moussaoui in the mosques and prayer halls of London in the 1990s. How could the two be so different? What was the appeal of the messages of Abu Qatada and Abu Hamza? What forces lead to very different interpretations of what it means to be Muslim? Much as different interpretations of Christianity have developed over time, so too has it happened with Islam. There are several trends occurring in Islam at the same time. Islamic revival movements have occurred and re-occurred throughout the history of Islam. In the present, Islam is going through a period of revitalization in the anthropological sense. This revitalization is an attempt to bring new meaning to life by returning with renewed commitment to the teachings of the Prophet. Revitalization movements occur when people see their lives as not fulfilling spiritually, and when current values of their society are rejected. Zacarias Moussaoui, whose family was achieving middle-class status by the time they were in Narbonne, was not a child of the banlieues. Although he experienced racism, he was not disadvantaged economically. He was not living in the circumstances assumed to be typical of the young who are drawn to jihadi Islam. The situation for Moussaoui was not like that described by Robert Leiken. Leiken said in a *Foreign Affairs* article on "Europe's Angry Muslims" (2005):

In Europe, host countries that never learned to integrate newcomers collide with immigrants exceptionally retentive of their ways, producing a variant of what the French scholar Olivier Roy calls "globalized Islam": militant Islamic resentment at Western dominance, anti-imperialism exalted by revivalism.

Although Moussaoui may express "resentment at Western dominance, anti-imperialism exalted by revivalism," he was not from a household of immigrants retentive of Maghrebi culture. He was instead seeking an identity and a connection to something larger than him. He was not a representative of Samuel Huntington's clash of civilizations. He was part of a Western culture and civilization until he emphatically rejected it.

An Islam with a global reach confronted the French Republic when the two French journalists were kidnapped in Iraq in 2004. Protesters in their support came together to unite with the French Republic in their demands for the release of the hostages. The shifting borders of otherness were, for a while, located in Iraq, but returned to France once the hostages were released later that year. The controversy over the wearing of religious items in French schools created an opportunity for observers to see the nation-state at work. The riots of November, 2005, revealed failing policies of the French state through the flames. By what principles are states created? Who can participate as a citizen? What role does and should the state have in determining the place of religion inside its borders? Islam, like Christianity and Judaism, exists across borders and without frontiers. Belief systems do not necessarily acquire statehood or citizenship. Zacarias Moussaoui's mother, Aïcha el-Wafi, wrote in a letter to her son Zacarias when he was in detention in New York, before his indictment in December, 2001. She said that:

Le seul Djihad qu'il nous demande sur terre est de nous battre contre le mal qui est en nous-mêmes afin de pouvoir vivre en harmonie dans le respect des uns et des autres, quelles que soient leur religion ou leurs idées. [The jihad we are asked to do on earth is to fight the evil within ourselves in order to be able to live in harmony with others, whatever their religion or their ideas.] (Chambon, 2001)

The jihad she had in mind bridges borders between people and cultures. But long before she wrote that letter, Moussaoui had chosen a different jihad.

7 BY WORD AND BULLET: LANGUAGE AND SYMBOLIC VIOLENCE

Islamic governments have never and will never be established through peaceful solutions and cooperative councils. They are established as they [always] have been
by pen and gun
　　　　　by word and bullet
　　　　　　　　　　by tongue and teeth.
(from a manual recovered in Manchester, England, by Metropolitan Police, *United States v. Moussaoui* Prosecution Exhibit AQ01677T)

The most brutal relations of force are always simultaneously symbolic relations. (Bourdieu, 1998a: 53)

LANGUAGE AND POWER

On May 4, 2006, the day Moussaoui was sentenced, Judge Brinkema told him: "You will never again get a chance to speak, and that is an appropriate and fair ending. This case is now concluded" (Markon and Dwyer, 2006d). The Moussaoui trial revolved around his use, and misuse, of speech. The government's case against him was based on the supposed impact of his lies on American vigilance, and on what the US could have done if only he had not lied. From his lies, to his words during pre-trial hearings, to his outrageous hand-written pleadings, to his refusal to speak with his lawyers, to his bizarre testimony and mocking statements at trial, the heart of the case was Zacarias Moussaoui's use of speech.

His words, both spoken and written, were often contradictory, often inflammatory, and often abusive. He did not use language as criminal defendants are expected to. He thought that Allah would help to make the government's case against him look ridiculous. He did not contest his guilt. He did not try to persuade the jury to be lenient. He did not defer to the judge. He did not admit the authority of the court to pass judgment on him. Even his body language was contrary, for he did not stand up when expected to. He seized the trial as an opportunity to make jihad on America. His only weapons were words, but he would use his words with effect. He used them to force the Justice Department to spend millions on a prosecution that did not result in the desired end, his death. He used those words to make Americans relive the horror and pain of 9/11, and he used them to mock America's grief. Above all, he used those words to show the world the contempt he and his Islamic brothers felt for America and the West.

Judge Brinkema was right. Zacarias Moussaoui has not been heard from since he was sentenced. But his silencing comes at a time of increasingly dangerous international relations, for there are many more Moussaouis who wish to be heard. What are they saying? What are they reacting to? What do they want? What should the nation-states of the West, particularly France (Moussaoui's place of birth), the United Kingdom (where Moussaoui learned the tenets of global jihad), and the United States (the target of his anger), learn from the Zacarias Moussaouis of Europe and North America?

The story of Moussaoui's life, as well as his courtroom language and behavior, presents us with a rare opportunity to see more clearly not only the causes of his anger – America's power, the seemingly unjust treatment of Muslims worldwide – but also the transition he made from what his family and friends said was a youthful admiration for the principles of Martin Luther King Jr. to the principles of global jihad. This is an opportunity to understand how acceptance of another set of values, social reality, and modernity, works, or at least, worked for Zacarias Moussaoui.

Why Jihad?

A 1999 Library of Congress study of terrorism (Hudson, 1999) reviewed a variety of reasons why people join terrorist movements. Each of them emphasized individual action and choice. These reasons were: rational choice on the part of the individual; frustration with the circumstances in which one has grown up, and heightened aggression because of those circumstances; negative identity ("No possibility of a university degree, so off I go to the training camps"); narcissistic rage ("Pay attention to me!"); and, last, an attractive separate subculture with its own set of values. Those reasons reflect some of the social and economic issues discussed, and in some cases, dismissed, in earlier chapters. True, Moussaoui was frustrated with life experiences while growing up, and to a degree he was blocked in his ambitions. But the last, an attractive subculture, comes the closest to a possible explanation for what attracted Moussaoui to al-Qaeda. Written before 9/11, the Library of Congress report does not give the role of religion the place it would have held if the report been written afterward.

Marc Sageman (2004) used social network analysis to understand how terror networks are formed. The al-Qaeda groups on which he focuses – the general staff of al-Qaeda, the core Arab, the Southeast

Asian, and the Maghreb clusters – had social bonds of friendship and family that linked members of each cluster together. Not only was each cohort linked by a common goal, but members of each cluster had prayed together at the same mosque, or lived together, fought together, and in some cases had kin relationships through marriage or by birth. This analysis is very useful in understanding the social bonds that link members of these groups. This analysis does not, however, explain the tenacity with which people such as Moussaoui persist in the face of the threat of death, or life in prison, far beyond those bonds of kinship and friendship. As Michael Scheuer (2005: 68) has pointed out, the role of religion in these choices must be better understood.

Moussaoui was not evil, crazy, or ineffectual. Nor can his choices be attributed solely to a clash of civilizations nor to structural economic conflict and unemployment. To what, then, can we attribute his choices? Why did he leave France for London? Why did he turn to a militant Islam in London? What role did his experiences in Afghanistan play in his firm adherence to al-Qaeda? And why was it so important to represent himself, and speak for himself, in Courtroom 700? His conversion experience was of course important to these choices, but how could a desire to speak in a courtroom be connected to transitions in religious belief and a desire to bring jihad to America?

A satisfactory explanation incorporates not only Zacarias Moussaoui's personal experience of social and racial exclusion in France and his emigration to London, but also the broader political and religious contexts in which he found himself from the time he left home in 1986. The political context is important to this explanation because militant jihad is an attempt to redress the wrongs perpetrated by nation-states, both inside and outside their borders. The religious context is important to this explanation because an Islam without borders offers the vision of a community of believers without borders. An Islam militant offers the vision of that community, with political barriers removed, and therefore without the abuses wrought by powerful nation-states working solely in their own self-interest.

The work of Pierre Bourdieu, the French sociologist-philosopher, provides a starting point for framing this discussion. Bourdieu understood, and tried to unravel, the complexity of relationships between individuals and the social settings within which they acted. Throughout his career, Bourdieu wrote cogently about the relationships between language and power. Drawing on Wittgenstein's ideas concerning language games, and the way in which meaning in language is worked out in social settings, Bourdieu (1990a) visualized human activity as occurring in social fields, or spaces. These fields could be households and families, or places of work, or courtrooms, or nation-states, or religions. The persons who act in those fields work out the rules and cultural practices acceptable to those fields. Bourdieu said that people acted out their lives as though they were playing on a field of action. He defined fields "as historically constituted areas of activity with their specific institutions and their own laws of functioning" (1990b: 87). Some of those fields are made of economic and social class relationships, where one group dominates another, and in which both the dominators and the dominated interact.

These actions of domination and being dominated are themselves actions of symbolic power, and as Thompson argues:

> To understand the nature of symbolic power, it is therefore crucial to see that it presupposes a kind of *active complicity* on the part of those subjected to it. Dominated individuals are not passive bodies to which symbolic power is applied, as it were, like a scalpel to a corpse. Rather, symbolic power requires, as a condition of its success, that those subjected to it believe in the legitimacy of power and the legitimacy of those who wield it. (Introduction in Bourdieu, 1991: 23)

Why do persons in a society conform to its norms, why do they not rebel, especially if those persons are a junior member of a firm or an excluded member of an underclass? For Bourdieu, this conformity was not brought about so much by the force of law or by the threat of physical violence; rather it was brought about through social action, especially through language and education. Language is therefore a vehicle for the exercise of power. He called this phenomena symbolic violence.

Symbolic Violence

Bourdieu argued that symbolic violence occurs in a wide range of social fields and in a wide range of relationships. It is the bond that joins members of a society one to another, so that they agree to submit to the society's rules, obey its customs, and accept its values. Unlike physical violence, symbolic violence is hidden behind a veil of normalcy and acquiescence.[1] Language enables that domination; it is the web of meaning that joins persons one to another. Bourdieu defined symbolic violence as "that form of domination which ... is only exerted *through* the communication in which it is disguised" (Bourdieu, 1977: 237), and in a later work, proposed that symbolic violence was a

> ... gentle, invisible violence, unrecognized as such, chosen as much as undergone, that of trust, obligation, personal loyalty, hospitality, gifts, debts, piety ... in a word, of all the virtues honoured by the ethic of honour, presents itself as the most economical mode of domination because it best corresponds to the economy of the system. (Bourdieu, 1990a: 127)

Though it be gentle, invisible, and unrecognized, symbolic violence has great coercive power, much as do the powers ascribed to magic, which works not so much through physical control but through mental control, through the belief that magic *does* have power. Both of these powers can work at a distance. The powers do not have to have a physical existence, instead they are learned, absorbed, and then carried around, ensuring that a person or a social group will behave in a particular, acceptable, way (Bourdieu, 1998a: 103). Those who are dominated in the context of symbolic violence do not necessarily recognize that violence. This misrecognition is: "the process whereby power relations are perceived not for what they objectively are but in a form which renders them legitimate in the eyes of the beholder" (Bourdieu and Passeron, 1977: xiii). Because of misrecognition, one does not see the arbitrariness of culture, or the unfairness of domination and power. At what point, therefore, do people move from misrecognition to recognition, from seeing that relations they had thought were legitimate are in fact otherwise? At what point did Zacarias Moussaoui make this transition, supplanting one social reality for another?

SOCIAL FIELDS OF ACTION

Major life experiences, such as divorce, illness, the loss of a spouse, even near-death experiences, can be turning points for a person. So too are conversion experiences. The first occasionally leads to the second; that is, a life-changing experience occasionally opens the door to conversion. These are two sets of events that enable one to move out of one social reality, to recognize the old rules and relations for what they are, and to create a new reality for oneself.

In Moussaoui's case there are four fields of action, or, to be less abstruse, times and places in his life when social relations were worked out in such a way that they created turning points in his life. This occurred in France, where he lived until his 20s; in London, the place of his transition to jihad; in Afghanistan and Chechnya, where he went through the training camps and experienced jihad; and in the courtroom, where he used his words on behalf of another kind of jihad. In each place he went through an experience, or experiences, that confirmed his desire to make a change or enter a new phase of his life. He might say that Allah led him through some of those transitional periods, or states. Another explanation would be that he learned to recognize the unsatisfactory nature of the racial, social, and political relations he and others experienced, that he saw the domination and symbolic violence of those relations, and he turned to something different.

France

Racism

There were social, racial, and political issues in Moussaoui's life in France that contributed to his decision to leave for London. Moussaoui's brother Abd Samad reported on the racial taunts and insults the Moussaoui boys experienced, both in school, on the streets, and in the nightclubs of southern France. The attitudes toward immigrants in France described in previous chapters were part of a growing concern for economic security in the 1990s. Those attitudes were linked with a similar concern for personal security, as terrorist attacks occurred in subways and on airplanes. Although the relationship between Moussaoui and his girlfriend was close, her parents' objections to him were evidence of the racial and social barriers that blocked him in France.

Social Relations

Although his mother had worked extremely hard to create a comfortable life, his relationship with her, according to Abd Samad, had apparently been problematic from his teenage years on. He had moved out by the time he was 18. He remained connected to his brother and sisters, and had a group of friends and a girlfriend. But the transition he underwent in London led not only to a separation from his girlfriend, it also made connections to his friends difficult. They were part of the social reality he had by then left behind. Moussaoui's friend Fabrice Guillen testified during the trial that, in 1997, on a return visit to France, Moussaoui told him about the deaths of Iraqi children he blamed on a US embargo. Guillen said Moussaoui broke off his conversation, telling Guillen: "You could not understand" (Gordon, 2006). That was the last time Guillen saw him, and the last time Moussaoui saw his family. He had cut his ties with that portion of his life.

Political Awakening

Moussaoui's sister Nadia noted that she and her brother would have long talks about the world, and that Moussaoui admired Martin Luther King Jr.'s role in the civil rights movement in the US. He felt strongly that wrongs toward black people should be righted. Later, when associating with students in Perpignan and Montpellier, he recognized the unfair relations of power in the world; in Bosnia, as Serbs attacked Muslims; in Kuwait, when imams preached against the American presence there during Desert Storm; in the United States which, unfairly in his view, exercised its economic power throughout the world. He dreamed of pursuing a life in the import–export business, but he would not be able to fulfill that dream in France. He would go to London to learn English, and try to follow that dream.

Symbolic Violence and the State

Jacques Derrida (Derrida and Dufourmantelle, 2000: 151–55) has discussed the peculiar aporia, or problem, of hospitality. As he saw it, if a host is to be hospitable to some, he must be inhospitable to others. This is the hospitality paradox, for if a value is placed on inclusion, then how can there be exclusion without undercutting that value? Furthermore, hospitality presupposes that someone – the host – is in charge. The host dominates the hospitality he offers, assuming control over who is welcome and who is not. Such domination occurs wherever hospitality is offered, whether in a house, or ethnic group, or in other domains, or fields of action; including nation-states. In France, the republican model does not necessarily admit to difference, diversity, and religious belief. And yet some are excluded, some continue to be foreigners, and some are deported. Without state recognition of such difference, the discussion perforce remains muted. Tariq Ramadan has therefore called on Europe's Muslims to claim European identities and to demand their rights as citizens. This would be, in his terms, a "silent revolution" (Ramadan, 2004: 4, 104).

States frame, control, and use concepts of domination, of inclusion and exclusion, through violence, both symbolic and physical. States use symbolic violence, which they exert through control of speech, of self-expression, of the press, of education. In France, the republican model controls, through its concern over the dangers of communautarisme, not only matters of distinction and difference, but also the discourse about that difference. The state contributes to that exclusion through denial of such categories of difference. The citizen then incorporates the state's control through the subjective habitus, by not wearing the headscarf, by not mocking town council members at Bastille Day commemorations. In the US, the UK, in France, and elsewhere, in courtrooms one is expected to acknowledge and submit to judicial and thereby state authority by standing for a judge, a jury, a sentencing. However, there is a point at which some trouble-makers, as they are considered to be, reject that control through dissidence, revolt, or terror. Therefore, states also claim control over physical violence, in their own use of force – through the military – and in the right to punish those individuals who use force without state authority – murderers, rapists, or terrorists.

London

Emigration

According to Moussaoui's mother and brother, Zacarias was not a practicing Muslim before he left France. This is confirmed by a friend of his mother. Craig Smith of the *New York Times* reported that while Moussaoui was in France, he was an adherent of the Muslim teaching group, Tablighi Jamaat, sometimes referred to in English as the "Preaching Party" (Smith, 2005). This teaching group is considered by some, including the FBI, to be a doorway to more militant Islam. A January 2005 MSNBC report said that Tablighi Jamaat is being closely watched in the United States because it has, in the view of the FBI, been infiltrated by those who endorse terrorism (Meyers, 2005). However, a source close to the Moussaoui case says there is no evidence to show that Moussaoui belonged to Tablighi Jamaat when he was in France.

Nil Plant, Moussaoui's friend from his first year at South Bank University, in 1992–93, said he was a regular attendee of Friday prayers. Mosques in London were at the time welcoming places, taking people in, and giving them a place to stay. Imam Baker of the Brixton mosque reported that Moussaoui stayed for several nights there at the mosque, and the Finsbury Park mosque also provided shelter for people. Given the limited evidence available, it is difficult to know just when Moussaoui moved from a moderate Islam to a more Salafist interpretation of Islam.

Emigration was a feature common to the young converts with whom Moussaoui associated in London. Moussaoui's own brother, Abd Samad, said: "Zacarias is a French man not at ease being French, a Moroccan who can't speak Arabic" (2003: 116). A student in the ethnically diverse university settings in Montpellier and Perpignan, Moussaoui found a place in France with students from North and West Africa as well as the Middle East, all of whom who were seeking alternative social fields of action, and then found a place in London with people of similar, transplanted, backgrounds.

The call to Islam initially connected him to the roots he did not have. The appeal of the more militant Islam he found in London would have resonated with his political concerns over events in Bosnia, Algeria, Kuwait, Iraq, and Afghanistan. The concept of a Muslim ummah does away with the nation-states that can cause harm through use and abuse of their powers. For him, such harm was perpetrated not only by the United States but also France and the UK, both places where he experienced some degree of exclusion.

The conversion state is the process through which one moves from one stage to another, leaving behind what, by the time conversion is accomplished, is seen to have been erroneous ways of thinking. Ali Köse (1996) reported of British converts to Islam that they wanted to move away from British society to a more satisfactory way of life. For these converts, Islam, or in the case of some in his sample, more particularly Sufism, offered a philosophy of life that gave value and meaning to their lives.

Conversion for Moussaoui allowed this transition to occur, that is, he moved, on his view, from misrecognition to recognition.

This new-found sense of self and new explanation of the world was invigorating. If one can feel so good, with this new knowledge, why then should one not try to tell others, try to convert them? Converts to Islam are not alone in this feeling, for converts to other religions experience a similar rush of good feeling. The conversion state leads converts to be more zealous practitioners than those who have grown up in that religion. The convert, however, has now acquiesced to a new form of symbolic violence, of a belief system that ensures one does not see its own domination. Moussaoui became a slave of Allah, and by doing so acquiesced in the symbolic violence of the Muslim jihad. He left behind the ways of thinking he had grown up using. He had now reintegrated himself into a new form of what Bourdieu would call misrecognition.

The very appeal of the new Islamic groups is the promise of a sense of belonging to *something* in a nation-state that has been complicit in the marginalization of many of its own citizens. As Abd Samad Moussaoui says: "Wahhabis have a vocabulary all their own, designed to forge a sense of group cohesion" (2003: 117). It is just this sense of cohesion that appeals, in a French nation-state which, because it does not admit of difference, does not see the racial discrimination and social exclusion that is so frequent in France (2003: 120). The Islam of an al-Qaeda offers not only a philosophy of life and a way of being, but also the promise of a religion beyond and across borders that could do away with the bureaucracy, the abuses of power, the control, and the domination that is used by nation-states to ensure that their citizens and residents will cooperate and keep the state going, without resistance.

Afghanistan and Jihad

Moussaoui said in court: "I'm grateful to be an al Qaeda member" (tr. March 27, 2006, page 2416, line 24). He also said that he was grateful that he was going to be the pilot of a fifth plane (tr. March 27, 2006, page 2416, line 25; page 2417, lines 1–2). What would lead him to say that he was grateful not only to be an al-Qaeda member but also to be a pilot on a mission that would lead to his death?

There is a growing literature on religious martyrdom; Juergensmeyer (2003) and Khosrokhavar (2005 [2002]) are two examples among many. The honor of martyrdom is reflected in the videos al-Qaeda has released depicting some of the 19 hijackers, and in the worshipful online discussions about Moussaoui's friend, the shaheed Xavier Djaffo, who died in Chechnya (see Adil, n.d.). There is less discussion about how this process actually works, since there is a usually a process undertaken to get to the state of agreeing to the act. Some people do indeed change their minds, some do not. It is difficult to know how far Moussaoui would have gotten in that regard, because he was caught before he, and the rest of us, had the chance to find out. But he said he was grateful to have the opportunity, and it is worthwhile knowing why. For many of the hijackers, and for Moussaoui, the decision was made while in Afghanistan.

Moussaoui testified that he went to Afghanistan in December of 1996. He said he landed in Karachi, Pakistan, then made his way to Peshawar, where he met Abu Zubaydah, who helped him to cross the border into Afghanistan in January 1997. At the time, Zubaydah managed travel arrangements, and selection for training, for potential al-Qaeda recruits from his Pakistani base. Moussaoui said of himself that he worked at a guest-house near the Kandahar airport, providing security for the guest-house. He said he also drove guests to meet with bin Laden at bin Laden's compound at the Kandahar airport.

A source knowledgeable about the case described the attraction of the call to jihad, and the attraction of al-Qaeda. A person, here Moussaoui, is alone and a bit adrift in a place like London, a large and, for some, an inhospitable place. A mosque provides not only a place to sleep and eat, but a community of welcoming people. The call to jihad is attractive because it offers a mission, an opportunity to do something to right wrongs. The training camps in Afghanistan, as with military training in nation-states, pull together a group of people through hard physical stress. Some cannot complete the course, and an empowering sense of accomplishment and worth is felt by those who do. To be a member of such a group, and to have the opportunity to learn to use lethal weapons, such as knives, guns, and explosives, is heady. Once a group of such like-minded people has been through a dangerous operation, such as those carried out in Chechnya, or Bosnia, or Afghanistan, they have completed the process of becoming a band of brothers who would die for each other and for the cause. To then meet Osama bin Laden, to have him offer guidance, to interpret one's dreams, and to ask one to go on a mission and become a martyr is indeed an honor, for which one is grateful. To know that, no matter what one does, no matter what problem one causes, as Moussaoui apparently did, one is still a member of the group, no matter what, is uplifting and gratifying. There can be no turning back.

Evidence at the trial described in some detail the training undertaken at the camps in Afghanistan. Mohammed Mani' al-Qahtani, who did not manage to get into the US to join the other 19 hijackers, described his experience in late 2000 and early 2001 at al-Farouq training camp. He said there were three levels of training, beginner, intermediate, and advanced. Students moved through training in a group. Each group was given a name. Students in the beginner group would wake in the morning, pray, and then do physical training. They would then have breakfast, and then undergo another training period from 9 a.m. until noon. At noon all the students would pray and eat lunch. Lunch was followed by more training, marching, and weapons training. The students prayed at sundown. They would then eat dinner and go to the mosque, where there were more prayers. After these prayers, students went back to their sleeping quarters, where there would be a headcount, and then they would go to bed. Sleep would on occasion be interrupted to go on night marches. Students learned to deal with hardship, sleeplessness, and risk of physical harm. Advanced training was required in order to move on to actual combat. Some chose not to do so, and were sent back to the guest-house. This process of pushing students to their physical limits – expecting more of them than they think they can accomplish – creates not only individuals who have managed to prove to themselves they can do what seems impossible, but also a cohesive group of committed soldiers.

Training camps developed different specialties. At the al-Matar complex one learned hijacking, disarming air marshals, explosives, body building, and basic English words and phrases. At al-Farouq, one trained with knives, learning to butcher sheep and camels, with the aim of learning to kill people, as well as how to storm cockpits, blow up trucks and buildings, and hijack trains (tr. March 27, 2006, page 2439, lines 24–25; page 2440, lines 1–3). Ahmed Ressam, who plotted to blow up the Los Angeles airport, claimed that he and Moussaoui trained at Khalden training camp in 1998. According to a Guantanamo Bay summary of evidence for an Algerian detainee, Khalden provided a speeded-up version of the training at al-Farouq. The training included training in light and heavy arms use, explosives, and topography (al-Qadir, 2005).[2]

The military training was important, but religious training also was considered an integral part of that training. Camps had mosques, and there were opportunities for individuals to discuss religious questions further if needed. Osama bin Laden would on occasion visit the camps and speak to the students about the importance of the cause. Students were encouraged to swear bayat to him. According to al-Qahtani, one could not become a mujahideen, a warrior, without swearing this oath of loyalty. From the Kandahar guest-house, one could visit bin Laden at his house, where one could swear bayat. It had to be done in person. According to Khalid Sheikh Mohammed, who said he did not swear bayat until after September 11, bayat follows the pattern of the oath of allegiance sworn to the Prophet Mohammed by tribal leaders. Mohammed reported that the oath was as follows:

I swear allegiance to you, to listen and obey, in good times and bad, and to accept the consequences myself; I swear allegiance to you, for jihad and *hijrah*, and to listen and obey; I swear allegiance to you, and to listen and obey; and to die in the cause of God. (tr. March 27, 2006, pages 2464, line 25; page 2465, line 1–4)

There were no penalties if one was disobedient, because, according to Mohammed, the oath was a matter "between the individual and God" (tr. March 27, 2006, page 2464, lines 13–15). One therefore offered submission, all at the same time, to a man, an organization, and to Allah.

The Courtroom

Moussaoui's jihad in the courtroom was an act of resistance that occurred at some personal cost to everyone involved in the case, including him. Before Moussaoui represented himself, he and Frank Dunham would often talk on Saturdays. Dunham wrote that his schedule on those days was to: "Drop off the dry cleaning, pick up the groceries, go to the bank, swing by the Alexandria Adult Detention Center." He said the two would talk about their lives, their different cultures, their families. They would talk sometimes in a meeting room, occasionally they would talk through the cell's food slot. On Friday, April 19, 2002, Dunham said: "Moussaoui looked at me kind of wistfully and asked if I was coming to see him the next day." Which Dunham did. But on April 22, 2002, the following Monday, Moussaoui fired his defense team (see Roth, 2002), and demanded the right to represent himself.

Moussaoui's case was an exercise in language use and power by Moussaoui, the court, and the lawyers for both sides. Not only did the case revolve around his lies to the FBI, but also his self-representation and the disputed access to witnesses rested on the right to be heard and to question others. Moussaoui insisted on representing himself, as he had a right to do, for more than a year during 2002 and 2003. He produced over 270 hand-written pleadings. As Raymond Patterson said during the trial, one of Moussaoui's stated goals was to work out ways to get into court and in front of the judge. He kept insisting that if he could speak, he could "clear up" 9/11 in a matter of minutes. His request to question witnesses important to his defense, first Ramzi bin al-Shibh, and then Khalid Sheikh Mohammed and Mustafa al-Hawsawi, was contested by the government, appealed to the Fourth Circuit Court of Appeals, and reversed in the name of national security.

Even after the judge revoked Moussaoui's right to represent himself, he insisted, during the trial, in making inflammatory statements each time he left the courtroom. During the trial he insisted on testifying twice, giving contradictory statements concerning his role in the 9/11 attacks. Apparently he thought he hadn't said enough. At the sentencing, Moussaoui said that the trial was "a wasted opportunity to know why people like me and Mohammed Atta undertake their opportunities" (Lewis and Stout, 2006). Then he told the court he would say no more, because America did not want to hear what he had to say. On May 8, 2006, Moussaoui's lawyers filed a motion, promptly denied by the judge, to withdraw his guilty plea of April 22, 2005. Moussaoui's accompanying affidavit said that his understanding of the American legal system was completely flawed, and that he now knew he could have had a fair trial. Solitary confinement had made him hostile to everyone, he said, and he "began taking extreme positions to fight the system." He pleaded guilty in April 2005, he said, because the Supreme Court had just denied his petition for a writ of certiorari, and he thought by pleading guilty the Supreme Court would therefore review the issue of the al-Qaeda witnesses. He learned that: "I can have the opportunity to prove that I did not have any knowledge of and was not a member of the plot to hijack planes and crash them into buildings on September 11, 2001." He wanted a new trial to prove his innocence of the September 11 plot (Docket No. 1857). On May 12, 2006, his lawyers appealed Judge Brinkema's denial of his motion to withdraw his guilty plea, as well as the final judgment and the sentence, to the Fourth Circuit (Docket No. 1860). Moussaoui was appointed new defense lawyers, who went to see him in October 2006. They began to prepare an appeal for the Slave of Allah.

French and American Reactions to Extra-State Symbolic and Physical Violence

The French have defined terrorism as "acts committed by individuals or groups that have as a goal to gravely trouble public order by intimidation or terror" (Shapiro and Suzan, 2003: 77). Immediately after 9/11, the European Commission looked to its own definitions, and proposed that they "cover groups with the aim of 'seriously altering ... the political, economic or social structure' of one or more countries and their institutions" (European Commission, 2001).[3] Furthermore, the French state developed a network of coordinated plans for vigilance against terrorist threats, each plan with its own focus, such as Vigipirate, Biotox (biological threats), Piratox (chemical), Piratome (nuclear), Piratair-Intrusair (airplane), Pirate-mer (ship), Piranet (internet) (Fiorenza, 2002). However, despite France's reputation as a centralized state, until recently the two divisions responsible for state security, the Direction de la surveillance du territoire (DST) and the Direction générale de la sécurité extérieure (DGSE) had little to do with each other. The French state has developed a method of control of would-be violent groups, which works as follows: magistrates handle much of the investigation into terrorism, operating from the Ministry of Justice in Paris. There, *tribunals de grand instance* appoint magistrates to handle investigations. These magistrates, or *juges d'instruction* ("investigating magistrates") specialize in particular types of terrorism (Basque, Breton, Islamic, etc.) (Shapiro and Suzan, 2003: 78), and are given cases depending on their own field of expertise. Cases are tried in various courts depending on the severity of the crime. For instance, in 2004 ten men accused of "association with a terrorist enterprise," a plan to blow up a Strasbourg Christmas market in 2000, were tried and convicted in a *tribunal correctionel* in which penalties of up to ten years in prison can be exacted (BBC, 2004).

The United States has found itself less prepared to face challenges from extra-state terrorism. After 9/11 thousands were rounded up in the United States, in Afghanistan, and in Pakistan, and hundreds of them were detained. What to do next with these "enemy combatants" was less clear. They have been held off-shore, in Guantanamo, Cuba, and at other unknown sites. The prosecution of the war on terror has had a bumpy ride in the United States. The United States has taken a number of these cases to federal district courts on the grounds that the defendant lied to US authorities. These are cases such as *US v. Moussaoui* and *US v. Awadallah*, Awadallah being a man who was accused of lying about whether he knew Khalid al-Mihdhar, a 9/11 hijacker (see Brick and Garland, 2006: A15). In the case of *US v. Hayat*, Hayat was an ice cream vendor in Lodi, California, accused of lying about whether or not his son attended a terrorist training camp in Pakistan (see Tempest, 2006). In Alexandria, Virginia, in the same federal district courthouse where Moussaoui was tried and in front of the same judge, Dr. Ali al-Tamimi was sentenced to life in prison for urging young men at a dinner party to go on jihad. The prosecution of these men relies primarily on their speech acts (lying and exhortation), and not on any specific physical act; no act of physical violence was committed by the persons prosecuted. Zacarias Moussaoui, because he lied, and then because he refused to remain silent during the years leading up to his trial, because of his decision to plead guilty to the six charges against him, because of his inflammatory speech in the courtroom, received six life terms, the longest sentence of them all, even though he had been in jail during the attacks of 9/11, and even though three members of the jury found that he had limited knowledge of the plans for those attacks.

Physical and Symbolic Violence beyond the State

On the view of al-Qaeda, Takfir wal Hijra, and related groups, the nation-state, not only but particularly in the West, is the very problem that Osama bin Laden and his followers are trying to overcome and dismantle. Lawrence Wright (2006) writes that, although comfortable with modern technology and science, Osama bin Laden and his followers try to replicate the life and the events in the life of the Prophet Mohammed, returning as best they can to the seventh-century ummah in their thoughts and actions. Bin Laden even follows the Prophet in his fasting and sitting positions (2006: 232–35). This is a compelling thought, and there is much that can be learned from understanding why someone would act in such a way. Wright depicts well that complex use of connection to the past, but it must be understood carefully. It is not uncommon to assume that groups considered different from the way the West is imagined to be are living in a past that the West has left behind.

There may well instead be, as Charles Taylor (2005) would have it, multiple modernities, and multiple social imaginaries. Those who would bring the ummah together, and who envision the dismantling of the borders of the world, do not necessarily envisage a return in time, a dismantling of modernity. Instead the desire is for a revitalization of what was considered to be a true community of like-minded believers. The difficulty is in getting other people to listen. In order to do this, as a training manual has said, the goal is to "establish Islamic governments by pen and gun, by word and bullet, by tongue and teeth" (Prosecution Exhibit AQ01677T). This view leads to armed insurgency, or terrorism. As Oliver Richmond has argued, terrorism has gone international. This is a "new terrorism," and it is not war in the usual sense:

> ... the new terrorism challenges value systems and legitimacy in a far more radical way than the older forms of terrorism that focused on recognition, and territorial and political control within the framework of the states-system ... terrorism and asymmetric forms of conflict are now perceived as "tools of diplomacy" and so have definitively entered the world of symbols, information, and communicative control which have marked the use and misuse of diplomacy. (Richmond, 2003: 292)

After 9/11, the French social theorist Jean Baudrillard wrote in *The Spirit of Terrorism* (2003) of the *symbolic* violence that the attack on the World Trade Center represented, and of the conflicts yet to come.[4] Similarly, Slavoj Žižek (2002) argued that the attacks of September 11 hit not the *symbol of capitalism* but the *symbol of virtual capitalism* – a capitalism that is spread throughout the world through intensively globalizing forces. Baudrillard and Žižek were thinking of a different form of symbolic violence from the one Bourdieu had in mind, but, as Friedman et al. (2001) argue, the tensions among both localizing and globalizing forces, and the violence that occurs as a result of those tensions, confronts nation-states with new understandings of the relationship between symbolism and action. Scholars in conflict and terrorist studies have, and should, take an interest in the complex interplay of symbol, meaning, language, action, and power. Terrorists, Richmond argues,

... increasingly tend to operate in a symbolic space in which symbols of power and control are targeted because civil insecurity is seen to be more effective and attainable through the spread of terror than via the stylized character and trappings of inter-state war. (2003: 296)

Logics of Practice: The State and Beyond

State domination through symbolic violence occurs through its educational institutions and its legislative and judicial bodies. Everyday practice reproduces the state. We think and act the state, and the state reciprocally thinks and acts us. The logic of practice beyond the state, in extra-state formations, has been less well formulated. Bourdieu touched on the place of neoliberalism in globalization, and argued that the dominant forces were to be found in a few institutions such as multinational corporations and banks. Power is accorded to these institutions through their seeming normality (see Bourdieu, 1998b). However, these institutions are not the only ones acting in the extra-state social field, even though these neoliberal institutions may have much of the extra-state economic power. Religion as a globalizing force has been present far longer than the nation-state; actions in the name of religious belief often "go without saying" and are not questioned. In this social field, it is not the state that is the universalizing force, or the entity that has a "monopoly of the universal" (1998b: 59) but the extra-state or transnational forces that are vying to create an Islam without borders.

8 WHAT THE WEST SHOULD LEARN FROM THE CASE OF ZACARIAS MOUSSAOUI

Then, having spoken for less than five minutes, he wrapped up: "You don't want to hear the truth."... He said Americans had wasted the opportunity of his trial to learn why he and other al-Qaeda members hate Americans. (Al Jazeera, 2006a)

I have nothing more to say. God curse America and save Osama bin Laden. You'll never get him. (Zacarias Moussaoui at his sentencing, May 4, 2006, in Riley, 2006c)

LESSONS FROM THE CASE

By September 5, 2006, Alberto Gonzales had succeeded John Ashcroft as US Attorney General. On that day, Gonzales met with reporters to speak about the Department of Justice's role in the war on terror in the US. The fifth anniversary of both 9/11, and soon thereafter, of Moussaoui's indictment, approached. Gonzales told reporters that the Moussaoui case demonstrated that terrorism cases are extremely hard to make. When asked why the Department of Justice and the administration had decided to try Moussaoui, the "most high-profile case" there has been, in a civilian court and not in a military tribunal, Gonzales responded:

The truth of the matter is, we all felt an obligation to know, was it possible to try a terrorist in an Article III (civilian) court where you might have to put at risk classified information, where that terrorist may insist on having direct access to someone that's being detained by the United States ... (Gordon and Rosen, 2006)

Gonzales said the administration and the Justice Department had wanted to see what sort of decisions federal judges would make concerning access by defendants to detainees who might have useful information concerning their cases. Now they knew.

In Moussaoui's case, Judge Brinkema had been ready to throw out the death penalty because the government denied Moussaoui access to those detainees. The Fourth Circuit Court had agreed that access to the witnesses was important for maintenance of the defendant's rights to a fair trial in a civilian court of law. But, for reasons of national security, the Fourth Circuit held that Moussaoui and his defense lawyers could not have direct access to the witnesses, neither in court nor through videotaped depositions. Instead, summaries of the witnesses' statements could be used, and the Fourth Circuit spelled out a procedure by which the summaries would be crafted from the detainees' responses to their interrogators' questions. Judge Brinkema would work with the lawyers for the government and for the defense to craft those summaries. The decisions of both the federal district court and the appeals court ensured that the statements from al-Qaeda detainees such as Khalid Sheikh Mohammed, Khallad, and Hambali would be made available to both Moussaoui and to the government.

The Zacarias Moussaoui case offers the United States, the West, and the world, lessons for the future. Some have been learned, others have not. Some of these lessons are obvious, others are obscure. In the United States, the administration, Congress, the courts, and the agencies in charge of justice, security, and intelligence are still working out some of those lessons. Outside the United States, the lessons learned are somewhat different. On the one hand, the Moussaoui case was reported as an instance of the US trying to do the right thing by bringing an al-Qaeda terrorist into a civilian court and giving him the rights granted to US citizens; on the other hand, it was reported as a case of the US trying to do the wrong thing, by treating him as a scapegoat, and by trying to execute him (Baudouin, 2006).

The case revealed the way in which the FBI and the US Department of Justice collected its evidence and built the case against Moussaoui. The case also revealed the dropped leads and lack of communication between intelligence agencies. The Bush administration learned that a trial such as this one can be cumbersome, lengthy, expensive, and embarrassing. More important, through analysis of Moussaoui's own statements and the evidence about him, we can learn about why Moussaoui made the choices he did, and we can learn what motivates people much like him.

Moussaoui's case reveals what the United States should have known before 9/11, what the world faces in the form of both symbolic and physical violence from newly radicalized Muslim militants, and what it could do to alter its policies to help lessen the appeal of the call to jihad. Horrified by the fact that 9/11 happened in the American homeland, the mantra became: "Never Again."[1] The world watched the trial, in some ways surprised by the apparent transparency of the proceedings, in others confirmed in what they already knew about American policies, both domestic and foreign. Five years after September 11, high-profile books continued to reveal the fallibility and remarkable memory lapses experienced by people who make life and death decisions for the rest of us (e.g. Ashcroft, 2006; Clarke, 2004; Suskind, 2006; Woodward, 2006).

WHAT DID THE UNITED STATES LEARN?

The US Department of Justice will never handle such a case in the same way again. The Justice Department learned that it was expensive and time-consuming to try a case like Moussaoui's. Although the cost of the trial has not been disclosed, certainly it cost millions of dollars. This, Gonzales said, is one reason why establishing military tribunals as an alternative to trying terrorism suspects is a better way to handle these sensitive cases. "I think it shows that these are very, very hard cases to make, if you think about the amount of money that was spent, the manpower used to bring [Moussaoui] to justice" (Gordon and Rosen, 2006). On the same day as Gonzales' press briefing, the Justice Department released a fact sheet. Titled "Department of Justice Anti-terrorism Efforts since Sept. 11, 2001," it listed important anti-terrorism trials, the creation of a new national security division, outreach efforts to Arab communities, and its work with Congress on immigration reform. But the Moussaoui case was nowhere mentioned (USDOJ, 2006d).

The Pain of 9/11

September 11 created pain for America and for the world. That pain is well documented in the hundreds of articles and books published since then. The family members and friends of victims of 9/11 dealt with the case of Zacarias Moussaoui in very different ways. Anger was directed at Moussaoui. Some were upset at the jury's decision. Debra Burlingame, sister of the pilot of American Flight 77, was angry with the family members who chose to be witnesses for Moussaoui's defense. Some of the defense witnesses and their families responded to the pain by working for peace and reconciliation efforts. Andrea LeBlanc, widow of Robert LeBlanc, the former professor of geography, and Phyllis Rodriguez, whose son Greg died in the World Trade Center, joined peace groups such as Peaceful Tomorrows and Stonewalk for Peace. Rodriguez formed a close friendship with Aïcha el-Wafi, traveling to France in the summer of 2006 to visit her in Narbonne and Paris.

Zacarias Moussaoui learned something as well. He was unrelenting in his apparent lack of remorse and concern for the victims and survivors. He appeared to pay little attention as family members spoke of their losses. Yet later he told Alan Yamamoto how moved he was by the testimony of the family members who spoke for the defense. These were people who had lost their children, husbands, sisters, fathers, wives, on September 11. Their message surprised him, according to Yamamoto. They were not vengeful; instead they testified for the healing power of life, and celebrated the lives of those they lost. He expected the witnesses who testified for the government to be angry toward him and toward everything he represented. He did not expect people to speak for hope and life and reconciliation (Townsend, 2006).

The attacks on the Pentagon and the World Trade Center damaged more than the people killed, their families, and the physical structure of the buildings. For those who worked in the Pentagon, the building represented an emotional home for its workers, and that home was damaged irreparably. The trial brought out both anger and reflection. One employee who escaped the Pentagon that day told me that employees would not be able to think about the building in the same way again. The employee said that it felt to employees there as though their place of work had been taken away from them. It was an honor to work there, the employee said, but now people feel more removed. It felt as though a national monument had been hit, wounding the building. It was almost physically painful.

Since the World Trade Center was totally destroyed, and other buildings close by damaged, there was no returning to places of work for many in downtown Manhattan, and businesses moved uptown and out of the city. The Moussaoui trial was a sad reminder of that day; some paid close attention, some did not. During the trial, Judge Brinkema remarked that fewer people were watching from the off-site courtrooms than anticipated.

The Press, Moussaoui, and al-Qaeda

The trial crystallized the interpretations of 9/11, and of the threat Americans now feel from groups such as al-Qaeda. In the end, the actual person who was and is Zacarias Moussaoui was obscured by the interpretations of him and of his activities leading up to his arrest in August 2001. Depending on their trial strategies, the lawyers painted different pictures of him. The defense depicted him as hapless, indiscreet, and ineffective. Furthermore, he had a bad childhood, and was schizophrenic, delusional, and psychotic. The government depicted him as evil incarnate, unremorseful, and a liar who caused the death of 3000 people.

At the trial, a BBC Arabic-language correspondent said to me that the Arab world was watching the proceedings with interest. Other Arabic-language correspondents said the same thing, even though the Western press reported that there was not much interest in the case in the Arabic-speaking world. The BBC correspondent remarked on the fact that Moussaoui was called "Mr. Moussaoui" by Judge Brinkema. The apparent fairness of the American legal system was worth noting, he thought. Moussaoui was not taken out and summarily hanged or shot. This, the correspondent said, was of note to the Arabic-speaking world. It was unusual from the Arab point of view, he said, that so much of the evidence and testimony was open to view. Although the proceedings were not televised, the court website provided access to the testimony, the pleadings, and the judge's orders. Arabic-language coverage was also provided by Al Arabiya and Al Jazeera television.

Reporters for the major American newspapers and broadcast media attended the trial daily. Reports for news services such as the Associated Press and Agence France-Presse passed on their stories to the rest of the world. The French press was there, particularly towards the end as interest grew in whether or not Moussaoui would get the death penalty. Some of the media focused on the terrorism beat. Soledad O'Brien, on CNN's *American Morning*, made sure that her viewers stayed put while receiving news of the trial: "And, of course, you'll want to stay with CNN day and night for the most reliable news about your security," she said (O'Brien, 2006). At the trial, one newspaper reporter said in jest that it was his job to keep his readers very afraid. But the reporters like him, who followed the proceedings closely, worked hard to present the complicated details of the case correctly. While the press tried to be balanced in reporting on this complex case, the opinion columnists and commentators picked and chose their interpretations of Moussaoui and the trial depending on their political sympathies, on their interpretations of what had happened in court that day, and on how they imagine al-Qaeda and its supporters to be.

The conservative right convicted Moussaoui long before he pleaded guilty. Mark Steyn, writing for the *Chicago Sun-Times*, railed against the expense the US taxpayers will incur by keeping Moussaoui alive in a federal prison (Steyn, 2006). Bill O'Reilly of Fox News congratulated President Bush on Congress's passage of the Military Commissions Act. He lamented that Moussaoui had not been sent to a military tribunal instead of a civilian court:

Well, we saw how that played out in the Moussaoui case. Four years, tens of millions of dollars to convict a guy who was involved with 9/11. Do the math: If every terror suspect lawyers up, they can cause chaos within the judicial system. (O'Reilly, 2006)

He said that "the only downside" of the Military Commissions Act was that waterboarding would no longer be allowed.[2] The conservative online magazines took that thought even farther. Although the jury decided Moussaoui had little knowledge of the plans for 9/11, a writer for the conservative *Frontpagemag.com* said Moussaoui was the 20th hijacker and praised the advantages of waterboarding. This technique of extracting information, Vasko Kohlmayer said, is more humane than using sleep deprivation. He thought it a pity it wasn't used on Moussaoui; that way, he said, lives would have been saved (Kohlmayer, 2006).

The press plays an important job in forming lines of communication between policy-makers and the public. Reporters who cover breaking news cannot do the in-depth coverage that is needed to give context to that news. They turn to experts from the law and academia for that context. But academics need time to think and reflect on events. That time does not work well with the sound-bites needed for the news. By the time the academics have reflected, the reporters have left the scene for the next breaking story, their cameramen have folded their tents and moved on (see Walker, 2005). The Moussaoui case was unusual in that it lasted four and a half years, enough time for the legal community and social scientists to think about what this case means. Strangely, that did not happen. Both the case, and Moussaoui as a person, were dismissed as oddities not to be repeated. Barring intervention by the US Supreme Court, in the future, cases such as this one will be tried in military tribunals. Much of the evidence will be classified or will disappear. The United States will not have an opportunity like this again.

The Fear of 9/11

Until 9/11, North America had experienced fewer terror attacks than most of the rest of the world. The thought that it could never happen here was one reason for the inability of intelligence agencies to adequately interpret the threat information picked up through the spring and summer of 2001. The grand scale of destruction, linked with the unexpected nature of the attacks, certainly got the attention of Americans. In true American style, a 9/11 industry has taken root in the charred soil left that day. Instant specialists, commentators, and researchers have been interviewed, published, and created websites analyzing that day, and covering the continuing threat from groups such as al-Qaeda.

A curious by-product of 9/11 is the formation of groups that question the official version of the attacks. These are the engineers, academics, and students who painstakingly study all the facts of the day to propose that explosives were brought into the twin towers ahead of time, to question whether a commercial aircraft ever hit the Pentagon at all, to claim that the description of the crash of Flight 93 was inaccurate. Such obsession is perhaps inevitable, given the enormity of the event and the fact that the military and intelligence agencies were perceived as somehow withholding information. If these powerful agencies withheld information as they did, the thinking goes, they must have been participants in these acts. After all, aren't they the most powerful agents in the most powerful country in the world?

Since 9/11, Americans have proceeded with an odd blend of business as usual and feeling as though there is a vague, horrible fear, thrown like a spider's web, over their everyday activities. Americans seem to specialize in victimization. Victims do not have agency, because they are victims. Therefore, they do not have to inspect the cause of the attack, because they have experienced it. The Enron case, involving American business practices, paralleled the Moussaoui case both in the timing of the indictments and the final jury trials. It frequently received more media coverage than did the Moussaoui trial. The Bush administration, particularly as the fifth anniversary of 9/11 and the mid-term elections approached, tried to bring Americans back to the message that the world is a dangerous place, and something must be done about it. The conservative supporters of the Bush administration's policies ("Never Again") dismissed liberal thinkers as blind, dazzled by their idealism. Hard policies are necessary, they said, in order to cope with dangerous men. The military, and military action, was needed in order to keep America safe.

WHAT SHOULD THE UNITED STATES LEARN?

Intelligence

The executive branch and the intelligence agencies should learn important lessons from this case. Once the Moussaoui trial was over, the Department of Justice's Office of the Inspector General (OIG) released its report on the FBI's role in the Moussaoui investigation. It had been withheld until the end of the Moussaoui trial. The account of dropped leads and lapsed opportunities was similar to that in the 9/11 Commission's final report. In fact, some of the Commission's own material had been drawn from this report. The frustrations of the Minneapolis FBI office in getting headquarters to pay attention to the agents' requests for permission to investigate Moussaoui more fully, the misinterpretation of the "wall" between criminal and intelligence investigations, and the impossibility of getting the FBI and CIA to exchange information were all described in detail (USDOJ, 2006b).

Lawrence Wright, in *The Looming Tower* (2006), chronicles the personal relationships of the employees of the CIA and FBI that led to the inability of American intelligence and criminal investigators to pass information to each other. FBI Agent Harry Samit's testimony during the trial illustrated some of those failures. Those failures have not ended. In September 2006, Attorney General Gonzales honored Justice Department employees, and others who worked with them, for their meritorious service. The Attorney General's Award for Excellence in Furthering the Interests of US National Security went to the lawyers, police, FBI and CIA agents who worked on the prosecution of Moussaoui. Robert Spencer, David Raskin, David Novak, and Aaron Zebley, all received awards, as did Special Agent James M. Fitzgerald of the FBI. FBI Special Agent Harry Samit, who had testified to the FBI's weaknesses before 9/11, did not receive an award (USDOJ, 2006c). In September 2006, the head of Samit's FBI Minneapolis office was called back to Washington when an internal investigation in the Minneapolis bureau was initiated. Unidentified sources said the investigation concerned a claim of workplace retaliation by Harry Samit (*St. Paul Pioneer Press*, 2006). Some of the lessons of 9/11 seem not to have been learned.

The Legal System

Martin Sabelli, a former federal public defender and an opponent of self-representation, said in 2002:

> It appears that Moussaoui is not competent to represent himself, because he doesn't seem to understand the fundamentals of the charges against him, but I am starting to feel that the rest of us are crazier – that is, we are not competent to construct a legal system in which lives are in the balance. For all our expertise and professionalism, we may let this man talk himself to death to soothe our sense of vulnerability. (in Hersh, 2002)

Five years after 9/11 this problem has not been satisfactorily resolved in the US. Focusing on the cost and time involved in the Moussaoui case indicates an unfortunate lesson learned, but it is a mistaken lesson. Future trials of "alien enemy combatants" will not be held on American soil unless held in secret military tribunals. In fact, during a stalemate in the Moussaoui proceedings, the government considered moving the case to a military tribunal. In November 2001, Bush had signed an Executive Order allowing military tribunals to try detainees. The validity of the order was litigated in the US courts. In June 2006, in the case of *Hamdan v. Rumsfeld*, the US Supreme Court ruled that the military tribunals violated both the Uniform Code of Military Justice and the Geneva Conventions. In consequence, the administration had to work with Congress on legislation that safeguarded the detainees' rights. This overthrown Executive Order was the same one that then-US Attorney General John Ashcroft had stumped for in a move to avoid highly expensive, well-publicized terrorism trials, trials exactly like the one Moussaoui's became.

By September 2006, President Bush was urging Congress to work out new legislation concerning the use of military tribunals to try detainees. In a surprising move, Bush also announced on September

6 that in August fourteen high-level al-Qaeda detainees had been moved out of secret prisons to Guantanamo Bay, Cuba. Khalid Sheikh Mohammed, Khallad, and Hambali, whose statements had been read in Moussaoui's trial, were in that group. Bush's announcement came several days before the fifth anniversary of 9/11. Throughout the month of September 2006, with mid-term elections approaching, Congress debated methods of interrogation, detention, and justice in order to cope with the problematic men held in Cuba. After heated debate, Congress authorized the military tribunals that the White House had wanted in the first place. The open proceedings of the Moussaoui trial will not be possible for the Guantanamo prisoners. Bush signed the Military Commissions Act of 2006 on October 17, 2006.

The most troubling piece of that legislation was the suspension of the detainees' right to habeas corpus, a right that is cherished as a bulwark against tyranny. This suspension meant that a detainee could not challenge in a court of law the reason why he or she was being held in detention. Another troubling piece of the legislation is the designation of an "alien enemy combatant." "Alien enemy combatants" are subject to trial in a military tribunal, not in a court of law. US citizens were exempted, but others are not. At a Washington press briefing in August 2006, one reporter had a question for David Welch, the Assistant Secretary of State for Middle Eastern Affairs about this issue. If people from the Middle East disagree with the American administration's policies, he wanted to know, will they be labeled as defenders of terror? Welch responded by saying that there is no cause that justifies violence (Welch, 2006). Welch's response avoids the question, and the worry persists. How will the administration sort out people who oppose its policies from those who would overthrow those policies by any violent means? What are the criteria? Who does the sorting out? Do nations such as the United States, France, or the United Kingdom have the right to do so? Nations assert that right in the name of self-defense. But do the requirements of self-defense justify this assertion?

WHAT SHOULD THE WEST LEARN?

In September 2006, the Bush administration made public portions of a classified National Intelligence Estimate titled "Trends in Global Terrorism: Implications for the United States." It is grim. The classified version speaks of the problems created by the invasion of Iraq, and the fact that global jihad has, in the words of one reporter, "metastasized" across the globe (Mazzetti, 2006). The unclassified version talks not only about the implications for the US but also for Europe:

The jihadists regard Europe as an important venue for attacking Western interests. Extremist networks inside the extensive Muslim diasporas inside Europe facilitate recruitment and staging for urban attacks, as illustrated by the 2004 Madrid and 2005 London bombings. (National Intelligence Estimate, 2006)

Other Western countries know this well. Before 9/11 they had worked on ways to cope with terrorist threats and attacks. This attention to security was not failsafe, as the Madrid 2004 and London 2005 bombings attested. Countries such as the Netherlands, proud of their tolerance for difference, have experienced murder in the street of a Dutch citizen by a Dutch citizen. Groups of people allegedly members of terror cells have been arrested in the UK, in Italy, and in Germany. The overarching question is: what should be done? Each nation answers that question slightly differently depending on its core values and the politics of the party in power.

The important lesson for the West to learn is that conceptual divisions of West and East, of North and South, are only moderately useful as categories. The West that was attacked on 9/11 in the US, on 3/11 in Madrid, and on 7/7 in London was not attacked by forces from outside the West. Hijackers on 9/11 used the United States as a training ground. Zacarias Moussaoui is a French citizen. The bombers of Madrid lived in Spain. The 7/7 bombers were British. Before and after 9/11 British, French, Dutch, Canadian, and American citizens have been arrested or deported for planning terrorist acts in the name of Allah. These issues are at once international and internal.

The Attraction of al-Qaeda

The global jihad attracts hundreds, even thousands, of people. The West should learn that people who join groups such as al-Qaeda do so for a reason. People like Moussaoui do not join the global jihad because they are wicked and want to do evil. They do not join the global jihad because they are crazy. Nor does al-Qaeda and related groups have much patience with doltish hangers-on. The "clash of civilizations" hypothesis and structural economic explanations do not satisfactorily explain Moussaoui's decisions. Dismissing the Moussaouis of the world as evil, crazy, or inadequate does nothing to explain the pull of the global jihad. Assuming that these are civilizations at war does not explain all the people who feel fully integrated into societies different from their birthplaces. Economic explanations are helpful, but they do not sufficiently get at the thoughts and needs that move a person to act. The tenacity with which Moussaoui held on to his beliefs through four and a half years of legal maneuvering, and in the face of death, shows that there is something deeper at work. The global jihad has meaning for its adherents. "I am al Qaeda," Moussaoui said.

And al-Qaeda was listening. Osama bin Laden's audiotape, released after the trial, was proof of that. In his sleepy voice he said he would talk first about "the honorable brother Zacarias Moussaoui" (MSNBC, 2006b). Moussaoui had kept bin Laden's confidence through his jihad in the American courtroom.

Part of the genius of networks such as al-Qaeda is that they offer opportunities for people to work out several different needs. One need is a place for the globalized emigrants who are far from family and familiar social connections. The social bonds of al-Qaeda and related groups reflect the attraction of friendship and family ties. Another is a need for young people to work out not only the inner struggle of jihad but also the physical, bodily struggle of jihad. The military units of the nation-states of the world have worked out ways of creating bands of brothers in arms. Groups such as al-Qaeda do the same. The training camps of Parris Island and Fort Bragg had their counterparts at Khalden and al-Farouq. Those training camps may be closed today, but there are others. Even more important is the place of religion in adherence to the cause of the Muslim community. The need for a meaningful life is offered by a religion that provides not only a message of social justice but also a complex philosophy of life and a connection with a greater being to whom submission brings rewards not only in this life but in the life hereafter.

Importance of Dreams

Reports of dreams and dreaming should not be dismissed as irrelevant to understanding motives for action. Contrary to some Western concepts that belittle the importance of dreams, dreams are given deference and consideration in Islam (e.g. Edgar, 2004). The Taliban and al-Qaeda consider dreams to be worthy of discussion and interpretation. In some cases they were considered accurate predictors of future events. Videotapes show bin Laden and his associates discussing dreams of planes flying into buildings that people had before 9/11. Dreams are acted upon. During the trial, evidence was submitted from several sources concerning Moussaoui's dreams. Moussaoui said he had a dream, which he revealed to bin Laden, of flying a plane into the White House. One of his plans was to demand the release of the "blind sheikh" from American custody. Bin Laden told him to follow his dream. Moussaoui tried to do so. Indeed, al-Qaeda and other groups have consistently called for the release of the "blind sheikh" and of the Guantanamo prisoners. Moussaoui also had a dream that he would be released by George Bush and flown back to London, where he would write a book. He is convinced of the accuracy of this dream. According to the mental health experts for the defense, his dream was evidence of a major thought disorder and of a mind out of touch with reality. And according to Western sensibilities, that dream does not represent reality. Moussaoui's dream of release reflects an Islamic reality, even if it is not an American reality.

Whose Responsibility?

Whose responsibility is it to use the information now at hand to prevent further atrocities like 9/11? Isn't there information sufficient for nation-states of the world to establish policies that do not engender murderous rage in the hearts of some members of their populations? To date, militaries use force, not only physical force but also symbolic force, through maintenance of high troop levels and an armed presence in strategic locations. Borders are patrolled and skies are scanned. The West has also responded to the global jihad by increasing its police and intelligence capabilities. These communities have enhanced and coordinated efforts to increase surveillance and gather more information about the threat from within and without. But do those responsible for the actions of the military, police, and intelligence communities appreciate and give due consideration to the information already before them? Do they give credence to the complex social imaginaries in which we all live? Will more information stop a determined suicide bomber from blowing herself up in a crowded subway? Who will use the information now available to establish workable policies which ensure that a suicide bomber will not arm herself in the first place? Is it the responsibility of governments? Is it the responsibility of academia? Is it the responsibility of schools? Is it the responsibility of mosques and churches? After four and a half years in the courtroom, many involved in the Moussaoui case were ready to have it come to an end. That case was concluded, as Judge Brinkema said. It is up to the rest of us to think about what it meant and to hear the lessons offered, not only of a United States trying, and occasionally failing, to do the right thing, but also of a determined Slave of Allah, trying, and sometimes failing, to get his message across. The desire to be part of something larger than oneself, to devote oneself to a transcendent cause, is very human. It is a desire that takes on formidable scope when a person adopts a cause as a rejection of the culture in which he was born. If we ignore the lessons that Moussaoui's trial teach – lessons of alienation, lessons of conversion, lessons of hatred – we do so at our peril.

NOTES

INTRODUCTION

1. The word "al-Qaeda," meaning "the base" in Arabic, has been spelt many different ways. Here, the spellings which appear in quotations are not changed from their original form, but, as with Arabic personal names, I have tried to consistently use the spelling "al-" as in "al-Qaeda" and "al-Shibh."
2. However, there was evidence, albeit dubious, that the planners had approached Moussaoui before the plan was decided upon. Moussaoui testified on March 27, 2006, that Osama bin Laden had asked him if he was willing to fly a plane into the White House on 9/11. Moussaoui contradicted this assertion with sworn testimony given both beforehand (when he changed his pleas to guilty on April 22, 2005), and afterwards (when he sought to withdraw his guilty plea after the conclusion of the trial).
3. Indeed, the only evidence at trial that he knew of the 9/11 attacks beforehand came from Moussaoui himself. At trial he testified that he knew that planes were to strike the World Trade Center sometime after August, and that he bought a radio so that he could listen to the news reports of the attack. If the government had found further evidence of Moussaoui's prior knowledge it would have been introduced at trial. The 9/11 Commission's report, which was not admitted into evidence, includes a statement that Ramzi bin al-Shibh, who had wired money to both Moussaoui and Mohammed Atta, thought Moussaoui might be one of the 9/11 hijackers. But bin al-Shibh was not informed of the detailed plans for the attack, and his statements were not admitted into evidence at the trial. The Minnesota FBI noted that, once detained, Moussaoui was eager to return to flight training. The 9/11 Commission report speculated that Moussaoui was being groomed to replace Ziad Jarrah, who had misgivings about the plan (Hamilton, 2006: 246–47). Ziad Jarrah was presumed to be the pilot of Flight 93, which crashed into a Pennsylvania field.
4. One employee of an intelligence agency told me Sageman's work was highly valued for its analysis of al-Qaeda's social networks.

1 THE LEGAL PROCESS BEGINS

1. All transcripts, prosecution exhibits, defense exhibits, and dockets relating to the Moussaoui case appear in the Bibliography under the entry *United States v. Moussaoui*.
2. From the author's notes on the trial.

2 SLAVE OF ALLAH: ZACARIAS MOUSSAOUI'S STRUGGLE TO REPRESENT HIMSELF

1. In that case, Egwaoje, the defendant, was allowed to represent himself. He was found guilty in federal district court, then appealed to the federal court of appeals claiming that he had been inadequately warned of the perils of self-representation. The appellate court affirmed the lower court's findings, whereupon the defendant asked for a hearing (through a writ of certiorari) in the US Supreme Court. That request was denied.

2. According to Denny, the word Islam is derived from *muslimun*, "submitter" (1977: 36). "Islam is the word for the faith found in the Koran 3:19. Words related to *''abada'* to serve, to worship, to be a slave or servant of" (1977: 42). *Ibada* is the work of the "submitters," the *muslimun* (1977: 43). The emphasis is on the work that must be done in order to worship.

3 COURTROOM 700, ALEXANDRIA, VIRGINIA

1. The counties of the Alexandria Division of the Eastern District of Virginia are Arlington, Fairfax, Fauquier, Loudon, Prince William, and Stafford.

2. I attended one day of the jury drawing, February 23, 2006; three days of the first, or eligibility phase, on March 21, 22, and 23, and three days of the second, or penalty phase, on April 18, 19, 20. I also had interviews and conversations with reporters and observers who had been there on other days when I was not present. Some descriptions therefore are drawn from my observations of the trial, and do not always have references to the court transcripts for those days. The transcripts are available through a website, www.exemplaris.com, which provides court transcripts for a fee.

3. A captain with a major American airline told me that it was indeed possible for someone with limited flight training, and with simulator training, to fly a jet such as a 747, although he did remark on the difficulty of being accurate in flying a plane into a target, even one the size of the World Trade Center.

4. In June of 2002 Moussaoui asked a number of times that the records of the FBI, CIA, and the "National Center of Communications" be checked for their surveillance of him, in Afghanistan and in London, via these telephone calls, and in Oklahoma and Minnesota. He apparently thought that these agencies were keeping track of him and of the 19 hijackers. He thought their records would show that he was not involved with the planning of 9/11. He also wrote during this time that there was a cover-up, particularly by the FBI, of the fact that they knew of the plans of the 19 hijackers. This cover-up would explain why the records were not forthcoming.

4 ZACARIAS, MY BROTHER: THE MAKING OF A TERRORIST

1. Drawn from the title of Zacarias Moussaoui's brother's biography, *Zacarias, My Brother: The Making of a Terrorist* (2003).

2. Wahhabi interpretations of Islam stem from the work of Mohammed ibn Abd al-Wahhab, an eighteenth-century Saudi theologian whose desire to return to an earlier purity of Islam was supported by Mohammed bin Saud. Saud's son married Wahhab's daughter. The close relationship between

Wahhabism and the Saudi rulers continues to this day. A related term, *salafi*, refers to the lives of the companions of the Prophets. Salafis call for a return to the purity of Islam as reflected by those lives. The Habashites are known for disputing the correctness of the Wahhabi interpretation of Islam. The Wahhabis dispute the good intentions of the Habashites. Several journalists have asked what Abd Samad meant to accomplish by writing his book about his brother (Barte, 2002; Ternisien, 2002). The struggles internal to French Islam hold some answers: the divisions between the Wahhabis and the Habashites are strongly felt. Websites warn people away from Habashite beliefs, saying they cloak their beliefs in good deeds and charity projects. Tariq Ramadan, a noted Muslim scholar, calls their teachings deviant and their discourse "extremely intransigent and closed" (2004: 30).

3. Ayman al-Zawahiri, second in command of al-Qaeda, is said to be Takfir. Joshua Gleis (2005: 1–4) writes that Sheikh Omar Abdul Rahman, the "blind sheikh" accused of the 1993 World Trade Center plot, is said to be a member of this group, although he has been spiritual leader of the Egyptian Islamic Jihad. The release of the sheikh is a goal of a number of groups affiliated with al-Qaeda. Moussaoui has said that one of his plans was to release the sheikh from prison in the United States. An August 1, 2001 daily presidential briefing to Bush said that an intelligence service had uncorroborated information that, in 1998, bin Laden was planning for such a release (CNN, 2004a). In a videotape released to the Al Jazeera television network in September 2000, bin Laden is shown calling for the release of the blind sheikh (MSNBC, n.d.).

4. Later, during the trial, Moussaoui agreed that there was friction between himself, Hambali, and Khalid Sheikh Mohammed. He said he never asked for 40 tons of ammonium nitrate. Concerning the Chinese businessmen, he said JI's planning was going nowhere and that they might as well be kidnapping said businessmen (tr. March 27, 2006, page 2390, lines 10–25; page 2391, lines 1–6).

6   ISLAM WITHOUT BORDERS

1. There is an exception, for Alsace and the department of Moselle are not bound by the same laws. Although those areas of eastern France became part of the Republic after 1801, the Concordat is still in place there, and crosses are still on Alsatian school walls (Boswell, 1999).

2. The Stasi Commission, and the Assembly, decided on the word "*ostensible*" (conspicuous or visible) as opposed to "*ostentoire*" (ostentatious). The decision therefore allows crosses and Stars of David to be worn as pendants if not visible, but the headscarf is, of course, visible. Bandanas are possible (Lerougetel, 2004).

7   BY WORD AND BULLET: LANGUAGE AND SYMBOLIC VIOLENCE

1. In French, the word "violence" does not always have the sense of physical violence that it has in English. In French the word is variously defined as "the quality with which (something) acts with force: the violence of fire, of wind, of evil, of pain or sorrow, of love." One can make violence against

a law, a text, giving that law or text a meaning contrary to its true spirit. Violence can be an effort made against oneself, through *"combat intérieur."* There can be sweet, or soft violence, it can be an action against someone who refuses to accept something (*Dictionnaire de la Langue Française*, 1883). In English, however, the word primarily has the sense of physical violence. In fact, the *Oxford English Dictionary* not only gives "the exercise of physical force ... " as its first definition, but the four other main definitions also include physical force. The sixth refers to "violation of some condition," as in "it is no breach of friendship, nor violence of paternal fondness."

2. Al-Qadir, an Algerian, had attended both Finsbury Park mosque and Brixton mosque. He had traveled from London to Pakistan, then to Afghanistan, in July 2001.

3. "... (t)he following offences (murder, bodily injury, kidnapping, etc.) which are intentionally committed by an individual or a group against one or more countries, their institutions or people with the aim of intimidating them and seriously altering or destroying the political, economic or social structures of those countries will be punishable as terrorist offences" (European Commission Framework for Combating Terrorism, Sept. 14, 2001).

4. "In dealing all the cards to itself, the system forced the Other to change the rules of the game. And the new rules are ferocious, because the game is ferocious" (Baudrillard, 2003).

8   WHAT THE WEST SHOULD LEARN FROM THE CASE OF ZACARIAS MOUSSAOUI

1. John Ashcroft (2006) reported that on September 12, 2001, President Bush had said the attacks of 9/11 should never happen again. The phrase "Never Again" became the title of Ashcroft's own book.

2. Waterboarding is a technique used to gain information. The person to be interrogated is bound hand and foot, then placed with her or his back on a board and tied to it. The foot of the board is then elevated 30 to 45 degrees. The questioner fills a large pail with water and the questioning begins. If the questioner does not like the response he pours water down the nose of the victim. The sensation for the victim is to feel that he or she is drowning, and some response is virtually assured.

BIBLIOGRAPHY

Adil, Abu. n.d. Shaheed Masood al-Benin: Islamic Awakening. http://www.
islamicawakening.com/viewarticle.php?articleID=412. Accessed August
8, 2006.

Aidi, Hisham. 2003. Let Us be Moors: Islam, Race, and Connected Histories.
Middle East Report No. 229. http://www.merip.org/mer/mer229/229_aidi.
html. Accessed October 30, 2006.

Alim, H. Samy. 2005. Hip Hop Islam. *Al Ahram Weekly Online.* July 7–13, No.
750. http://weekly.ahram.org.eg/2005/750/feature.htm. Accessed October
30, 2006.

Al Jazeera. 2005. Moussaoui Says He Wants to Plead Guilty. Al Jazeera.net. News
Global, April 22. http://english.aljazeera.net. Accessed October 23, 2006.

—— 2006a. Moussaoui's Parting Shot at US. Al Jazeera.net. Posted May 5.
http://english.aljazeera.net/NR/exeres/7BA2DC68-625F-44A0-BBC9-
E72A51B281A4.htm. Accessed September 30, 2006.

—— 2006b. Moussaoui May Serve Life in France. Al Jazeera.net. Posted May
4. http://english.aljazeera.net/NR/exeres/EB0FD024-CF57-4E65-9999-
63E66A516BC2.htm. Accessed June 25, 2006.

Amara, Fadela. 2005. Moi, fille d'immigrés, pour l'égalité et la laïcité. *Libération.*
Posted March 2. http://sisyphe.org/article.php3?id_article=1603. Accessed
November 5, 2006.

Arena, Kelli. 2006. Confronting Terror. CNN.com. Aired March 3. http://
transcripts.cnn.com/TRANSCRIPTS/0603/03/lol.01.html. Accessed August
28, 2006.

Arthur, Bill and Nadine Elsibai. 2006. Moussaoui Grew Up in Violent Home,
Social Worker Says (Update2). Bloomberg. Posted April 17, 2006. http://
www.bloomberg.com/apps/news?pid=10000103&sid=aaAQYFwbBDq8&r
efer=us. Accessed September 1, 2006.

Asad, Talal. 1993. *Genealogies of Religion: Discipline and Reasons of Power
in Christianity and Islam.* Baltimore, MD and London: Johns Hopkins
University Press.

Ashcroft, John. 2001. News Conference Regarding Zacarias Moussaoui,
December 11. US Department of Justice. http://www.fas.org/irp/
news/2001/12/agremarks12_11.htm. Accessed September 14, 2006.

—— 2006. *Never Again: Securing America and Restoring Justice.* NY: Warner
Faith/Center Street.

Associated Press. 2006a. Jury Takes Up Moussaoui's Fate. *USAToday.* Posted
April 24. http://www.usatoday.com/news/nation/2006-04-24-moussaoui_
x.htm. Accessed September 26, 2006.

—— 2006b. Moussaoui Formally Sentenced, Still Defiant. Posted May 4. http://
www.msnbc.msn.com/id/12615601/. Accessed September 26, 2006.

Astier, Henri. 2005. French Struggle to Build Local Islam. BBC. Posted November 14. http://news.bbc.co.uk/2/hi/europe/4430244.stm. Accessed October 30, 2006.

Austin-Broos, Diane. 2003. The Anthropology of Conversion: An Introduction, pp. 1–12, in Andrew Buckser and Stephen D. Glazier, eds. *The Anthropology of Religious Conversion.* Lanham, MD: Rowman and Littlefield Publishers, Inc.

Baker, Abdul Haqq. 2005. Videotaped Testimony, November 10, 2005. Defense Exhibit 002.V2.

Banjoko, Adisa. 2005. Islam, Hip-hop, and Black America. Lecture at Harvard Islamic Society. From Holla at a Schola!! http://www.netweed.com/lyricalswords/2005_08_07_lyricalswords_archive.html. Accessed October 30, 2006.

Barte, Yann. 2002. Aïcha, la rage au ventre. *Rédac chefs* website. Posted April. http://www.redacnomade.com/article.php3?id_article=4. Accessed August 6, 2006.

Baudouin, Patrick. 2006. Guilty, but a Scapegoat. *Le Monde Diplomatique.* February. http://mondediplo.com/2006/02/05moussaoui. Accessed November 3, 2006.

Baudrillard, Jean. 2003. *The Spirit of Terrorism, and Requiem for the Twin Towers,* 2nd edn. London: Verso (*Le Monde,* 11 November, 2001).

BBC. 2001. Moussaoui "Slipped Through Net." BBC News. Posted December 12, 2001. http://news.bbc.co.uk/2/hi/americas/1706326.stm. Accessed October 24, 2006.

—— 2002. Obituary: Chechen Rebel Khattab. Posted April 26. http://news.bbc.co.uk/2/hi/europe/1952053.stm. Accessed October 21, 2006.

—— 2004. Jail for Strasbourg bomb plotters. BBC News. Posted December 16. http://news.bbc.co.uk/2/hi/europe/4102023.stm. Accessed November 10, 2006.

—— 2006. Deportation Row on French Flight. BBC News. Posted August 26. http://news.bbc.co.uk/2/hi/europe/5299062.stm. Accessed October 29, 2006.

Beale, Jonathan. 2006. The Strange Case of Zacarias Moussaoui. BBC News. Posted May 3. http://news.bbc.co.uk/1/hi/world/americas/4944626.stm. Accessed November 30, 2006.

Beaud, Stéphane and Olivier Masclet. 2002. Un passage à l'acte improbable? Notes de recherche sur la trajectoire sociale de Zacarias Moussaoui. *French Politics, Culture and Society* 20(2): 159–70.

Beriss, David. 1990. Scarves, Schools, and Scapegoats: The Headscarf Affair. *French Politics and Society* 8(1).

Boëldieu, Julien and Catherine Borrel. 2000. La Proportion d'immigrés est stable depuis 25 ans. *INSEE Première* No. 748. November. http://www.insee.fr/fr/ffc/ficdoc_frame.asp?ref_id=ip748. Accessed October 29, 2006.

Borrel, Catherine. 2006. Inquêtes annuelles de recensement, 2004–2005. *INSEE Première* No. 1098. August. http://www.insee.fr/fr/ffc/ipweb/ip1098/ip1098.html#inter7. Accessed October 29, 2006.

Boswell, Laird. 1999. Franco-Austrian Conflict and the Crisis of National Sentiment during the Phony War. *Journal of Modern History* 71(3): 552–84.

Bourdieu, Pierre. 1977. *Outline of a Theory of Practice.* Richard Nice, trans. Cambridge: Cambridge University Press.

—— 1990a. *The Logic of Practice*. Richard Nice, trans. Stanford, CA: Stanford University Press.

—— 1990b. *In Other Words: Essays Towards a Reflexive Sociology*. M. Adamson, trans. Stanford, CA: Stanford University Press.

—— 1991. *Language and Symbolic Power*. J.B. Thompson, ed., G. Raymond and M. Adamson, trans. Cambridge, MA: Harvard University Press.

—— 1998a. *Practical Reason: On the Theory of Action*. Stanford, CA: Stanford University Press.

—— 1998b. *Acts of Resistance: Against the New Myths of our Time*. Richard Nice, trans. Cambridge: Polity Press.

Bourdieu, Pierre and Jean-Claude Passeron. 1977. *Reproduction in Education, Society, and Culture*. London: Sage.

—— 1979. *The Inheritors*, Richard Nice, trans. Chicago: University of Chicago Press.

Bowen, John R. 2004a. Does French Islam Have Borders? Dilemmas of Domestication in a Global Religious Field. *American Anthropologist* 106(1): 43–55.

—— 2004b. Beyond Migration: Islam as a Transnational Public Space. *Journal of Ethnic and Migration Studies* 30(5): 879–94.

Brick, Michael and Sarah Garland. 2006. After Mistrial, Another Prologue Begins in Epic Perjury Case Related to 9/11. *New York Times*, May 6, p. A15.

Bright, Martin, Anthony Barnett, et al. 2001. The Secret War. *The Observer*. Posted September 30. http://observer.guardian.co.uk/waronterrorism/story/0,,560787,00.html. Accessed September 18, 2006.

Brinbaum, Yaël. 2005. Immigration in France: Concepts, Measurements, and Surveys. Posted September 9. http://www.pch.gc.ca/pc-ch/pubs/diversity2003/brinbaum_e.cfm#table1. Accessed October 30, 2006.

Brooks, David. 2005. Gangsta, in French. *New York Times*, November 10, p. A31.

Buckser, Andrew and Stephen D. Glazier, eds. 2003. *The Anthropology of Religious Conversion*. Lanham, MD: Rowman and Littlefield Publishers, Inc.

Bulliet, Richard. 1978. First Names and Political Change in Modern Turkey. *International Journal of Middle East Studies* 9(4): 489–95.

Burrell, Ian, Andrew Gumbel, and Kim Sengupta. 2001. The "20th Hijacker" Had Been a Suspect for Years – But He Was Ignored by Intelligence Agencies. *Independent News*. Posted December 11. http://news.independent.co.uk/world/americas/article148403.ece. Accessed October 10.

Bush, George W. 2006a. Statement by the President on the Zacarias Moussaoui Jury Sentence. Prepared statement issued May 3. http://www.whitehouse.gov/news/releases/2006/05/20060503-11.html. Accessed June 25, 2006.

—— 2006b. President Discusses Global War on Terror. Press Release, September 5. http://www.whitehouse.gov/news/releases/2006/09/20060905-4.html. Accessed September 6, 2006.

Button, James. 2005. Paris Heat not from Muslims. *The Age*. Posted November 7. http://www.theage.com.au/news/world/paris-heat-not-from-muslims/2005/11/07/1131212007304.html. Accessed November 3, 2006.

Camus, Jean-Yves. 2004. Islam in France. Institute for Counter-Terrorism, Israel, May 10. http://www.ict.org.il/articles/articledet.cfm?articleid=51. Accessed November 3, 2006.

Chambon, Frédéric. 2001. Entre New York et Narbonne: l'échange épistolaire d'Aïcha et Zacarias Moussaoui. *Le Monde*, November 19, p. 1.

Chambon, Frédéric, Jean-Pierre Langellier, and Eric Leser. 2001. Itinéraire d'un apprenti terroriste. *Le Monde* 57(17680), November 28, p. 16.

Chirac, Jacques. 2003. Discours prononcé par M. Jacques Chirac, Président de la République, relatif au respect du principe de laïcité dans République. http://www.elysee.fr/elysee/interventions/discours_et_declarations/2003/decembre. Accessed 23 March 2005.

Citron, Suzanne. 1987. *Le Mythe national: l'histoire de France en question*. Paris: Editions Ouvriers/Etudes et Documentation Internationales.

Clarke, Richard A. 2004. *Against All Enemies: Inside America's War on Terror*. New York: Free Press.

CNCZ. 2005. Hijab and Academic Freedom, Blogistan. Posted March 30. http://www.blogistan.co.uk/blog/mt.php/2005/03/29/hijab_and_academic_freedom. Accessed October 29, 2006.

CNN. 2004a. Bin Laden Determined to Strike in US. Transcript of presidential daily briefing, Posted April 10. http://www.cnn.com/2004/ALLPOLITICS/04/10/august6.memo/. Accessed September 18, 2006.

—— 2004b. Investigators Name Suspects in Spain Attack. CNN.com. Posted March 16. http://transcripts.cnn.com/TRANSCRIPTS/0403/16/lol.05.html. Accessed September 1, 2006.

cooke, miriam and Bruce B. Lawrence, eds. 2005. *Muslim Networks: From Hajj to Hip-hop*. Chapel Hill: University of North Carolina Press.

Cohen, Andrew. 2006. Major Gov't Blunder Inexcusable in Moussaoui Trial. CBS. Posted March 13. http://www.cbsnews.com/stories/2006/03/13/opinion/courtwatch/main1397691. Accessed August 23, 2006.

Collinson, Stephen. 2006. Jury to Decide if Moussaoui "Killed by Lying." IOL. Posted March 29. http://www.int.iol.co.za/index.php?set_id=1&click_id=&art_id=qw1143647641293B223. Accessed September 23, 2006.

Coroller, Catherine, Thomas Calinon, and Mourad Guichard. 2006. Les Musulmans investissent la rue. *Libération*. 2006. Posted February 13, 2006. http://www.liberation.fr/actualite/evenement/evenement1/1464.FR.php. Accessed November 20, 2006.

Cotterill, Janet. 2003. *Language and Power in Court: An Analysis of the O.J. Simpson Trial*. New York: Palgrave Macmillan.

CourtTV. 2002. Attorney Unable to Meet with Moussaoui. Posted June 3. http://www.courttv.com/archive/news/2002/0603/attorney_ap.html. Accessed November 29, 2006.

—— 2005. Judge Accepts Moussaoui's Guilty Plea. Posted April 22, 2005. http://www.courttv.com/trials/moussaoui/042205_ap.html#continue. Accessed August 20, 2006.

Cratty, Carol. 2006. Moussaoui Penalty Jury Pool Down to 86. CNN.com. http://www.cnn.com/2006/LAW/02/24/moussaoui.jury/. Accessed October 25, 2006.

De Galembert, Claire. 2006. Islam and Local Protagonists: Between Uncertainty and Recourse to Public Authority. *Les Cahiers de la Sécurité* No. 62. Institut National des Hautes Etudes de Sécurité. http://www.inhes.interieur.gouv.fr/fichiers/RECH_62CSIinternet.pdf. Accessed November 4, 2006.

Deloire, Christophe and Christophe Dubois. 2004. *Les Islamistes sont déjà là*. Paris: Albin Michel.

Denécé, Eric. 2005. Le Développement de l'Islam en France: aspects sécuritaires, economiques, et sociaux. *Rapport de recherche* 1(Sept.) http://www.cf2r.org/download/rapports_recherche/RR1-Islam.pdf. Accessed November 3, 2006.

Denny, Frederick Mathewson. 1977. Some Religio-communal Terms and Concepts in the Qur'an. *Numen* 24(Fasc.1) April: 26–59.

Derrida, Jacques and Anne Dufourmantelle. 2000. *Of Hospitality*. Rachel Bowlby, trans. Stanford, CA: Stanford University Press.

Désir, Harlem. 1990. Interview. *Le Debat* (Paris) 61 (Sept.–Oct.): 42–58.

Desjardins, Thierry. 1996. *Lettre au Président à propos de l'immigration*. Paris: Fixot.

—— 1999. *Lettre au Président sur le grand ras-le bol des Français*. Paris: Fixot.

Dogonay, Cennet. 2004. IslamOnline.net. Posted October 13. http://www. islamonline.net/livedialogue/english/Browse.asp?hGuestID=gOg7Xd. Accessed October 29, 2006.

Dominus, Susan. 2003. Everybody has a Mother. *New York Times*, February 9, Section 6, p. 37.

Donahue, Katherine C. 1997. The Language of Violence: Race, Racism, and Culture in France. In B. Dieckmann, C. Wulf, and M. Wimmer, eds. *Violence: Nationalism, Racism, Xenophobia*, pp. 187–203. European Studies in Education, Vol. 5. New York: Waxmann.

—— 2005. Nomad Souls across Time and Space: West African Musicians as Ethnographers. *Journal of the Society for the Anthropology of Europe* 5(2): 2–12.

Downey, Sarah. 2001. Who is Zacarias Moussaoui? MSNBC.com. Posted December 14. http://www.msnbc.msn.com/id/3067363/. Accessed October 24, 2006.

DST. 2003. *Processus de l'enrolement de jeunes musulmans dans le jihad*. Paris: DST.

Dunham, Frank. 2004. When Yasir Esam Hamdi Meets Zacarias Moussaoui. *Richmond Journal of Global Law and Business* 4(March): 30. http://law. richmond.edu/global/website/PubliSteps/doc_display.php?docid=35. Accessed November 28, 2006.

Dwyer, Timothy. 2006. One Juror between Terrorist and Death. *Washington Post*, May 12, p. A01. http://www.washingtonpost.com/wp-dyn/content/ article/2006/05/11/AR2006051101884.html. Accessed August 28, 2006.

Edgar, Iain R. 2004. The Dream Will Tell: Militant Muslim Dreaming in the Context of Traditional and Contemporary Islamic Dream Theory and Practice. *Dreaming* 14(1): 21–29.

Egwaoje v. United States (No. 03–691), 2004 (petition for writ of certiorari to the United States Supreme Court from the Seventh Circuit Court of Appeals).

Eickelman, Dale F. 1977. Time in a Complex Society: A Moroccan Example. *Ethnology* 16(1): 48–50.

—— 2002. *The Middle East and Central Asia: An Anthropological Approach*. Upper Saddle River, NJ: Prentice Hall.

Engler, Marcus. 2005. Country Profile: France. *Focus-Migration* 2(April). http:// migration-research.org/dokumente/focus-migration/CP02_-_France.pdf. Accessed October 29, 2006.

Erikson, Erik. 1980. *Identity and Life-cycle*. New York: Norton.

Esposito, John L. 1998a [1988]. *Islam: The Straight Path*. New York: Oxford University Press.

—— 1998b. *Islam and Politics*. Syracuse, NY: Syracuse University Press.

—— 2002. *Unholy War: Terror in the Name of Islam*. New York: Oxford University Press.

—— ed. 2003. Abd. *Oxford Dictionary of Islam. Oxford Reference Online.* Oxford University Press. http://www.oxfordreference.com/views/ENTRY.html?sub view=Main&entry=t125.e1. September 6, 2006.

European Commission. 2001. Framework for Combating Terrorism, Sept. 14, 2001. http://www.statewatch.org/news/2001/sep/14eulaws.htm. Accessed November 10, 2006.

Faretta v. California, 422 U.S. 806, 1975.

Fiorenza, Nicolas, 2002. Plan Vigipirate: France Reinforces Anti-terrorism Efforts in the Wake of 9/11. *Armed Forces Journal International* 139(9): 23–24.

Fox News. 2001. Justice Department Appoints Defense Team for Moussaoui. Associated Press. Posted December 13. http://www.foxnews.com/story/0,2933,40775,00.html. Accessed September 10, 2006.

—— 2006. Bin Laden: Moussaoui Wasn't Sept. 11 Conspirator. FoxNews.com. Posted May 24. http://www.foxnews.com/story/0,2933,196682,00.html. Accessed October 5, 2006.

Friedman, Jonathan. 2001. Impaired Empire. In "Civilization, Vulnerability and Translation: Reflections in the Aftermath of September 11th," special issue, *Anthropological Quarterly* 75(1): 93–202.

fzer0. n.d. http://www2.usenetarchive.org/Dir33/File158.html. Accessed November 4, 2006.

Geertz, Hildred. 1979. The Meanings of Family Ties. In Clifford Geertz, Hildred Geertz, and Lawrence Rosen, eds. *Meaning and Order in Moroccan Society,* pp. 341–56. New York: Cambridge University Press.

Ghannoushi, Soumaya. 2005. The Corrosive Division in France. Al Jazeera.net. http://english.aljazeera.net/NR/exeres/DFF6CC7D-792F-4E22-8A3C-D281DEC0C964.htm. Accessed November 27, 2005.

Gideon v. Wainwright, 372 U.S. 335, 1963.

Gleis, Joshua L. 2005. National Security Implications of Al-Takfir wal-Hijra. *Al-Nakhlah* (Fletcher School Online Journal for issues related to Southwest Asia and Islamic Civilization) spring; Article 3, pp. 1–4. http://fletcher.tufts.edu/al_nakhlah/archives/spring2005/gleis.pdf. Accessed September 1, 2006.

Goldberg, Jonah. 2006. Globalization for Losers. *National Review Online.* Posted April 28. http://www.nationalreview.com/goldberg/goldberg200604280604.asp. Accessed November 3, 2006.

Gonzales, Alberto. 2005a. Prepared Remarks. April 22. http://www.usdoj.gov/ag/speeches/2005/prepared_remarks_042205.htm. Accessed September 6, 2006.

—— 2005b. Prepared Remarks for Alberto R. Gonzales at the Council of Foreign Relations. December 1. http://www.usdoj.gov/ag/speeches/2005/ag_speech_051201.html. Accessed October 3, 2006.

Gordon, Greg. 2006. Witnesses Testify about Moussaoui's Upbringing, Mental State. McClatchy Papers, Scripps-Howard News Service. Posted April 17. http://www.shns.com/shns/g_index2.cfm?action=detail&pk=MOUSSAOUI-04-17-06. Accessed August 10, 2006.

Gordon, Greg and James Rosen. 2006. Attorney General Gonzales Supports Military Tribunals. McClatchy Papers. Posted September 5. http://www.realcities.com/mld/krwashington/15445975.htm. Accessed September 30, 2006.

Guitta, Oliver. 2005. The French Counter-terrorism Model. *Frontpagemag.com.* Posted September 8. http://www.frontpagemag.com/Articles/ReadArticle. asp?ID=19403. Accessed November 3, 2006.

Hamilton, Lee. 2006. *The 9/11 Commission Report.* New York: Barnes and Noble Publishing. (See also 9/11 Commission Report, 2004. http://www. gpoaccess.gov/911/index.html. Accessed October 15, 2006.)

Hemmer, Bill. 2005. Questions Over Moussaoui's Competency. CNN.com. Aired April 21. http://transcripts.cnn.com/TRANSCRIPTS/0504/21/ltm.06. html. Accessed November 29, 2006.

Heneghan, Tom. 2004. French Pro-hijab March Branded Dangerous. *Muslim News.* Posted July 1. http://www.muslimnews.co.uk/news/news. php?article=6670. Accessed November 3, 2006.

Hermansen, Marcia. 2004. Genealogy. *Encyclopedia of Islam and the Muslim World* Vol. 1, pp. 272–73.

Hersh, Seymour. 2002. The Twentieth Man. *New Yorker,* September 30. Posted September 23. http://foi.missouri.edu/terrorbkgd/twentieth.html. Accessed March 11, 2007.

Hill, Eleanor. 2002. US Senate Intelligence Committee Statement. October 17. http://intelligence.senate.gov/0210hrg/021017/hillunclass.pdf. Accessed November 29, 2006.

Hill, Jonathan D. and Thomas M. Wilson. 2003. Identity Politics and the Politics of Identities. *Identities: Global Studies in Culture and Power* 20: 1–8.

Hirschkorn, Phil. 2002. Moussaoui Spurns Court-appointed Lawyer. CNN.com. Posted June 18. http://archives.cnn.com/2002/LAW/06/18/moussaoui.trial/ index.html. Accessed November 29, 2006.

—— 2006a. Moussaoui Dreamed of Flying Plane into White House. CNN. com. Posted March 9. http://www.cnn.com/2006/LAW/03/08/moussaoui. trial/. Accessed October 11, 2006.

—— 2006b Giuliani Describes 9/11 Horrors. CNN.com. Posted April 8. http://www.cnn.com/2006/LAW/04/06/moussaoui/index.html. Accessed November 1, 2006.

—— 2006c. Moussaoui: "No Remorse" for 9/11. CNN.com. Posted April 13. http://www.cnn.com/2006/LAW/04/13/moussaoui.trial/. Accessed November 1, 2006.

—— 2006d. Jury Deliberations Begin in 9/11 Trial. CNN.com. Posted April 24. http://www.cnn.com/2006/LAW/04/24/moussaoui.trial/index.html. Accessed August 21, 2006.

—— 2006e. "Aggravating" Stumps Moussaoui Juror. CNN.com. Posted April 28. http://www.cnn.com/2006/LAW/04/28/moussaoui.trial/. Accessed September 26, 2006.

—— 2006f. Jury Spares 9/11 Plotter Moussaoui. CNN.com. Posted May 3. http://www.cnn.com/2006/LAW/05/03/moussaoui.verdict. Accessed May 3, 2006.

Hopquin, Benoît. 2004. Négociations diplomatiques, reprise en main des services, mission parallèle: 124 jours de tractations. *Le Monde,* December 23.

Hudson, Rex A. 1999. *The Sociology and Psychology of Terrorism: Who Becomes a Terrorist and Why?* Washington, DC: Federal Research Division, Library of Congress. http://www.fas.org/irp/threat/frd.html?o=0. Accessed November 20, 2005.

194   *Slave of Allah*

Huntington, Samuel P. 1993. The Clash of Civilizations? *Foreign Affairs* 72(3): 27–45.

—— 1997. *The Clash of Civilizations and the Remaking of World Order.* New York: Touchstone.

Husbands, C.T. 1991. The Mainstream Right and the Politics of Immigration in France: Major Developments in the 1980s. *Ethnic and Racial Studies* 14(2): 170–98.

Israel, Simon. 2004. MI5 Courted Terror Suspect. Channel 4 News. Posted 23 March. http://www.channel4.com/news/ftp_images2/2004/03/week_4/23_document.pdf. and http://www.channel4.com/news/2004/03/week_4/23_qatada.html. Accessed September 2, 2006.

Jackman, Tom. 2002. Moussaoui Allowed to Defend Himself. *Washington Post,* June 14, p. A01.

Jelen, Christian. 1996. *La France éclatée ou les reculades de la République* (France Shattered, or the Retreat of the Republic). Paris: Nil Éditions.

Johnson, Kevin. 2006. Moussaoui Vows to be Free Again. *USAToday.* Posted May 4. http://www.usatoday.com/news/nation/2006-05-04-moussaoui_x.htm. Accessed October 2, 2006.

Johnson, Kevin and Alan Levin. 2006. Sanction Makes Moussaoui Case "Impossible," Feds Say. *USAToday.* Posted March 15. http://www.usatoday.com/news/nation/2006-03-15-moussaoui_x.htm. Accessed August 23, 2006.

Juergensmeyer, Mark. 2003. *Terror in the Mind of God,* 3rd edn. Berkeley: University of California Press.

Karam, Azza, ed. 2004. *Transnational Political Islam: Religion, Ideology, and Power.* London: Pluto Press.

Kelley, Sarah and Jason McLure. 2006. Witness Flap Calls Doubt on Call for Death in Moussaoui Case. *Legal Times,* March 21.

Kepel, Gilles. 1997. *Allah in the West.* Stanford, CA: Stanford University Press.

Khedimellah, Moussa. 2005. L'Islam industriel. Oumma.com. Posted December 6. http://oumma.com/spip.php?article1812#_ftn2. Accessed October 25, 2006.

Khosrokhavar, Farhad. 1997. *L'Islam des jeunes.* Paris: Flammarion.

—— 2002. *Les Nouveaux Martyrs d'Allah.* Paris: Flammarion.

—— 2003. Terrorist Networks in Europe. Conference on Muslims in Europe Post 9/11: Understanding and Responding to the Islamic World. 25–26 April. http://www.sant.ox.ac.uk/princeton/pap_khosro.shtml. Accessed July 12, 2006

—— 2004. *L'Islam dans les prisons.* Paris: Balland.

—— 2005. *Suicide Bombers: Allah's New Martyrs.* London: Pluto Press. (Published in 2002 as *Les nouveaux martyrs d'Allah.* Paris: Flammarion.)

Kohlmayer, Vasko. 2006. The Case for Waterboarding. *Frontpagemag.com.* Posted September 29. http://www.frontpagemag.com/Articles/ReadArticle.asp?ID=24653. Accessed September 30, 2006.

Köse, Ali. 1996. *Conversion to Islam: A Study of Native British Converts.* London: Kegan Paul International.

Leahy, Patrick. 2003. Statement of the Honorable Patrick Leahy, United States Senator, Vermont. October 21. http://judiciary.senate.gov/member_statement.cfm?id=965&wit_id=2629. Accessed July 20, 2006.

Leiken, Robert S. 2005. Europe's Angry Muslims. *Foreign Affairs* July/August. Posted July 7. http://www.foreignaffairs.org/20050701faessay84409/robert-s-leiken/europe-s-angry-muslims. Accessed November 4, 2006.

Le Monde. 2005. Une forte hausse des quartiers-ghettos. November 10. http://www.lemonde.fr/web/vi/0,47-0@2-3226,54-709033,0.html. Accessed November 11, 2005.

Le Pen, Jean-Marie. 2002. Profile: Jean-Marie Le Pen. BBC. Posted April 23. http://news.bbc.co.uk/1/hi/world/europe/1943193.stm. Accessed October 30, 2006.

Lerougetel, Antoine. 2004. The Islamic Headscarf Ban: A French Teacher's View. World Socialist Website. Posted March 23. http://www.wsws.org/articles/2004/mar2004/head-m23.shtml. Accessed November 27, 2006.

L'Est Républicain. 2005a. Villepin reprend la main. Posted November 26. www.estrepublicain.fr. Accessed November 26, 2005.

—— 2005b. Appendix: Retour sur neuf nuits de violence dans le Doubs. Posted November 16. http://archives.estrepublicain.fr/. Accessed November 26, 2005.

Lewis, Neil. 2006. Moussaoui's Lawyers Focus on Troubled Childhood. *New York Times.* Posted April 17. http://www.nytimes.com/2006/04/17/us/17cnd-moussaoui.html. Accessed July 31, 2006.

Lewis, Neil A. and David Stout. 2006. Moussaoui is Defiant at Formal Sentencing. *International Herald Tribune, Americas,* May 5. http://www.iht.com/articles/2006/05/04/america/web.0504trialcnd.php. Accessed May 7, 2006.

Livesey, Bruce. 2005. The salafist movement. *Frontline.* Posted January 25. http://www.pbs.org/wgbh/pages/frontline/shows/front/special/sala.html Accessed September 1, 2006.

Lorcerie, Françoise. n.d. Ecole et apparenances ethniques: que dit la recherche? CNRS. http://www.recherche.gouv.fr/recherche/fns/lorcerie.pdf. Accessed October 29, 2006.

Malik, Abd al. 2005. Interview. http://www.grainesdecitoyens. Accessed November 14, 2005.

Malkin, Michelle. 2006. No Tears for Moussaoui. Posted April 18. http://michellemalkin.com/archives/005012.htm. Accessed July 31, 2006.

Markon, Jerry and Timothy Dwyer. 2006a. Moussaoui Unfazed as 9/11 Attacks Detailed. *Washington Post,* March 8, p. A07. http://www.washington-post.com/wp-dyn/content/article/2006/03/06/AR2006030600781.html. Accessed October 21, 2006.

—— 2006b. Federal Witnesses Banned in 9/11 Trial. *Washington Post,* March 15, p. A01. http://uniset.ca/terr/news/wp_moussaoui_witnessban.html. Accessed November 30, 2006.

—— 2006c. Horror Takes the Stand at the Moussaoui Trial. *Washington Post,* April 7, p. A1. http://www.washingtonpost.com/wp-dyn/content/article/2006/04/06/AR2006040600818.html. Accessed October 22, 2006.

—— 2006d. Some Saw Moussaoui as Bit Player, Juror Says. *Washington Post,* May 5, p. A0l. http://www.washingtonpost.com/wp-dyn/content/article/2006/05/04/AR2006050400715.html. Accessed October 25, 2006.

Matthies, R. John. 2006. Kicking the Anthill (Un coup de pied dans la fourmilière). Conference on Islam in the European Public Sphere, Brigham Young University. http://kennedy.byu.edu/partners/CSE/islam/pdfs/matthies-paper.pdf. Accessed November 5, 2006.

Mazzetti, Mark. 2006. Spy Agencies Say Iraq War Worsens Terrorism Threat. *New York Times*. Posted September 24. http://www.nytimes.com/2006/09/24/world/middleeast/24terror.html. Accessed October 26, 2006.

McCrummen, Stephanie, 2005. A Mix of Ordinary, Drama at Courthouse. *Washington Post*, April 23, p. A11. http://www.washingtonpost.com/wp-dyn/articles/A10404-2005Apr22.html. Accessed August 20, 2006.

McKenna, Terence. 2004a. Interview with Abd-Samad Moussaoui. CBC News, The National. Posted March 16. http://www.cbc.ca/national/news/recruiters/abdsamad_interview.html. Accessed September 1, 2006.

—— 2004b. The Recruiters. CBC News, The National. Posted March 16. http://www.cbc.ca/national/news/recruiters/moussaoui.html. Accessed September 1, 2006.

Meek, James Gordon. 2006. Al Qaeda Big Wig's War Cries. *New York Daily News*, July 28. http://www.nydailynews.com/front/story/438829p-369631c.html. Accessed July 29, 2006.

Meyers, Lisa. 2005. FBI Monitors Islamic Group for Terror Ties. MSNBC.com. Posted January 18. http://msnbc.msn.com/id/6839625/. Accessed November 8, 2006.

Moussaoui, Abd Samad, with Florence Bouquillat. 2003. *The Making of a Terrorist*, Simon Pleasance and Fronza Woods, trans. New York: Seven Stories Press.

Moussaoui, Jamila. 2005. Videotaped Testimony, December 7. Defense Exhibit 010.V2.

Moussaoui, Nadia. 2005. Videotaped Testimony, December 17. Defense Exhibit 011.V2.

Moussaoui v. United States, 161 L. Ed. 2d 496, 2005. (US Supreme Court's refusal to hear case, March 21, 2005).

MSNBC. n.d. Al-Qaida: Timeline of al-Qaida Statements, The Hunt for al-Qaida. http://www.msnbc.msn.com/id/4686034/page/2/#storyContinued. Accessed September 18, 2006.

—— 2006a. Moussaoui Offered to Testify against Himself. Posted March 28. http://www.msnbc.msn.com/id/12036777/. Accessed October 21, 2006.

—— 2006b. Osama bin Laden Tape Transcript. Posted May 23. http://www.msnbc.msn.com/id/12939961/. Accessed October 7, 2006.

Muslim Population Statistics. 2006. http://www.ilaam.net/Intl/PopStats.html. Accessed November 3, 2006.

National Intelligence Estimate. 2006. Declassified Key Judgments of the National Intelligence Estimate "Trends in Global Terrorism: Implications for the United States," dated April 2006. http://www.dni.gov/press_releases/Declassified_NIE_Key_Judgments.pdf. Accessed September 30, 2006.

National Statistics. 2001. Religion in Britain. National Statistics Online. http://www.statistics.gov.uk/cci/nugget.asp?id=293. Accessed March 11, 2007.

National Strategy for Combating Terrorism, September 2006, page 15. http://www.whitehouse.gov/nsc/nsct/2006/nsct2006.pdf. Accessed September 6, 2006.

N'Dour, Youssou. 2004. *Egypt*. CD. Nonesuch.

Newman, Dina. 2001. Interview on BBC: Moussaoui "Slipped Through Net." BBC News. Posted

Novak, David. 2002. Letter Regarding the Moussaoui Trial. February 26. http://www.giveyourvoice.com. Accessed October 19, 2006.

Novak, Viveca. 2003. How the Moussaoui Case Crumbled. *Time* 162(17), October 27. http://foi.missouri.edu/secretcourts/moussaouicase.html. Accessed November 30, 2006.

O'Brien, Soledad. 2006. Transcript. *American Morning.* CNN. Aired March 27. http://transcripts.cnn.com/TRANSCRIPTS/0603/27/ltm.05.html. Accessed October 26, 2006.

O'Reilly, Bill. 2006. The Terror War Meets the Culture War. *The O'Reilly Factor.* Posted September 29, 2006. http://www.foxnews.com/story/0,2933,216557,00.html. Accessed November 2, 2006.

Peugeot. 2006. http://www.peugeot.com/tradition/histoire/en/entreprise_1960. htm. Accessed October 25, 2006.

Pialoux, Michel and Stéphane Beaud, 2000. *Retour sur la condition ouvrière.* Paris: Fayard.

Plant, Nil. 2005. Videotaped Testimony, November 15, 2005. Defense Exhibit 012.V2.

Pontaut, Jean-Marie and Eric Pelletier. 2002. Ce que le DST a transmis au FBI. *L'Express.* Posted June 13. http://lexpress.fr/info/monde/dossier/benladen/dossier.asp?ida=339131. Accessed August 8, 2006.

Powell, Stewart M. 2006. Moussaoui Banned from Court Ahead of Jury Selection. *TimesUnion.com.* http://www.timesunion.com/AspStories/story.a sp?category=&storyID=450868&BCCode=&newsdate=2/15/2006. Accessed October 25, 2006.

Power, Carla. 2005. Welcome to the Hip-hop Ummah. *Time Europe.* Posted October 23. http://www.time.com/time/europe/html/051031/music.html. Accessed October 30, 2006.

al-Qadir, Mohamed Abd. 2005. Unclassified Summary of Evidence for Administrative Review Board. March 7. Department of Defense, Guantanamo Bay, Cuba. http://www.dod.mil/pubs/foi/detainees/csrt/ARB_Factors_Set_1_944-1045.pdf. Accessed November 8, 2006.

Ramadan, Tariq. 2004. *Western Muslims and the Future of Islam.* Oxford: Oxford University Press.

—— 2005. Fear Will Only Fuel the Riots. *The Guardian.* Posted November 12. http://www.guardian.co.uk/comment/story/0,,1640802,00.html. Accessed October 30, 2006.

Reed-Danahay, Deborah. 2005. *Locating Bourdieu.* Bloomington: Indiana University Press.

Reid, Tim. 2006. White House a Target, Says 9/11 Plotter. *The Times* (London). Posted March 28. http://www.aclufl.org/news_events/alert_archive/Index.cf m?action=viewRelease&emailAlertID=1752. Accessed November 3, 2006.

Richmond, Oliver. 2003. Realizing Hegemony? Symbolic Terrorism and the Roots of Conflict. *Studies in Conflict and Terrorism* 26: 289–309.

Riley, Alan. 2004. Headscarves, Skullcaps, and Crosses. Muslim Lawyers Net. Posted May 17. http://www.muslim-lawyers.net/news/index.php3?aktion =show&number=248. Accessed October 29, 2006.

Riley, John. 2006a. FBI "Can't Put Him With" Hijackers. *Newsday.com.* Posted March 8. http://www.newsday.com/mynews/ny-usmous-084654382mar08,0,3567496.story. Accessed October 21, 2006.

—— 2006b. A Martyr in the Making? *Newsday.com.* Posted March 29. http://www.newsday.com/mynews/ny-usmous294679837mar29,0,5135777.story. Accessed September 23, 2006.

198 *Slave of Allah*

———— 2006c. An Appropriate and Fair Ending. *Newsday.com*. Posted May 5. http://www.newsday.com/mynews/ny-usmous054729867may05,0,7565204.story. Accessed November 5, 2006.

Rotella, Sebastian, 2005. In Bleak Projects, Emerging Culture. *Los Angeles Times*. Posted September 27. http://www.latimes.com/news/education/la-fg-projects27sep27,1,6110050.story?coll=la-news-learning. Accessed October 30, 2006.

Rotella, Sebastian and David Zucchino. 2001. Embassy Plot Offers Insight into Terrorist Recruitment, Training. *Los Angeles Times*. Posted October 22. http://www.norwalkadvocate.com/news/nationworld/sns-worldtrade-embassyplot-lat,0,3646484.story?page=4&coll=sns-newsnation-headlines. Accessed September 1, 2006.

Roth, Siobhan. 2002. Strange Twists Come with the Territory when You're a Lawyer for the "20th Hijacker." *Legal Times* 22 July.

Sabouraud, Corine. 2001. Les jeunes années perpigno-audoises de Zacarias Moussaoui terroriste presume. *Midi Libre* (*L'Indépendant*), September 18. http://www.midilibre.com/dossiers/moussaoui/jeune.html?num=1015791800. Accessed October 1, 2006.

Sandalow, Marc. 2005. Bush Warns of "Radical Islamic Empire." *San Francisco Chronicle*. Posted October 7. http://www.sfgate.com/cgi-bin/article.cgi?file=/c/a/2005/10/07/MNGLQF42PD1.DTL. Accessed August 20, 2006.

Sageman, Marc. 2004. *Understanding Terror Networks*. Philadelphia: University of Pennsylvania Press.

San Antonio Express News. 2006. Albader Alhazmi: They Thought He Was the Enemy. Posted September 9. http://www.mysanantonio.com/news/metro/stories/. Accessed September 10, 2006.

Scheuer, Michael. 2005. Militant Islam, on the Wane or on the Rise? In *Al Qaeda Now: Understanding Today's Terrorists*, pp. 61–60. Cambridge: Cambridge University Press.

Schimmel, Annemarie. 1989. *Islamic Names*. Edinburgh: Edinburgh University Press.

Searle, John R. 1995. *The Construction of Social Reality*. New York: Free Press.

Seper, Jerry. 2006. Judge Ousts Moussaoui Again. *Washington Times*. Posted 15 February. http://www.washtimes.com/national/20060214-110943-6030r.htm. Accessed September 21, 2006.

Serrano, Richard A. 2006. 9/11 Phone Drama Replayed at Moussaoui Sentencing Trial. *Los Angeles Times*. Posted April 12. http://www.sfgate.com/cgi-bin/article.cgi?f=/c/a/2006/04/12/MNG95I7P2G1.DTL&feed=rss.news. Accessed October 13, 2006.

Shapiro, Jeremy and Bénédicte Suzan. 2003. The French Experience of Counter-terrorism. *Survival* 45(1): 67–98.

Shenon, Philip. 2002. Interview with Gwen Ifill: The Moussaoui Case. *Online News Hour*, June 13. http://www.pbs.org/newshour/bb/law/jan-june02/moussaoui_6-13.html. Accessed September 6, 2006.

Silverman, Maxim. 1991. Citizenship and the Nation-state in France. In Robert Miles and Jeanne Singer-Kerel, eds. *Migration and Migrants in France*, Special Issue of *Ethnic and Racial Studies* 14(3): 333–49.

Silverstein, Paul A. 2004. *Algeria in France: Transpolitics, Race, and Nation*. Bloomington: Indiana University Press.

Singer-Kerel, Jeanne. 1991. Foreign Workers in France, 1891–1936. In Robert Miles and Jeanne Singer-Kerel, eds. *Migration and Migrants in France*, Special Issue of *Ethnic and Racial Studies* 14(3): 279–93.

Smith, Craig. 2005. French Islamic Group Offers Rich Soil for Militancy. *New York Times* April 29, p. A15.

Smith, Robert. 2006. The (Untelevised) Trial of the Century. National Public Radio, April 3. http://www.npr.org/templates/story/story.php?storyId=5319395. Accessed August 23, 2006.

Sniffen, Michael. 2006a. Jury Pool Grows for Moussaoui Sentencing. Forbes.com. Posted February 17. http://www.forbes.com/work/feeds/ap/2006/02/17/ap2536544.html. Accessed September 15, 2006.

—— 2006b. Judge Unexpectedly Halts Moussaoui Trial. ABC News. Posted March 13. http://abcnews.go.com/US/LegalCenter/wireStory?id=1719239. Accessed September 27, 2006.

Special Immigration Appeals Tribunal. 2004. Open Judgement. January. http://www.channel4.com/news/ftp_images2/2004/03/week_4/23_document.pdf. Accessed September 2, 2006.

St. Paul Pioneer Press. 2006. Head of FBI Office Is Reassigned in Probe. TwinCities.com. Posted September 23, 2006. http://www.twincities.com/mld/pioneerpress/news/local/15587629.htm. Accessed September 24, 2006.

Steele, John, Sean O'Neill, Richard Alleyne, and Sue Clough. 2003. Police Seize Weapons in Mosque Raid. *The Telegraph*. Posted January 21. http://www.telegraph.co.uk/news/main.jhtml?xml=/news/2003/01/21/nmosq21.xml. Accessed September 2, 2006.

Stein, Lisa. 2006. Crazy or Not Crazy? Timesonline. 25 April. http://www.timesonline.co.uk/article/0,,28009-2150898,00.html. Accessed August 30, 2006.

Steyn, Mark. 2006. Moussaoui Gets Life, the Terrorists Win. *Chicago Sun-Times*. Posted May 7. http://www.freerepublic.com/focus/f-news/1628144/posts. Accessed October 28, 2006.

Sublet, Jacqueline. 1991. *Le Voile du nom: Essai sur le nom propre arabe*. Paris: Presses Universitaires de France.

Suskind, Ron. 2006. *The One Percent Doctrine*. New York: Simon and Schuster.

Swedenburg, Ted. 2002. Aki Nawaz, Natacha Atlas, and Akhenaton. In Tony Mitchell, ed. *Global Noise: Rap and Hip-hop Outside the USA*. Hanover, NH: UPNH/Wesleyan University Press.

Taylor, Charles. 2005. *Modern Social Imaginaries*. Durham, NC: Duke University Press.

Taylor, Guy. 2005. Moussaoui Pleads Guilty. *Washington Times*. Posted April 30. http://www.washtimes.com/national/20050422-114701-1729r.htm. Accessed October 23, 2006.

Tempest, Rone. 2006. US to Retry Lodi Father in Terrorism Training Case. *Los Angeles Times*. Posted May 5. http://ktla.trb.com/news/ktla-lodiretrial,0,6827002.story?coll=ktla-news-1. Accessed November 20, 2005.

Ternisien, Xavier. 2002. Les Quatre Principales Familles de l'islam militant. *Le Monde*, January 25.

Thompson, John B. (1991) Introduction. In *Language and Symbolic Power*. J.B. Thompson, ed., G. Raymond and M. Adamson, trans. Cambridge, MA: Harvard University Press.

Todorov, Tzvetan. 1989. *Nous et les autres: la réflexion française sur la diversité humaine*. Paris: Seuil. (Published in English in 1993 as *On Human Diversity: Nationalism, Racism, and Exoticism in French Thought*. Catherine Porter, trans. Cambridge, MA: Harvard University Press.)

Townsend, Peggy. 2006. Onetime Watsonville Resident, Attorney Reflects on Work with "20th hijacker." SantaCruzSentinel.com. Posted September 10. http://www.santacruzsentinel.com/archive/2006/September/10/local/stories/02local.htm. Accessed October 20, 2006.

Turley, Jonathan. 2006. Interview with Soledad O'Brien on *American Morning*. Transcript. CNN. Aired March 27. http://transcripts.cnn.com/TRANSCRIPTS/0603/27/ltm.05.html. Accessed October 26, 2006.

UPI. 2006. France Steps Up Immigrant Deportations. Posted September 3. http://www.upi.com/NewsTrack/view.php?StoryID=20060903-015528-8069r. Accessed November 4, 2006.

United States v. Moussaoui. 2001. Indictment of Zacarias Moussaoui. December 11. http://www.usdoj.gov/ag/moussaouiindictment.htm. Accessed August 22, 2006.

—— Transcript of Arraignment. January 2, 2002. http://cryptome.org/usa-v-zm-arr.htm. Accessed September 14, 2006.

—— Hearing Transcript. April 22, 2002. http://cryptome.org/usa-v-zm-ht1.htm. Accessed September 14, 2006.

—— Hearing Transcript. July 18, 2002. http://cryptome.org/usa-v-zm-071802.htm. Accessed September 14, 2006.

—— Hearing Transcript. July 25, 2002. http://cryptome.org/usa-v-zm-072502.htm. Accessed August 23, 2006.

—— Hearing Transcript. August 29, 2002. http://cryptome.org/usa-v-zm-082902.htm. Accessed November 29, 2006.

—— Transcript of Plea Hearing. April 22, 2005. (Defense Exhibit 954). http://www.vaed.uscourts.gov/notablecases/moussaoui/exhibits/defense/954.pdf. Accessed November 30, 2006.

—— Hearing Transcript. February 14, 2006. http://cryptome.org/usa-v-zm-021406-01.htm. Accessed November 29, 2006.

—— Hearing Transcript. March 6, 2006a. http://cryptome.org/usa-v-zm-030606-01.htm. Accessed March 8, 2007.

—— Hearing Transcript. March 6, 2006b. http://cryptome.org/usa-v-zm-030606-02.htm. Accessed March 8, 2007.

—— Transcript, March 8, 2006. Testimony of Bafana. http://cryptome.org/usa-v-zm-030806-02.htm. Accessed October 11, 2006.

—— Transcript, March 9, 2006. Testimony of Harry Samit. http://www.law.umkc.edu/faculty/projects/ftrials/moussaoui/zmsamit.html. Accessed September 22, 2006.

—— Transcript, March 9, 2006. Testimony of Clarence Prevost. http://www.law.umkc.edu/faculty/projects/ftrials/moussaoui/zmprevost.html. Accessed September 22, 2006.

—— Transcript, March 27, 2006. Exemplaris.com. Accessed March 29, 2006.

—— Prosecution Exhibit AQ01677T. Manual Recovered in Manchester, England, by Metropolitan Police. http://www.vaed.uscourts.gov/notablecases/moussaoui/exhibits/prosecution/AQ01677TA.pdf. Accessed November 30, 2006.

—— Prosecution Exhibit MN00151. Copy of Email. May 23, 2001. http://www.vaed.uscourts.gov/notablecases/moussaoui/exhibits/prosecution/MN00151.pdf. Accessed November 30, 2006.

—— Prosecution Exhibit MN00601. WHS Notebook. http://www.vaed.uscourts.gov/notablecases/moussaoui/exhibits/prosecution/MN00601.pdf. Accessed November 29, 2006.

—— Prosecution Exhibit MN00666. WHS Notebook. http://www.vaed.uscourts.gov/notablecases/moussaoui/exhibits/prosecution/MN00666.pdf. Accessed November 29, 2006.

—— Defense Exhibit 56. Email, dated August 22, 2001, Rowley/Pointer, Re Query. http://www.vaed.uscourts.gov/notablecases/moussaoui/exhibits/defense/056.pdf. Accessed November 30, 2006.

—— Defense Exhibit 59B. FBI Legat Memo re French Information. http://www.vaed.uscourts.gov/notablecases/moussaoui/exhibits/defense/059B.pdf. Accessed November 30, 2006.

—— Defense Exhibit 332. Email. August 28, 2001. http://www.vaed.uscourts.gov/notablecases/moussaoui/exhibits/defense/332.pdf. Accessed November 29, 2006.

—— Defense Exhibit 810. FBI Letterhead Memo Drafted by Samit, August 31, 2001. http://www.vaed.uscourts.gov/notablecases/moussaoui/exhibits/defense/810.pdf. Accessed March 11, 2007.

—— Defense Exhibit 922. Inventory of Items Seized from Moussaoui. http://www.vaed.uscourts.gov/notablecases/moussaoui/exhibits/defense/922.pdf. Accessed November 30, 2006.

—— Defense Exhibit 941. Substitution for Testimony, Khalid Sheikh Mohammed. http://www.vaed.uscourts.gov/notablecases/moussaoui/exhibits/defense/941.pdf. Accessed November 30, 2006.

—— Defense Exhibit 943. Substitution for Testimony, al-Hawsawi. http://www.vaed.uscourts.gov/notablecases/moussaoui/exhibits/defense/943.pdf. Accessed November 30, 2006.

—— Defense Exhibit 944. Substitution for Testimony, al-Qahtani. http://www.vaed.uscourts.gov/notablecases/moussaoui/exhibits/defense/944.pdf. Accessed November 30, 2006.

—— Defense Exhibit 945. Substitution for Testimony, Khallad. http://www.vaed.uscourts.gov/notablecases/moussaoui/exhibits/defense/945.pdf. Accessed November 30, 2006.

—— Defense Exhibit 946. Substitution for Testimony, Hambali. http://www.vaed.uscourts.gov/notablecases/moussaoui/exhibits/defense/946.pdf. Accessed November 30, 2006.

—— Defense Exhibit JV002.1T. Decree for Admission to Childhood Welfare Services. http://www.vaed.uscourts.gov/notablecases/moussaoui/exhibits/defense/JV002-1T.pdf. Accessed March 11, 2007.

—— Defense Exhibit JV002.5T. Court Decision, St. Vincent de Paul. http://www.vaed.uscourts.gov/notablecases/moussaoui/exhibits/defense/JV002-5T.pdf. Accessed March 11, 2007.

—— Defense Exhibit JV002.7T. St. Vincent de Paul Register. http://www.vaed.uscourts.gov/notablecases/moussaoui/exhibits/defense/JV002-7T.pdf. Accessed March 11, 2007.

—— Defense Exhibit JV002.12T. Divorce Judgment. http://www.vaed.uscourts.gov/notablecases/moussaoui/exhibits/defense/JV002-12T.pdf. Accessed March 11, 2007.

—— Defense Exhibit JV002.17T. Family History, M.J. Burckard, Social Worker. http://www.vaed.uscourts.gov/notablecases/moussaoui/exhibits/defense/JV002-17T.pdf. Accessed March 11, 2007.

—— Defense Exhibit JV002.18T. Letter from DSS to Judge. http://www.vaed.uscourts.gov/notablecases/moussaoui/exhibits/defense/JV002-18T.pdf. Accessed March 11, 2007.

—— Defense Exhibit JV002.20T. Letter from DSS Placing Children in Homes. http://www.vaed.uscourts.gov/notablecases/moussaoui/exhibits/defense/JV002-20T.pdf. Accessed March 11, 2007.

—— Defense Exhibit JV002.21T. Release Form for Nadia and Jamila. http://www.vaed.uscourts.gov/notablecases/moussaoui/exhibits/defense/JV002-21T.pdf. Accessed March 11, 2007.

—— Defense Exhibit. JV002.24T. Letter to Judge re Mr. El-Kadi. http://www.vaed.uscourts.gov/notablecases/moussaoui/exhibits/defense/JV002-24T.pdf. Accessed March 11, 2007.

—— Defense Exhibit JV002.28T. Ruling, Omar Moussaoui Guilty. http://www.vaed.uscourts.gov/notablecases/moussaoui/exhibits/defense/JV002-28T.pdf. Accessed March 11, 2007.

—— Defense Exhibit JV002.29T. Report Card for ZM 1988–1990. http://www.vaed.uscourts.gov/notablecases/moussaoui/exhibits/defense/JV002-29T.pdf. Accessed March 11, 2007.

—— Defense Exhibit JV002.37T. Report Card for ZM 1980–91. http://www.vaed.uscourts.gov/notablecases/moussaoui/exhibits/defense/JV002-37T.pdf. Accessed March 11, 2007.

—— Defense Exhibit JV002.45T. Trimester Bulletin for ZM 1983–84. http://www.vaed.uscourts.gov/notablecases/moussaoui/exhibits/defense/JV002-45T.pdf. Accessed March 11, 2007.

—— Defense Exhibit JV002.46T. Trimester Bulletin for ZM 1983–84. http://www.vaed.uscourts.gov/notablecases/moussaoui/exhibits/defense/JV002-46T.pdf. Accessed March 11, 2007.

—— Defense Exhibit JV002.61T. Court Extract, Omar Moussaoui. http://www.vaed.uscourts.gov/notablecases/moussaoui/exhibits/defense/JV002-61T.pdf. Accessed March 11, 2007.

—— Defense Exhibit JV002.67T. Psychiatric Interview, Omar Moussaoui. http://www.vaed.uscourts.gov/notablecases/moussaoui/exhibits/defense/JV002-67T.pdf. Accessed March 11, 2007.

—— Defense Exhibit JV002.68T. Medical Records, Jamila Moussaoui. http://www.vaed.uscourts.gov/notablecases/moussaoui/exhibits/defense/JV002-68T.pdf. Accessed March 11, 2007.

—— Defense Exhibit ZM010. ZM God Curse the Queen. http://www.vaed.uscourts.gov/notablecases/moussaoui/exhibits/defense/ZM010.pdf. Accessed November 30, 2006.

—— Docket No. 88. Order as to Website. http://notablecases.vaed.uscourts.gov/1:01-cr-00455/docs/64827/0.pdf. Accessed November 29, 2006.

—— Docket No. 89. Notice of Intent to Seek Death Penalty. http://notablecases.vaed.uscourts.gov/1:01-cr-00455/docs/64851/0.pdf. Accessed November 14, 2006.

—— Docket No. 94. Motion for Relief from Conditions of Confinement, April 12, 2002. http://notablecases.vaed.uscourts.gov/1:01-cr-00455/docs/64929/0.pdf. Accessed November 30, 2006.

—— Docket No. 95. Order Granting in Part Motion for Relief. April 12, 2002. http://notablecases.vaed.uscourts.gov/1:01-cr-00455/docs/64941/0.pdf. Accessed November 30, 2006.

—— Docket No. 112. Motion to Dismiss Counsel. April 22, 2002. http://notablecases.vaed.uscourts.gov/1:01-cr-00455/docs/65403/1.pdf. Accessed November 30, 2006.

—— Docket No. 186. Order as to Zacarias Moussaoui. June 17, 2002. http://notablecases.vaed.uscourts.gov/1:01-cr-00455/docs/65954/0.pdf. Accessed November 29, 2006.

—— Docket No. 228. Documents Filed by Bro. Charles Freeman. June 25, 2002. http://notablecases.vaed.uscourts.gov/1:01-cr-00455/docs/66373/0.pdf. Accessed November 29, 2006.

—— Docket No. 241. Motion by Zacarias Moussaoui. June 27, 2002. http://notablecases.vaed.uscourts.gov/1:01-cr-00455/docs/66424/1.pdf. Accessed November 30, 2006.

—— Docket No. 243. Motion by Zacarias Moussaoui. June 27, 2002. http://notablecases.vaed.uscourts.gov/1:01-cr-00455/docs/66430/1.pdf

—— Docket No. 272. Motion for Independent Expert Test Fan. July 3, 2002. http://notablecases.vaed.uscourts.gov/1:01-cr-00455/docs/66590/0.pdf. Accessed November 30, 2006.

—— Docket No. 314. Motion for Pre Contempt of Leonie Brinkema. July 11, 2002. http://notablecases.vaed.uscourts.gov/1:01-cr-00455/docs/66807/0.pdf. Accessed November 30, 2006.

—— Docket No. 340. Second Superseding Indictment, July 18, 2002. http://notablecases.vaed.uscourts.gov/1:01-cr-00455/docs/66826/0.pdf

—— Docket No. 369. Motion by Zacarias Moussaoui. July 20, 2002. http://notablecases.vaed.uscourts.gov/1:01-cr-00455/docs/66950/0.pdf. Accessed October 19, 2006.

—— Docket No. 772. Motion to Access Witness El-Hadi. March 4, 2003. http://notablecases.vaed.uscourts.gov/1:01-cr-00455/docs/68313/1.pdf. Accessed November 30, 2006.

—— Docket No. 794. Motion to Stop the Pervert Game of the Fascist Bureau. March 25, 2003. http://notablecases.vaed.uscourts.gov/1:01-cr-00455/docs/68383/4.pdf. Accessed November 30, 2006.

—— Docket No. 796. Motion to Force Ashcroft and FBI to Produce Mohammed. March 25, 2003. http://notablecases.vaed.uscourts.gov/1:01-cr-00455/docs/68389/1.pdf. Accessed November 30, 2006.

—— Docket No. 803. Motion for Access to Brother Mohammed. March 31, 2003. http://notablecases.vaed.uscourts.gov/1:01-cr-00455/docs/68410/1.pdf. Accessed November 30, 2006.

—— Docket No. 832. Order as to Zacarias Moussaoui. April 14, 2003. http://notablecases.vaed.uscourts.gov/1:01-cr-00455/docs/68499/1.pdf. Accessed November 29, 2006.

—— Docket No. 847. Motion to Force Fat Megalo Dunham. April 21, 2003. http://notablecases.vaed.uscourts.gov/1:01-cr-00455/docs/68546/1.pdf. Accessed November 30, 2006.

—— Docket No. 853. Renew Motion to Force Fat Megalo Dunham ... April 22, 2003. http://notablecases.vaed.uscourts.gov/1:01-cr-00455/docs/68564/1.pdf. Accessed November 30, 2006.

—— Docket No. 972. Motion: Wanted in the Tyran Court. July 14, 2003. http://notablecases.vaed.uscourts.gov/1:01-cr-00455/docs/68936/1.pdf. Accessed November 30, 2006.

—— Docket No. 1024. Motion for Clarification. August 15, 2003. http://notablecases.vaed.uscourts.gov/1:01-cr-00455/docs/69102/1.pdf. Accessed November 30, 2006.

—— Docket No. 1082. Motion for Reconsideration. October 7, 2003. http://notablecases.vaed.uscourts.gov/1:01-cr-00455/docs/69288/1.pdf. Accessed November 30, 2006.

—— Docket No. 1117. Motion for Reconsideration. November 12, 2003. http://notablecases.vaed.uscourts.gov/1:01-cr-00455/docs/69403/1.pdf. Accessed November 30, 2006.

—— Docket No. 1120. Order; Request to Represent Self is Vacated. November 14, 2003. http://notablecases.vaed.uscourts.gov/1:01-cr-00455/docs/69412/0.pdf. Accessed November 30, 2006.

—— Docket No. 1264. Statement of Facts. April 22, 2005. http://notablecases.vaed.uscourts.gov/1:01-cr-00455/docs/70543/0.pdf. Accessed November 29, 2006.

—— Docket No. 1277. Letter Motion. Ineffective Assistance of Defence Counsel. May 3, 2005. http://notablecases.vaed.uscourts.gov/1:01-cr-00455/docs/70582/0.pdf. Accessed November 30, 2006.

—— Docket No. 1314. Motion to Strike Notice of Intent to Seek Death Penalty. June 24, 2005. http://notablecases.vaed.uscourts.gov/1:01-cr-00455/docs/70695/0.pdf. Accessed November 29, 2006.

—— Docket No. 1346. Government's Memorandum in Opposition to Trifurcation. October 14, 2005. http://notablecases.vaed.uscourts.gov/1:01-cr-00455/docs/70793/0.pdf. Accessed September 30, 2006

—— Docket No. 1372. Order Granting Motion for Separate Hearing. November 14, 2005. http://notablecases.vaed.uscourts.gov/1:01-cr-00455/docs/70873/0.pdf. Accessed September 30, 2006.

—— Docket No. 1377. Defendant's Motion for a Separate Hearing ... November 16, 2005. http://notablecases.vaed.uscourts.gov/1:01-cr-00455/docs/70764/1.pdf. Accessed September 30, 2006.

—— Docket No. 1508. Memorandum Opinion. February 3, 2006. http://notablecases.vaed.uscourts.gov/1:01-cr-00455/docs/71289/0.pdf.

—— Docket No. 1509. Order. February 3, 2006. http://notablecases.vaed.uscourts.gov/1:01-cr-00455/docs/71292/0.pdf

—— Docket No. 1617. Filed Under Seal. (But see Docket No. 1686. Order re Aviation Witnesses.) March 17, 2006. http://notablecases.vaed.uscourts.gov/1:01-cr-00455/docs/71868/0.pdf. Accessed November 30, 2006.

—— Docket No. 1857. Defendant's Motion to Withdraw Guilty Plea. May 8, 2006. http://notablecases.vaed.uscourts.gov/1:01-cr-00455/docs/72453/0.pdf. Accessed November 30, 2006.

—— Docket No. 1860. Notice of Appeal. May 12, 2006. http://notablecases.vaed.uscourts.gov/1:01-cr-00455/docs/72465/0.pdf. Accessed November 24, 2006.

United States v. Moussaoui. Fourth Circuit Court of Appeals No. 02-4571, Opposition to Petition. http://fl1.findlaw.com/news.findlaw.com/hdocs/docs/moussaoui/usmouss72402mndop.pdf

—— Fourth Circuit Court of Appeals. 333 F.3d 509, 517 (4th Cir. 2003). (Decision that the appeal was interlocutory.)

—— Fourth Circuit Court of Appeals. 365 F.3d 292 (4th Cir. 2004) (April 22, 2004 decision concerning death penalty and access to witnesses.)

—— Fourth Circuit Court of Appeals. 382 F.3d 453 (4th Cir. 2004). (Decision of September 14, 2004.)

USDOJ. 2006a. A Brief History. US Attorney's Office, Eastern District of Virginia. http://www.usdoj.gov/usao/vae/ourhistory.html. Accessed October 2, 2006.

—— 2006b. *A Review of the FBI's Handling of Intelligence Information Related to the September 11 Attacks (November 2004)*. http://www.usdoj.gov/oig/special/s0606/final.pdf. Accessed October 27, 2006.

—— 2006c. Attorney General's Annual Awards Recipients Announced. http://www.usdoj.gov/jmd/ps/54thAGAwardsRecipients2006.pdf. Accessed November 10, 2006.

—— 2006d. Fact Sheet: Department of Justice Anti-terrorism Efforts since Sept. 11, 2001. #06-590. Posted September 5, 2006. http://www.usdoj.gov/opa/pr/2006/September/06_opa_590.html. Accessed November 10, 2006.

Van Natta, Don and Benjamin Weiser. 2001. Compromise Settles Debate Over Tribunal. December 12. *New York Times*.

el-Wafi, Aïcha. 2006. (with Matthias Favron and Sophie Quaranta). *Mon fils perdu: La mère de Zacarias Moussaoui parle*. Paris: Editions de Noyelles, Plon.

Walker, Edward S., Jr. 2005. Does Anyone in Washington Listen to Academics and Think Tanks? Transcript. Middle East Institute Publications. March 31.

Washington Post. 2006. Detainee Biographies. http://www.washington-post.com/wp-srv/nation/documents/DetaineeBiographies.pdf. Accessed September 11, 2006.

Welch, David. 2006. Middle East Update. Foreign Press Center Briefing, August 15. http://fpc.state.gov/fpc/70654.htm. Accessed November 3, 2006.

Wieviorka, Michel, ed. 1997. *Une société fragmentée?* Paris: La Découverte.

Willing, Richard. 2002. "Westernized Kid" Grows into 9/11 Radical. *USAToday*. Posted June 25. http://www.usatoday.com/news/world/2002/06/25/cover.htm. Accessed September 20, 2005.

Woodward, Bob. 2006. *State of Denial*. New York: Simon and Schuster.

Woodward, Will. 2001.Hijack Suspect was South Bank Student. *The Guardian*. Posted October 6. http://www.guardian.co.uk/wtccrash/story/0,,564459,00.html. Accessed August 29, 2006.

Wright, Lawrence. 2006. *The Looming Tower: Al-Qaeda and the Road to 9/11*. New York: Knopf.

al-Zayyat, Montasser. 2004. *The Road to al Qaeda*. Ahmed Fekry, trans., Sara Nimis, ed. London: Pluto Books.

Zeman, Ned, David Wise, David Rose, and Bryan Burrough. 2004. The Path to 9/11. *Vanity Fair* 531: 326–403.

Žižek, Slavoj. 2002. Welcome to the Desert of the Real! *South Atlantic Quarterly* 101(2): 385–40.

INDEX

Note: Names which begin with al- and el- have been alphabetized by first letter of the word following. For instance, "al-Shibh, Ramzi" is to be found under the letter "S", "el-Wafi, Aïcha" is to be found under the letter "W".